TRACING GANDHI

This book traces the journey of Mahatma Gandhi, from being a simple and truth-seeking human being, a *satyarthi*, to a committed, conscious and social human being, a *satyagrahi*. It specifically looks at this critical transformation during the time Gandhi was in South Africa. The central argument of the book is that Gandhi evolved from being a *satyarthi* to a *satyagrahi* in South Africa. Subsequently in India, he consolidated his orientation with an emphasis on praxis, by developing his ideas as instruments for social and individual struggles. Marked by a series of events, this period was an intense quest of self-realization and understanding, and shows his journey from being Mohandas Karamchand Gandhi to being Mahatma Gandhi.

The book discusses various elements of Gandhian thought and praxis – morality, wisdom, non-violence, truth, social justice, dharma, trusteeship, education, sarvodaya, *Hind Swaraj*, swadeshi, and social service – and interprets the relevance of Gandhi's thought in the modern world by highlighting its unique significance for social transformation and change.

Lucid and accessible, the book will be useful to scholars and researchers of Gandhi studies, Indian political thought, modern Indian history, and political studies.

Samir Banerjee is an independent researcher based in Bengaluru, India. Besides long-standing involvement in the non-formal sector on issues such as sustainable development, environment, organic farming, watershed development, technology, adult literacy, and slum habitats, he has taught, written, and published on the significance of Gandhian thought and praxis. His last published book was *Notes from Gandhigram: Challenges to Gandhian Praxis* (2009).

TRACING GANDHI

Satyarthi to *Satyagrahi*

Samir Banerjee

LONDON AND NEW YORK

First published 2020
by Routledge
2 Park Square, Milton Park, Abingdon, Oxon OX14 4RN

and by Routledge
52 Vanderbilt Avenue, New York, NY 10017

Routledge is an imprint of the Taylor & Francis Group, an informa business

© 2020 Indian Institute of Advanced Study (IIAS), Shimla

The right of Samir Banerjee to be identified as author of this work has been asserted by him in accordance with sections 77 and 78 of the Copyright, Designs and Patents Act 1988.

All rights reserved. No part of this book may be reprinted or reproduced or utilised in any form or by any electronic, mechanical, or other means, now known or hereafter invented, including photocopying and recording, or in any information storage or retrieval system, without permission in writing from the publishers.

Trademark notice: Product or corporate names may be trademarks or registered trademarks, and are used only for identification and explanation without intent to infringe.

British Library Cataloguing-in-Publication Data
A catalogue record for this book is available from the British Library

Library of Congress Cataloging-in-Publication Data
A catalog record for this book has been requested

ISBN: 978-0-367-13758-8 (hbk)
ISBN: 978-0-367-28011-6 (pbk)
ISBN: 978-0-429-29921-6 (ebk)

Typeset in Bembo
by Apex CoVantage LLC

CONTENTS

Preface		*vi*
1	Invoking Gandhi: recalling an interlocutor's paradigm	1
2	A *satyarthi* in South Africa	14
3	Gandhi: a *satyagrahi*	29
4	*Satyagrahi* Gandhi returns to India	51
5	Morality and wisdom: brahmacharya, satya, ahimsa, satyagraha	66
6	Religion: case, brief, and argument	108
7	Towards a world view: sarvodaya, *Hind Swaraj*, swadeshi, social service	145
8	Gandhi is gone, but Gandhian thought remains	180
Glossary		*194*
Bibliography		*197*
Index		*203*

PREFACE

Reading Gandhi has never been easy, and as time passes, it gets even more difficult. To understand his thoughts and actions is a demanding task made more difficult by the simplicity and the overarching nuances, sometimes disconcertingly bordering on the naiveté, with which he presents them. From the sagacious to the downright evasive is how one feels treading Gandhi's path. The famous dialogues, some of which he himself penned, the political disagreements, the showmanship, the trying to draw a line on the sands of time, all the while trying to retain relevance, integrity, and tradition, make for an interesting tapestry of thought, praxis, and hope. Most of us might find insight in the weave of such intricacies while others will most probably remain preoccupied with his busts, specs, portraits, and *lathi*. However, Gandhi himself, given his deep concern regarding the way we dirty our pristine pure blanket (*maille chadar audh ke aaya: nirgun bhajan*) would have rued at how he had soiled the blanket. Just reading his agreements and disagreements with a whole host of enormously competent contemporaries, stretching from Tagore, Nehru, Ambedkar to Jinnah, Rajagopalachari and Bose, is a job in itself. Since then many thinkers have tried to help us comprehend the 'essential Gandhi'. Gandhi himself spoke just about everything: economics, politics, culture, gender, and nature, including our personal nature.

So how does one respond? I took my clue from Gandhi and tried to 'listen to that little voice within'. This I hope will permit me my preferences and references while allowing me to be critical and creative in my analysis of events regarding Gandhi and his thoughts and actions. But then there is this small problem: I am to an extent aware how Gandhi has impacted me; but how will I impact Gandhi? This might sound a bit pompous. But take a closer look and you realize that Gandhi today is what we have made of him. His import to us is what makes him mahatma and not what Gandhi thought he was; the solemnity is in what we construct of Gandhi to facilitate our aspirations. However, while Gandhi did what he thought he should do, he would want us to set the terms of reference in order to understand him. He would certainly not want to engage with us about our judgment of him. For him Gandhism itself is to be avoided. Further it is not for anybody to say as to why he should or will be remembered; why his actions will be reconsidered in the future as memories to aid our tryst with civilization. Gandhi prophesied that for 30 years after his death, his ideas would be largely forgotten, but that, generations later, the *tapas* of millions would bear fruit and that out of his ashes 'a thousand Gandhis will arise'.[1] This is the abiding promise of Gandhi; a promise which intrigues and attracts. And as with all attractions, this too runs into a quaint problematic: to remember Gandhi, where should one begin? Should it begin from its inception, or from its impact?

In the case of Gandhi this can be a difficult task. The transition of a simple truthful human being, from a *satyarthi* to a *satyagrahi*, from a person fearful of the dark outside world to a person fearful of the ambiguousness within his own self, from Mohandas Karamchand Gandhi to Mahatma Gandhi is a narrative of conversion which is much more complex than proceeding from the passable to the consummate. It was an intense quest of self-realization, of recognizing and being at peace with ahimsa and satya. And in the process, Gandhi evolved from being just a leader, to Mahatma, a soubriquet his fellow Indians bestowed upon him. This journey from a simple *dehin-atma* to a *mahan-atma* is a narrative marked by a series of engagements both profound and perfunctory. It is this *jugalbandi* of the obligatory and the reflective which holds both enormous insights and intriguing fascination. Perhaps it is this suppleness which creates the belief that Gandhi was an event masquerading as a man. Conceivably Gandhi was wary of being squeezed between the contending propensities of internationalism and *vasudaiva kutumbakam*.

For Gandhi, a fundamental concern, one which he recognized could not be ignored is the notion of development, more precisely who is developed, who is underdeveloped, and who has the authority over the discourse of development. He also accepted that as far as this business of development is concerned, while caution is acceptable, wavering can be disastrous. For him development has all the ingredients of the doom he would not deem. Moreover, development is premised on change, a notion accompanied by the enormously debatable choice. Likewise, while the old is resilient and will not just fade away, it is perilous to debunk the ethos of the prevailing hegemony because it is essentially not very different from our allegedly progressive ideas. In social transformation for large sections of society, there pervades an element of determinism; this comes with an element of despair because it engenders an end of the comfortable 'known'. Faced with such contradictions, in Gandhi we look for a genuineness which could point toward alternatives to the so-called inevitable. Khadi for him was one such necessity which could propose alternatives not only to unemployment and the labour and technology conflict but also to the problematic of technology itself.

I started with the impact approach, that is by trying to analyze social movements oriented by Gandhian thought such as the *bhoodan*, *sampoornakranti*, and *chipko* movements. Simultaneously, I tried to understand the significance of institutions such as Gandhigram Trust, Dindigul[2] and ShramBharati, Khadigram, Jamui,[3] which had Gandhian thought as the world view driving them. One element common to all was the dominating presence and influence of interlocutors straddling these activities, who considered themselves to be in the Gandhian mode. These were events initiated and articulated by Gandhian interlocutors using Gandhian thought to consciously intervene in processes of social transition and transformation. For the interlocutors of such events, selecting between processes of social change and continuity, knowing that these are subjected to chance and necessity, meant supporting choices which they felt adhered to a Gandhian world view. Since the processes were complex, original, and innovative, the nature and quality of these efforts depended profoundly on the competence and credibility of the interlocutors, particularly on the ability to attract more and more interlocutors. This meant making *satyagrahis* out of *satyarthis* and as involvement, a synthesis of means and ends.

The task was never easy, and it was made difficult by an abiding Gandhian problematic: even a good thing cannot be forced; forcing involvement of any variety undermines the possibility of ahimsa, deference, and inviolability. For an event, in this case involvement, to be genuine it has to respect the possibility that those whom it proposes to benefit might choose not to accept it. Gandhi's satyagraha drew the line between genuine involvement and involvement under benevolent premises. People should be bound to the involvement through personal pledge and not some form of overt commitment. Involvement must not be confused with virtue. The issue is clarity regarding purpose and agency of action and how imperious action is towards morality and truth. Besides asserting the goodness of the effects of action, the correctness of the action needs to be intrinsic to the action itself. This entails an organic intimacy of purpose and agency. In actuality, this means not only the why, how, where, and when, but also regarding whom. Such a narrative requires clarity about ideas and concepts configuring such thoughts. What then is Gandhian thought, or more explicitly, the praxis which aspires to measure up to such stringent demands? This study seeks to elaborate and hopefully understand what I fondly call clarity regarding the above. I must hasten to add that this clarity is not about the relevance of Gandhi. It is about the way we give expression and bind together this relevance and what it means both as an idea and a way of life. Above all, it is about the interlocutor and ethics; about the autonomy of imagination, and a dare to think differently. The text and narrative traces two themes: Gandhi's transition and transformation from a *satyarthi* to a *satyagrahi*, and the various elements which initiated, nurtured, and conspicuously evolved into what we now know as the Gandhian world view.

This book has been possible because of a fellowship given by the Indian Institute of Advanced Study, Shimla. I must thank Chetan Singh, my co-fellows, and the staff of the Institute for their unstinted help and cooperation. For information, ideas, suggestions, and comments I must thank Moloy Bannerjee. Sundar Sarukkai, Sabyasachi Bhattacharya, Kaustav Chakrabarty, Anand Kumar, Gawhar Yaqoob, Jagdish Davar, Shekhar Pathak, Aditya Pratap Deo, Imrana Quadeer, Dunu Roy, Udayan Misra, Tilottama Misra, and Rupin Maitreyee. I thank the reviewers whose comments helped improve the text. Last, but certainly not least, I have been fortunate to benefit from the competence, efficiency, and professionalism of everyone with whom I have interacted at Routledge.

Notes

1 *TEWMG* (1991, 39).
2 Banerjee (2009).
3 Banerjee (1999).

1
INVOKING GANDHI
Recalling an interlocutor's paradigm

Many of us as individuals have often found ourselves quite confused and as a group also somewhat lost. Often many have been turning to Gandhi, sometimes from choice and at other times from necessity. Of course many others have also turned to Gandhi out of conviction. Of the confused lot, while many turned to Gandhi with reverence, there were others who did it with reluctance all the while disliking the idea. Lately egged on by the question 'what it means for an Indian to be an Indian', this urge seems to be taking a serious turn. It seems this urge is evolving and is no more just a simple question of patriotism and its precocious twin, nationalism. It now concerns identity and issues such as language, region, colour, caste, and sect and so on. The moot question somehow still seems to remain an innocent elemental sounding 'who am I', and Gandhi seems to be the most competent person to go to for advice. Perhaps Gandhi can help the 'perfect Indian' find a place between a pristine past and a parody of the modern west?

But then Gandhi is not someone given to indulging anybody. While he is all for experiments and being critical and creative, he is also all for discarding ideas which have reached their expiry date, and for leaders who seek to operate beyond their level of incompetence. While this does not mean any indiscriminate rejection of the past, it certainly means a commitment to the present and its exceptional unity in diversity. Further, it also means that meaningful or constructive thinking and timely action are inseparable twins. Gandhi's oceanic circles are akin to the waves which stretch out when you drop a stone in a placid lake. But then again, we are not the only ones dropping stones. There are others doing the same. And we also know that when one set of waves meets another, they seem to try and clamber over each other. We notice turbulence in the smooth constant amplitude of the sine curve our stones have generated; we take notice of this and respond not by taking away the right of others to drop a stone, but by trying to see as to how together we can drop stones to watch an unbroken inclusiveness of waves desisting from clambering over each other, perhaps enjoying how these micro swells fold and spill over themselves. Some of course will consider this as a dilettante's muse.

Gandhi with his ahimsa avoids such self-goals. Ahimsa or *krōdh tyāg* encourages us to desist from making anger integral to problem solving. By enlightening us about the violence within society and the violence this violence encourages, ahimsa inspires us to engage with it through seeking freedom from insecurity which is the root cause of fear. In a way ahimsa has a way of charming everything. True: but behind this soothing ethos, ahimsa can point out via belonging, the particularities of and between, being and becoming. You either don't throw stones or throw them together. And this is no muse, because we humans when disillusioned can easily decide to throw stones at each other.

Trying to understand ahimsa is an act of humility. It is an act with which we try to approach the anger within us, thereby creating a conducive personal ethos. Anger represents the volatility between destruction and rejuvenation, qualities present in every act of living which every human being seeks to recognize and come to terms with. Ahimsa as an inclination encourages a middle path of reconciliation and consolidation. Gandhi in South Africa recognized that he and his fellow Indians were at the threshold; they were outsiders wanting to get inside as equals. But then there were others who too had just come and were not just reluctant to share their new home, but were downright hostile to even tolerate the idea of thinking about sharing it with anybody, including the locals. Gandhi's journey starts with this insider-outsider debate which for him evolves into a discourse regarding being '*at the threshold*'. He begins with an insider-outsider dialogue with himself, extends it to his fellow Indians in South Africa, and then moves over to India to continue with fellow Indians. Along the way perched at his threshold, he ends up inviting everyone to join the narrative. Doubts are raised, questions asked, suggestions and solutions offered: *aap he dandi, aap taraju, aap he baitha tolta*, you are the measure, the measured, and the measurer, as Kabir suggests. Ahimsa, tyaag, conflict resolution, confrontation, reconciliation, consensus, fear, freedom, and various other elements of Gandhi's discourse while offering a range of potentialities, perhaps also suggest that the threshold is a systemic location to initiate and sustain interrogation of social transformation processes. This interrogation can in turn help us come to terms with the problematic of the duality of being and becoming: being as given and becoming as potentially consciousness-driven arrival.

Walking with Gandhi

It is apparent that Gandhi is relevant. If our Marxist comrades can appropriate the nuances of satyagraha and bhook-hartal, our saffron mentors vouch by swadeshi, swachh, and swaraj, and if NGO activists get busy debunking globalization and the deleterious impact of technology, then surely the Gandhian weltanschauung must be holding some promise.

The problem is how should one approach a study of Gandhi? "To deduce one final supervening Gandhi from his life and work would be both anti-Gandhian and self-defeating".[1] But then the next set of complications emerges. Should our questions be posed to Gandhi the politician, or the person, the *bairagi*, or should it be posed to his policies, philosophy, and practice i.e. to Gandhism? He himself would have dissuaded us from 'Gandhism': "I do not know myself who is a Gandhian. Gandhism is a meaningless word for me. An ism follows the propounder of a system. I am not one, hence I cannot be the cause for any ism. If an ism is built up it will endure, and if it does it will not be Gandhism. This deserves to be properly understood".[2] But whatever he might say, or not say, Gandhi remains an enigma.

Perhaps one way could be to try and invoke his legacy where we in the first place have to dig deep into our collective wisdom wherein problem solving is an abiding concern, an involvement in itself. Maybe in the Gandhi as praxis as Rajmohan Gandhi (1995), as Rajni Bakshi (1998) and others have suggested, we can find the wisdom that has the potential to help us as committed social beings articulate non-sectarian, non-exploitative, and abiding equanimous alternatives for meaningful social transformation? Perhaps "*majboori ka naam* Mahatma Gandhi": "compulsion thy name is Mahatma Gandhi" is a cynically coinage? Maybe it was because he at times did tend to withdraw his publicly announced agitations. However it does make a lot of sense particularly because compulsion has this element of helplessness. While helplessness informs necessity, it also abets humility. Humility sometimes derided as cowardice can be very energizing and self-respecting because it encourages a search for collective social wisdom, a sure remedy to overcome dependence. Perhaps this is why Gandhi beckons. Tagore had insightfully written, "He (Gandhi) stopped at the thresholds of the huts of the thousands of the dispossessed, dressed like one of their own. He spoke to them in their own language; here was living truth at last, and not quotations from books. For this reason the 'Mahatma', the name given to him by the people of India, is his real name".[3] But to reiterate humility can be a surrogate to debility and many know it as such! And therefore, a question should be asked: 'why this invocation of Gandhi'? Invocation after all comes loaded with elements of mediation and mendication. Moreover who will be doing this invocation? Further in a more problematic mode we will need to invoke Gandhi simultaneously at the personal and the social levels because it is nearly impossible to separate 'I' the personal, from 'Me' the social in Gandhi. Perhaps this refers to that liminal call, 'the small voice' of Gandhi which urges us to not surrender our memories. Through Gandhi we can hope to invoke our personal and social memories.

Invoking Gandhi

Invoking is to call forth with earnest desire. You seek recall not to eulogize but to sensitize yourself. During invoking the 'I' seeks to both acknowledge and hail the 'ME'. Premised on the credibility of tradition, invoking aspires to inculcate an element of creative recall into the possessive nature of tradition. Always aware that individuals make traditions, the act of invoking albeit biased towards reifying tradition, by creating a feeling of appropriateness and disclosing intentions, initiates '*shraddha*', thereby making the self, receptive. In effect, along with meditation it becomes a process of mediation, wherein creative and contemporary insights, guided by traditions, can contemplate upon the '*siddha*' and the '*sadhya*' and thereby encourage alternatives, all the while underscoring the extent to which deference should be accorded to tradition vis-à-vis aspirations. Since invoking accompanies and/or follows contemplation, it can facilitate a dialogue between the existing and the possible. In effect, invoking can be the first step in coming to terms with ambivalence; as such while it is inseparable from contemplation it can also encourage action which is the ontology of truth.

Invoking thus is a process. It is both the art and the act of an interlocutor. An interlocutor is somebody who has an opinion, listens to the opinion of others, and tries to collate all these various opinions into a common discourse or platform. Most often invoking begins with contemplation and, mediated by creative, critical, and contemporary insights, it progresses towards clarity and commitment. This arguably is Gandhi's method of involvement and *Hind Swaraj, Satyagraha in South Africa, From Yervada Mandir, Ashram Observations in Action*, are classic examples. My invocation of Gandhi starts with contemplation and proceeds through an engagement with a wide range of critical and contemporary views and opinions. It might read like a joint appeal or a tired sigh of a confused person. It might even sound like the rattling of a ragbag of disparate ideas. But that I am afraid is the interlocutor's raison d'être: be participatory, listen, and proceed, always mindful that choice can be very arbitrary. The interlocutor seeks to explicate a method, the context being his essential calling. While we may not talk of context or even method in isolation, the focus of the interlocutor's paradigm is method and context. This in turn leads to contemplation.

Contemplation is an adjunct of invocation. Moreover contemplation is a continuum. It is a continuum in that it is not just a progressive series of linear and ascending clarity. It is varied, heterogeneous, and always at the crossroads beset with the demands of conflicting choices. However, it is a continuum since elements always pop up between elements. Memory, metaphor, perceptions, and events coexist. And as the mathematician would like to remind us, just like a number always exists between two numbers, similarly between the origin and the tentative point of arrival, essentials will always exist which we might have never noticed. Contemplation has this very nice quality of allowing withdrawal into the self while keeping one's eyes fully open. It permits a comfortable feeling of mental indulgence albeit with an element of restraint. Moreover it is not demanding in the sense of necessitating decisions or action. As such contemplation is about truth, but is not truth itself. Since contemplation has a very binding internal quality, it only creates an ambience and in so doing helps recognize the necessary conditions which could lead to truth. It remains issue biased. Even if it is a stray abstract thought, contemplation has to be about something. Most of the time the content of contemplation is not necessarily solemn as the term might indicate. It can be rather mundane, covering issues such as personal predicaments, social contingencies, social events and relationships, desired consequences, etc. The list can be unending. The significance, however, is in our engagement with contemplation and the way this influences our consciousness and action.

In a way at the time of origination inner contemplation-dialogues might not have any compelling utilitarian value. What remains engaging, however, are the ways in which such thinking processes emerge, the obvious dialogical-ness of notions influencing them and an intriguing urge to defy both servility and anonymity? Further their obvious dialogical nature makes them potent subconscious yearnings, which in turn can manifest into concrete actions. The adage 'listen to your self' has a lot of meaning. Contemplating the adjunct, urges the invocation to go beyond and manifest as action. But this can create problems. It can end up trying to construct knowledge and wisdom out of dreams; or in short become a dilettante's dalliance with Gandhi for instance as the *Vidushak* where the wise jester is a 'reckless innocent'? Perhaps it encourages us to surreptitiously replace the wise jester!

My contemplation brings me to a stereotype in the manner of a Gandhi: '*budhau*' old man. *Budhau* is much more than just an old man. Informed, responsible, concerned, visionary with a bagful of views, a *budhau* is a 'wise old man', a man who can discriminate, who has an insight, and above all can harmonize his, others, and society's good. He in other words can be relied upon to advice with humility and sincerity. Aware that wisdom is a matrix of happiness and morality, he is also conscious that while more morality reduces happiness, the opposite holds too; more happiness reduces morality. Morality is also about consciousness and not just principles. So regarding my quest for social clarity and whether one should engage with Gandhi, *budhau* cautions: remember that while you are going to a wise person, you nevertheless are equally wise. Moreover, Gandhi's penchant for a hands-on-approach might encourage me to author a narrative and be part of the text too; i.e. be a chronicler and an activist simultaneously. This can be problematic. We know that doubts and clarity are always at a handshaking distance albeit oblivious of each other. Questions will emerge from doubts but the statement of these doubts will be interrogative in nature. This in turn can bring in the problematic of causality and intentionality. Moreover every debate has some ground rules. Perhaps a reading of the *Prasna Upanishad* could help.

The *Prasna Upanishad* presents a very interesting study about the demanding nature of method in analysis and talking with wise men. The Upanishad starts with six wise seers recognizing that they needed more clarity about some issues. They approach an equally if not wiser seer who they think can help them. Pipplada on being approached tells them "stay here another year in fervent ardour, chastity and faith. You may then ask us questions according to your desire. If we know, we shall, indeed, answer them all". In effect, he makes it clear that he will try, but the questioners must contemplate and be clear about their queries. Further his explanations will by necessity be within his ability. Nevertheless, when Sukesa one of the seers asks a question, the import of his clarification becomes vague:

> Then Sukesa, son of Bharadvaja, asked him: Venerable Sir, Hiranyanabha, a prince of the Kosala Kingdom, came to me and asked this question:

'Bharadvaja, do you know the person with sixteen digits?' To the prince I made this reply: 'I know him not. If I knew him, why shouldn't I tell you? To his roots does he wither who tells a lie. Therefore, it behoves me not to tell an untruth.' In silence he mounted his chariot and went away. I ask you about the self-same person: Where is he?[4]

That Sukesa wants to know and is inclined to ask a valid question is one thing; but this introduction of the possibility of untruth, holding back, and doubt while involved in teaching and learning as indicated in the response of the prince is significant. Why does the Upanishad reintroduce this caveat/caution between the teacher and the taught when Pipplada has already said that a teacher/savant can answer only if he knew? Is it to draw attention to the distinction between conscience and consciousness or ethics and awareness? Perhaps it is indicating that ultimate clarity is a matter of conjuncture i.e. a state of affairs, and that maybe there never is 'the last word'. In effect can any teacher or world view for that matter be absolutely definitive? In effect the anguish of the wisest indicates that method cannot shake off intentionality altogether.

Lastly, we are informed that debate even between seers has to be informed by integrity, openness, perseverance, and transparency, and not just curiosity. The getting-to-know period is indicative of this. What can one deduce from all this to inform our present context? Well, knowledge is both a personal and a social endeavour. In other words when a method is used to analyze Gandhi, the logic should hold for evaluating us too. The intellectual or for that matter a social worker, a consciously created being, supposedly more mature than an ordinary person, is an adjunct of the individual. When provided with an independent world view, this adjunct which is an addition can easily turn contingent, a dependent on uncertainty. A product of conviction, the adjunct can take over from the individual. The person egged on by the adjunct can then end up being an opinionated purveyor of philosophies, concepts, and dogmas. Did this happen to Gandhi? Can this happen to us? It can. As for us seeking clarity from Gandhi, we have reached a threshold, and a threshold is a problematic.

As a location, the threshold where Tagore finds Gandhi is a complex and intriguing site. The threshold is an individual's access to a thoroughfare. In a house it is a place of departure and entry. For an individual it is the point where the personal and the social encounter. As a site of engagement, it can underscore change and continuity, being and becoming and even hope and despair as also of clarification and yearning. But for all its flux, the threshold exists as the given launching site of every 'moment' which is the initiation of our relentless transformation. Gandhi recognizes this as the place where the 'I', 'me', 'other', and the 'we' come together and transact. This is where Gandhi as a social server (worker) by taking a stand against the various binaries engaging him, sought to initiate a discourse which would harmonize his personal subjective sacrifice with the relationship of that personal struggle to the larger normative ideals of public good. While the openness of the site made him intrepid, the relatively intermittent nature of the site made him conscious of the significance of specific moments of vigour which evolve into awareness events.

Since the process is never easy Gandhi attempted to combine the individual, institution, and events into a *darshana (path)*, *niti (ethics)*, and *dharma (duty)*. And towards this he sought to bring together the 'I' and the 'me' while emphasizing the 'me'. But then the 'me' comes with its longing for the 'other' thus locating the 'other' both inside and outside as family, friends, and enemies. Maybe this is why he preferred the 'Isa Vasyam' and its invocation mantra:

> *Purnam adah, purnam idam, purnat purnam udacyate,*
> *purnasya purnam adaya purnam evavasisyate.*

> That is complete, this is complete, from completeness comes completeness,
> if completeness is taken away from completeness only completeness remains.

The mantra teaches the wisdom of *samata* and *samatvam* and cautions against easy interpretations and predicating of analysis on a primordial 'I'. As such, for Gandhi being a *satyagrahi* was not acquiring a qualification; it was recognizing the individual's transition and being at ease with one's own self. Perhaps due to his adjunct the *satyagrahi*, at times he mistook the threshold to be a *Laxman-rekha*. His conceptualization of 'brahmacharya' immediately comes to mind. For the individual the threshold remains a site under seize.

Gandhi and Gandhian thought

Gandhian thought is not comprised of just some simple rules and norms of do's and don'ts. The lure of Gandhi is more complex. This becomes more compelling when we recognize how significant Gandhi and his thoughts have become to the functioning of civil society in India and the inability of the state to shake him off. Gandhi himself was not enamoured with the term 'Gandhism'. But he did accept that he worked to a purpose and had some thoughts which informed his purpose. Over the years of his involvement in society these thoughts crystallized, and now we refer to them as 'Gandhian thoughts' if not Gandhism. While many swear by these, others are ready to recognize their significance, while still others consider them as mere homilies and good, albeit misplaced intentions. Interestingly even among those who don't hold by Gandhian thoughts, some of his practices seem to have taken root: hartal, non-cooperation, dharna, fasts, and swadeshi, to name some. From the right to the left of the political spectrum, from the employer to the employee and particularly the unemployed, from youth to women to the organized working classes all seem to be drawing something or the other from what Gandhi stood for, expounded, and practiced. And most of the time such borrowings seem to have a salutary influence in the respective engagements and emerging narratives. Perhaps we can say, 'down with Gandhism, long live Gandhi'.

Gandhi lived tradition. And tradition is a corpus of mentalities, intentions, social structures, and processes, which is both a collage and a scripting of change and continuity. Above all it is an endowment which makes and mars our entitlements. For Gandhi, this tradition is something always in the making: a memory, a script, and a narrative. Essentially tradition is neither in the giving of somebody nor can it be an off-the-shelf commodity. It is in this sense that we find civil society being inexorably drawn to Gandhi and his seminal concepts. Civil society groups seek to articulate a community's tradition as a continuum both as a narrative and as a memory of the community. But they are clear that the script is not in the giving of anybody, and that it is also a demanding undertaking. As Gandhi had put it, "Opposition to mills or machines is not the point. What suits our country most is the point. I am not opposed to the movement of manufacturing machines in this country. I am only concerned with what these machines are meant for".[5] The issue therefore is, 'why do we do what we do?' This is an engagement where Gandhi comes in and is a question of involvement.

A churning

With independence, the nature of the Indian milieu changed radically. The details and the nature of the emerging discourse between the oppressor, the oppressed, and the interlocutor changed. The Mahatma was assassinated and it was up to the interlocutors to continue with the nation's truncated aspirations of satya, swaraj, sarvodaya, satyagraha, and ahimsa. However, in a post-independence changed milieu, the interlocutors had to redefine their role and philosophy. As Ramamurti, one such interlocutor was to latter put it, "it was a question of power: capturing power, generating power and exercising power"; the interlocutor's role was to generate power.[6] In an emerging democracy the issue was to help people exercise authority. It is another matter that the business of capturing power became central to everything.

Six weeks after Gandhi's assassination some of his leading followers gathered at Sevagram, Wardha to try and come to terms with a couple of issues: with Bapu gone whom would they go to with the questions that independent India was asking, and what were they to do? The discussions were intense, introspecting, and illuminating.[7]

J.C. Kumarappa, trying to understand the emerging role of the interlocutor, felt that they were not able to "utilize the energies of these youths as we should have".[8] Kishorelal Mashruwala was more pointed, reasoning "that we do not now have the strength of character which our work requires",[9] and the Gandhians had to rediscover themselves and their roles as interlocutors.[10] While all of them wanted to deliver justice to the people, particularly the poor people of India for whom independence was just the first step, it was left to Nehru to clarify and who was honest enough to accept, "Until now the role of Congress was to oppose the British government; but that role is now over and done with – it has been fulfilled, in a manner of speaking. Congress has now to *govern*, not to oppose government. So it will have to function in a new way, staying within politics".[11] And he cautioned,

"In politics, one looks at the advantage of the moment. But what really matters is this: whether or not a certain action yields immediate advantage, it must be right in itself. This is a fundamental principle in all areas of life".[12] But then a narrative wherein the 'advantage of the moment' and 'right in itself' is expected to be in harmony is easily expressed, but not that easily bound together.

Once Nehru had separated the role of the state it was for Jayprakash Narayan to clarify the role of the Gandhian interlocutor. He summed it up, "Governments work within constraints. It is beyond the power of any government to undertake and complete constructive activities to their fullness. Such work requires freedom and independence of means. It requires research, experimentation and field work. Without these, constructive work will not acquire meaning. All this is beyond the ambit of governments. These are fields in which people have to get interested and involved directly".[13]

Subsequently other than those who wanted to associate with the state, many Gandhians went to various places all over the country and established organizations, institutions, and even initiate movements such as Sarva Seva Sangh, Gandhigram, khadigram, Bhoodan, Chipko, and so on. Essentially Gandhian, each of these nevertheless had a distinct import and learning curve. And each of them has left behind, or is still carrying, a distinct narrative.

Some concepts

At the core of Gandhian praxis is conscious involvement and participation along with prudence of ethics. Involvement is premised around three parameters: vision and mission; interlocutor, activist, or cadre; and lastly programme, that is intervention structures and processes logistics. In post-independence democratic India the role of non-state initiatives to influence and mediate socio-economic processes had been considerable. From the radical notion of democracy to what it means to call oneself an Indian, and to feel that one has both a right and a duty to think about one's personal and social destiny was the noble gift of independence. While those who wanted to exclusively work with the state went their way, there were others who felt that participation and involvement had to be broad based and organic to the process of nation building. And this meant conscious and explicit participation of each and every citizen in the structures and processes of making swaraj. While on the one hand it was recognized that independence did not remove the age-old oppressor – oppressed – interlocutor discourse, those who wanted to go beyond the state hegemony were acutely aware of the possibility of a new breed of 'Englishman' taking over and creating an *Englishtan*. And they also recognized that the most efficacious way in a democracy to question and oppose such threats lay in consciously making such reservations a part of the citizens nation building discourse. Consequently, while nation building in India has been a truly messy affair, to our merit this discourse has been a rejuvenating bedlam of the creative, the experimental, the confusing, and the opportunistic. It has been a vibrant organic argumentative narrative. That we continue to remain a vibrant democracy is ample tribute to an all-round alertness amongst all concerned: activists, academics, politicians, and of course the citizen. It is in reference to this clutter of 'alert nation building' that the seminal role of Gandhian thought and praxis stands out. The question is "'can Gandhian orientation be picked up and used for say nation building all by itself'", particularly since these thoughts are a product of a whole life of involvement, that is, they always seem to come with a practitioner? Moreover these had actually emerged as a consequence of struggles in South Africa. But then again, brahmacharya, ahimsa, satyagraha, swaraj, sarvodaya are ideas which are not exclusive innovations of Gandhi. They have been part and parcel of Indian psyche. However, it must be accepted that Gandhi not only revised, elaborated, and worked with them in South Africa; he subsequently expanded and expounded about them right through his involvement with the Indian independence struggles. This usage and engagement with the same concepts in very distinct and dissimilar social milieu has to be recognized before their efficacy in the Indian context is appraised. Moreover Gandhi himself insisted that over the years he, his practices, and his ideas did not remain the same and stagnant. Essentially while he sustained his core orientation, details were adjusted and modified. As far as he was concerned, for any analysis of his concepts, in case differences were discovered, his latest statement or position should prevail. Accordingly to grasp the rich nuances necessitates understanding the import of these concepts as used by Gandhi himself, first in South Africa and then in the India context during the independence struggle. But then it is not the ultimate arrival or product; the journey is equally important because the product and the process are inseparable. To quote Gandhi to Gandhi, how can we separate the means from the end; after all, no intervention comes without expectations? Ironically while Gandhi developed his concepts while struggling on behalf of a section of colonizers to acquire a better share of the colonial haul, latter he refined and enriched the same concepts to struggle on behalf of the colonized to oust the colonizers.

This will require clarity at three integrated levels. Firstly, how transformational were these concepts regarding the evolving personality of Gandhi himself, considering that while the concepts matured, he himself changed significantly? Secondly, while the efforts in South Africa were only implicitly political in that their narrative was not independent of the notion of power, after coming to India Gandhi had to explicitly respond to the political demands of the independence struggles and the issue of empowerment of Indians. We need to understand how these concepts responded to the necessity of having to adapt to new and radical demands. Lastly it will be useful to understand the value of these concepts as thought and praxis not just as a legacy, but also as conceptual instruments of social analysis and intervention. However it will be unfair to ignore Gandhi's unambiguous qualification. Gandhi while delivering a lecture about constructive work on 22 February 1940 to the Gandhi Seva Sangh, which he felt could do a lot of what he called post-graduate work and research for the various organizations he was associated with, asserted, "I love to hear the words: Down with Gandhism. An 'ism' deserves to be destroyed. I am eager to see Gandhism wiped out at an early date.... You should not give yourself over to sectarianism".[14] "I did not belong to any sect. I have never belonged to any sect. If any sect is established in my name after my death, my soul would cry out in anguish".[15] Later, on 16 March 1940 he again elaborated, "I have an horror of 'isms', especially when they are attached to proper names; more so because ahimsa abhors sects".[16] Gandhi was very heedful of the brooding menace of 'isms', an ism can easily replace an 'I' and 'we' with a hierarchic dominance prone 'us'.

Accordingly while the overall thrust has to be on trying to historically appraise how Gandhi conceptualized, elaborated, and worked with brahmacharya, satyagraha, swaraj, ahimsa, sarvodaya, industrialization, education, and trusteeship, first in South Africa and then in India, to explore and comprehend the seminal significance of Gandhi's thought and praxis, the analysis has to reveal it's intentionality. Therefore we first hope to trace Gandhi's personal progress from being what we refer to as a '*satyarthi*' to becoming a consummate '*satyagrahi*'; how an honest human being consciously evolves from being a truthful human being focused on living an honest life to a socially committed individual aspiring to help everyone live an honest life. Obviously this process drew inspiration from a vibrant ethos and was anchored on resilient concepts. As we proceed we will focus separately on the various concepts which aided Gandhi in formulating his praxis. Essentially we will try to recognize how and why Gandhi's ideas made him into an 'intrepid itinerant social worker' and not a political hegemon.

In a way this is where the notions of invocation and contemplation help. For Gandhi the daily prayer was not a ritual; it is recognition of the presence of the past in the present. For Gandhi the topic, the institution, and the individual all have to respond to *darshan, dharma,* and *niti* that is path, duty, and ethics. Not surprisingly we find him resonating with the savant of Varanasi, Kabir: '*Kabeera khada baazar; pooche sabka khair; na kesise dosti na kesise bair*' (Kabir stands in the marketplace with good wishes for all; he has no friends and has strife with none). For Gandhi: "Fighters do not always live at the barricade. They are too wise to commit suicide. The barricade life has always to be followed by the constitutional. That front is not taboo for ever".[17]

For Gandhi: "Every deviation from the straight path has meant a temporary arrest of the evolutionary revolution";[18] and "A non-violent revolution is not a programme of 'seizure of power'. It is a programme of transformation of relationships ending in a peaceful transfer of power".[19] The site, the agency, the engagement, the revelation, the vision, the mission, the sight and the insight, the being, the becoming, the knowing, and the known are all located within you. It manifests as the community, the self, self-realization and selfishness. Since social transformation and transition is a matrix of change and continuity, mankind is encumbered with the problematic of choice: of what, how, where, when, by whom, and of course the most contentious why. Above all the process of living is not just a mere cause-effect continuum. Social transformation is a complex transition influenced by an overabundance of ideas and individuals. Streamlining these is a process of continuity and change, wherein chance, necessity, and choice all play a considerable role which is both competitive and accommodative. Various streams of appealing world views and visions vie with each other and either consolidates or fades away depending on how they appeal essentially to the hegemonic authority and in a democracy, possibly the people. Gandhi's concepts seek to come to terms with the extremely capricious mix of change, continuity, chance, and choice that society engenders. The *satyarthi* to *satyagrahi* transformation is broadly a process from perception and assessment to appreciation and revaluation.

Chapter scheme

To begin we ask why we need to understand and draw inspiration from Gandhi, his thoughts and his praxis. While Gandhi's life can be divided into four phases, childhood and student life, *satyarthi* phase and *satyagrahi* phases in South Africa, and as a *satyagrahi* in India; we will study the last three phases. In Chapters 'A *satyarthi* in South Africa', 'Gandhi: a *satyagrahi*' and '*satyagrahi* Gandhi returns to India', we trace Gandhi's transformation from what we call a '*satyarthi*' to a '*satyagrahi*'. Given that while in South Africa Gandhi had to learn from unique conditions of having to relate to a constantly evolving combination of imperialism, indentured semi-slavery, migration, and apartheid, in these chapters, the effort is to recognize the indicators of form, spirit, and meaning of this transition. In these chapters we chronicle the history and also the travails of a conscientious person. Gandhi sought to reject pretentions; more precisely he sought to recognize the contradictions within these pretensions which are a part of our lifestyles offered gratis by society. In a subtle twist we actually find Gandhi sympathetic to the dilemmas of the pretender while disagreeing to the pretensions. The details of the transition indicate how nuanced and even individualistic the process of transition from *satyarthi* to *satyagrahi* can be.

During his stay in South Africa Gandhi tried to systematically understand and conceptualize the nature and nuances of his nascent but rapidly evolving orientation. Satya, ahimsa, brahmacharya, satyagraha, sarvodaya are markers he recognized and elaborated.

While he evolved from a *satyarthi* to a *satyagrahi* in South Africa, later in India he elaborated and consolidated his orientation. Chapters 'Morality and wisdom: brahmacharya, satya, ahimsa, satyagraha', 'Religion: case, brief, and argument' and 'Towards a world view: sarvodaya, *Hind Swaraj*, swadeshi, social service', focus on the concepts which Gandhi developed as a *satyagrahi* first in South Africa and then in India. Gandhi honed these through actual praxis. To be sensitive to this praxis we analyze the broad contours of the concepts with a distinctive thrust. To illustrate, ahimsa will be understood as *krodha tyāg* where *tyāg* is giving up of something only to acquire some other thing. Similarly, brahmacharya will be *trishna tyāg* i.e. renouncing longing of secure relationships of which celibacy is just one element. Sarvodaya we will argue seeks to sort out the quaint anomaly of how our entitlement of freedom a natural ability comes as if circumscribed with an endowment of fear, which is an apprehension of losing our possession, power and progeny. The last chapter takes a look at how people who accepted his ideas responded after his demise and also suggest alternatives for social transformation along Gandhian lines.

Overall our fundamental quest will remain on trying to explain the significance of the interlocutor's role in social transformation. An interlocutor's is a two-fold act: the first is to reveal, that is, to uncover, make apparent, and announce, while the second is to become involved in the apparent, that is become an activist; an activist in the Gandhian mould will have to be an interlocutor sensitive to the essential core of Gandhi's method and matrix, ahimsa, and satya. In other words engage and find peace with the natural and the man-made world.

Notes

1 Nandy (1992, 129).
2 *MGTEW* (2008, 20).
3 Bhattacharya (1997, 76).
4 Gupta (1991, 422).
5 Parel (2009); Dasgupta (1996).
6 Banerjee (1999).
7 Gandhi and Snell (2007); Sewagram Rachnatmak Karyakram ka vivaran: 1948.
8 Ibid. (30).
9 Ibid. (35).
10 Ibid. (34–35).
11 Ibid. (61).
12 Ibid. (71).
13 Ibid.
14 *MPWMG*, Vol. I (1986, 423).
15 Ibid.
16 Ibid. (61–64).
17 Ibid., Vol. II (1986, 446).
18 Ibid. (443).
19 Ibid.

2

A *SATYARTHI* IN SOUTH AFRICA

Mohandas Karamchand Gandhi was forty five years old when he returned to India from South Africa where he had stayed for twenty of his most formative years. His life in South Africa was one of learning, teaching, reflecting, and above all 'consciously practising' what he thought and taught. Sometimes we forget that while he might have been a mahatma to many, he was not a mahatma to himself. Life for him was not just a given, nor was he ready to accept it as just a matter of living. Perhaps this was because of the work he did, that by the time he was twenty five he was already one of the leaders of the expat Natal Indians exercising considerable influence among his compatriots. For him his role soon became a responsibility, an obligation. It was also an involvement which had to be respected as something which you undertake and make a part of yourself. In the process while he met many with whom he struck lasting friendship, he also had to relate with many adversarial others, relating with whom he had to create within himself the courage to defy and face antagonistic circumstances head-on. This defiance meant he had to confront and at times compromise with well-entrenched regressive ideas and practices. Some of these were at the individual level, while others were more systemic in nature. And to do this, he not only made hard choices, but also came up with ground-breaking pioneering ideas and concepts. While some were a re-working of older existing social values and ideas, many were profoundly original. The concepts which he employed, redrafted, and shaped such as satya, Seva, satyagraha, ahimsa, brahmacharya, and swaraj were infused with features and considerations which made them exceptional. For him, when he came back to India for good, these ideas and concepts were clear and apposite. In India he wanted to practice them, of course with the qualification that practice should keep teaching the adept to adopt and keep improving. The question is who is an 'adept' in serving the people and the nation? Broadly his definition would be one who is courageous, selfless, poised, and who inspires through dedication to social service. And these are qualities to acquire which requires '*sadhana*'– dedicated striving. But more importantly Gandhi's advancement from a timid boy, to an unflinching *satyagrahi* was due to his initiatives, activities, and what he called experiments in South Africa: a *karmabhoomi* chance and necessity chose for him; and further how this 'chance and necessity' guided him particularly in the first phase of his stay in South Africa.[1]

In South Africa he started as a professional lawyer who had come on a short assignment. He however stayed back and gained considerable monetary success. But he soon restricted the monetary aspect of his practice to focus on helping his fellow Indians. Later he gave up his law practice altogether. He simultaneously started to radically redesign his life style. He was acquiring a calling. Not surprisingly by January 1897 when he was returning back to South Africa from India he would claim, "I do not return here with the intention of making money, but of acting as a humble interpreter between the two communities [of Europeans and Indians]. There is a great misunderstanding between the two communities, and I shall endeavour to fulfil the office of interpreter as long as both the communities do not object to my presence".[2] Clearly he was already aspiring to be more than just a professional migrant lawyer.

The 20 years that he lived in South Africa can be separated into two phases: the *satyarthi* phase from 1893 to about 1903 and the *satyagrahi* phase from 1904 until his return to India in 1914. Sustaining these were emerging ideological convictions such as tyaag, satyagraha, brahmacharya and so on. These initiatives were experiments wherein he sought to fine-tune, consolidate, and proclaim his own convictions and also help likeminded to walk a similar, if not the same path. Broadly the first decade of his stay from 1893 to 1903 was spent seeking clarity about the nature of social and personal problems at a personal level i.e. what these meant to him. Maybe we could say he acquiring a world view! This was what can be called his '*satyarthi phase*'.

This was a period when he was reorienting and cautious. All his involvement revolved around his profession, self, family, and the local Indian community. His activities influenced by chance and necessity began with him needing a job and chance (he of course was qualified) offering him one in South Africa. However this period also found him involved in a concatenation of 'awareness building events' which made him personally sentient about his personal and social life and living. These events had an enormous bearing on his subsequent orientation both as an individual and as a member of a community. To illustrate, in the Dada Abdulla case he suggested that the cousin who had lost the case should be allowed to pay in instalments, failure of which in the first place was the reason behind the litigation. He soon became an activist of the Indian community's political cause, respected not only for his competence in drafting but also for seeking compromise rather than stretching litigation. Essentially this decade was a period when he was becoming clear about what being social meant for him as distinct from both personal and social life in general. He now had a set of problems which neededsorting out.

The next ten years beginning from about the end of 1903 to 1914 when he left South Africa for good, were what can be termed the '*satyagrahi phase*'. During this period he actively sought and implemented solutions to the problems the earlier phase had posed. In the earlier phase the Pietermaritzburg incidence helped him recognize a problem. During this phase he actively sought to both unravel the cause behind the problem and suggest abiding solutions. Towards this we find him leading agitations, going to jail, conceptualizing satyagraha, writing *Hind Swaraj* and so on. While in the earlier phase the matrix of chance and necessity was restricted to offering opportunities and perhaps helping recognize problems, not necessarily resolving them, he now personally started to actively work on alternative modules to meaningfully influence social transformation processes. This of course had to encompass both the personal and the social. As a *satyagrahi* he hoped to inform history.

This phase started with him launching the journal *Indian Opinion* and announcing it as the voice of the Indian community. The Indian Opinion was to be a platform to carry news for Indians in South Africa and help others know Indians. While this was an effort to unite all Indians in South Africa, the Phoenix Settlement which he established in 1904 was meant to engage more actively with community living and cultivating community spirit. The narrative of this phase became more complex with Gandhi trying to be within it, i.e. actively participating in the unfolding of the narrative and outside it i.e. directing the discourse as a mentor. He was himself becoming a *satyagrahi* while facilitating and encouraging others to become *satyagrahis*; a complex task in which he often overlooked that while he himself was charting an unknown course, others might still have to first go through their individual *satyarthi* phase at their own pace. At a personal level he cut down his law practice, simplified his personal needs by accepting an ascetic life style, got involved in spiritual discourses mediating between the transactional and the transcendental, accepted brahmacharya, began experimenting and working out a care and cure regimen for a healthy life style and so on. At the social level within months after involving in raising an ambulance corps during the Zulu rebellion we find him getting involved in 'passive resistance' against the Transvaal Asiatic Registration Act requiring all Asiatic to re-register. Later this essentially reactive passive resistance was transformed into the more dynamic and ahimsa permeated satyagraha: not just resistive action against exploitation, but active mutual resolving of exploitation without resorting to violence. In the *Hind Swaraj* he writes, "passive resistance is a method of securing rights by personal suffering: it is the reverse of resistance by arms. When I refuse to do a thing that is repugnant to my conscience, I use soul-force".[3] Perhaps Gandhi was seeking to go beyond passive transactional processes of conflict resolution.

This was a phase when he as a *satyagrahi* was offering solutions to personal and social problems with a certain degree of certainty. This was also a phase when he understood and came to terms with the true import of possession, possessiveness and tyāg, equability and self-control, truth, ahimsa and brahmacharya. One would naturally ask the question: why then did he leave South Africa? One reason could be that in this *satyagrahi* phase, in his pre-occupation, he unintentionally was not sympathetic enough to the requirement of many of his colleagues who although involved with him, might have been requiring a *satyarthi* period of individual preparation. It must be understood that he was interacting with a very heterogeneous and disparate group. Another reason could be that while an ashram can be a site for the orientation training of *satyarthis*, it might not be the right place as the headquarters of 'satyagraha' as a movement. Perhaps there were also some postulations that ashram norms were the most conducive for a *satyagrahi*.

On 19 December 1914 Gandhi left South Africa for good. His condition when he left is aptly described by C. F. Andrews,

> His work in S. Africa is *done*. . . . He must go, both for his own sake and for the community's. Yes! For the community's: for if he stays on he will dwarf everyone else and there will be no leaders here for at least another generation. . . . He does everything – he *will* do everything: and people simply get to lean on him more and more and the selfish ones take advantage of his goodness. . . . He is one of the best men in the world! . . . He has made the noblest fight that has been made for years, and I cannot bear to think that it should all end in some great and huge mistake made in haste . . . but persisted in because of a mind distracted or outworn.[4]

Within this deeply perceptive analysis are some very unsettling but pertinent questions. Can the *agraha*/obsession of satyagraha become a handicap? What could Andrews an academic and a priest committed to a lifetime of service have meant when he says, 'if he stays on he will dwarf everyone else and there will be no leaders here for at least another generation'? Why did the *satyagrahi* land up in a situation where 'He does everything – he will do everything: and people simply get to lean on him more and more and the selfish ones take advantage of his goodness'? Is it possible that Gandhi had still to comprehend the contingent nature of a *satyagrahi's* role? Do we see a mixing up of serving-for-a-cause with serving per se? Is it possible that '*aparigraha*' by enjoining *tyaag* of material possession inadvertently encourage 'possessiveness' of some other perhaps psychological kind? Did Gandhi mix up solving conflicts with resolving contradictions because the satya or truth of solving a conflict can very well be the illusion of resolving the contradiction behind the conflict?

Andrews' missive to Gokhale is in many ways an indication of some very complex issues. Getting people to understand about social problems is one thing; getting them to come together to struggle to solve the problem is altogether different. Change and continuity in social transformation is an engagement with authorities who along with hegemony have a world view of their own. Satyagraha could be the means, but the ends have to reflect a contestation with authority. The problem is how should this dialogic process be mediated? Gandhi's satyagraha did unsettle and discountenance those in authority. But in all this the local African people were missing! As a struggle between one set of outsiders with another, struggles inevitably mean a contest of 'access to the spoils'. Complicating everything was the fact that the Indian community was not a homogeneous bloc.

The transition of Gandhi configures around three fundamentals: the question of the personal and the social, distinct but mutual; on why Gandhi needed Ashrams; and the issue of tyāg and the ambience and expectations it generates. Our effort will be to comprehend these very demanding and complex questions along with the significance of the *satyarthi* and *satyagrahi* as distinct phases in the emergence of Gandhi as an *itinerant intrepid social-worker*. The evolution from *satyarthi* to a *satyagrahi* is the process of enablement of the conscious to conscientiousness that is awareness to scrupulousness. This is a deliberate movement from passive acceptance of the duality of the personal and the social within oneself, to seizing the significance of this duality. It is a complex process of evolving instincts, natural tendencies, racial and communal memories, and individual sensitization and maturing of perceptions which instigate deliberate efforts; it is a movement towards individual praxis. However, an individual never becomes a complete *satyagrahi*. The individual's being and becoming are re-rendered by the individual's matutinal conscious, maturing. Perhaps this is why Gandhi remained process oriented in his involvements.

While Gandhi believed that people were essentially truthful at a personal level, from personal experience he found that, at a social level this being truthful acquires a more complex and demanding nature. Moreover given the contradictory and contentious nature of society, wanting to be truthful might not be enough. It needs being clear about what being truthful entails, and while imbibing this ethos, making it an intimate quality of oneself. Further it is quite possible that 'being consciously truthful' and not just truthful by nature or default is a step beyond the existential needs of living. Thought, experience, and the senses can between them throw up conflicting processes of obtaining knowledge about truth. Moreover, in complex societies this discourse about truth – existential, perceived, or theorized – and having to take positions is either due to compulsions or choice. Complicating everything further, for the individual, this truth manifests distinctly as personal and social cognition which need not be in conformity.

Satyarthi: a phase

While a lot has been written, analyzed, and conceptualized about satyagraha and the *satyagrahi*, and rightly so, we know relatively very little about the urge, compulsions, and concerns of the people who become a *satyagrahi*. Who are the people who want to be a *satyagrahi*? What is the requisite background of such an individual? What are the compulsions which urge them to take up such arduous life time commitments? Are they products of various spontaneous, sporadic social events, where such events are awareness creating social episodes or incidents for the concerned individuals? Do such dedications require specific competences, credibility, and commitments? Obviously underlying all this is another reality: not everybody wants to become a *satyagrahi* even while accepting the qualities of openness, receptivity, and sharing as a personal credo. Lastly perhaps for the *satyagrahi* this stage becomes a prelude to becoming a sadagrahi where self-liberation becomes self-realization: an open-minded blending of the personal and the social.

While many such questions come up, a *satyagrahi* essentially evolves through a demanding process from being just an element of the social milieu. It can begin when a person is exposed to, involved in, or affected by some awareness events. Active association in events with other people over a period of time in turn leads to an increase in knowledge about the milieu which leads to introspection. Past events become a corpus of memory. This memory becomes the first step which makes the individual recognize the tense interdependence of the personal/private and the social/political that expresses one's being. Perhaps this is also when the individual recognizes the sharp distinction between the intuitive and the conscious which manifest as the '*I-Me* and the *We-Us*' interface. While becoming critical the individual simultaneously starts understanding the systemic nature of social issues and problems: systemic in that the causes and resolutions of such issues and problems are not necessarily in the individuals doing or undoing because the individual still remains heavily dependent on chance and necessity. The enhanced consciousness however also indicates that social transition and transformation are processes of change and continuity impact both the personal and the social. Further while the matrix of change and continuity unfolds both at the personal and the social level, a simmering tension continues between them. Engaging with this simmering tension the individual soon gets involved in a complex discourse between innocent seeming binaries such as ends and means, rights and duties, wants and needs, what should change and what should continue and so on. In effect the individual starts trying to come to terms with 'personal intentionality'. Such a person it can be argued, becomes a '*satyarthi*': one for whom 'experience provides the vantage point for making epistemological moves' first at the level of the self and then beyond.

A *satyarthi* is one who is seeking truth as a personal ethos. Grappling with seemingly personal issues which also seem to have an apparent social bearing, her question is: what is wrong? The query as yet is not as to what is correct or what should be the nature of response to whatever is wrong. Of course the person can look for readymade solutions, adapt and adopt. Generally solutions are sought alone by oneself or with others facing similar problems. But for a *satyarthi*, it necessitates critically and consciously abjuring the urge to accept readymade solutions. The word '*satyarthi*' is a compound of '*satya*' with '*arthi; arthi* means seeking after (in this case truth) and its significance for the individual. While truth can caution us, particularly against exclusivism, and help us establish a harmonious relationship between the personal and the social, two perpetually contending facets of our being, for the *satyarthi*, the nucleus of motivation is first an appraisal by the personal the personal, and then by the social. Of particular importance for a *satyarthi* is the significance of seeking and clarity. In effect this indicates bipolarity: 'I know' and 'I know that I know.' This 'I know that I know' is what has the potential to motivate the person towards further conscious action. But the 'I know' can be a restriction on the critical creativity of the sagacious 'I know that I know', which can offer meaningful insights. These need elaboration.

Individuals tend to try and balance the distinct but conjoined facets of their being: the personal and the social. Specific social events and the experiences of these events influence and demarcate individual attitudes and understandings. Such understandings make an individual appreciate the real nature and implication of the conjoining of the personal and the social, both as a lived comprehension and as a prospective potentiality. Living then becomes a continuum of events, experiences, and alert response in a helical cycle with the vector firmly directed towards personal well-being.

An individual's daily existence is a continuous process of interacting and contending with the dominant hegemonic discourse, a process which seeks to construct the individual. This in a way is the 'spirit of involvement' which makes the individual a social being. For the individual this spirit of involvement indicates that while the individual experiences events wherein the personal seeks to outmanoeuvre the imperatives of the social, the social continues to remains partial to the social protocol. In effect, in the occurrence of such events, individuals start finding their contemporary location in relation to the milieu. But in the process of trying to outmanoeuvre the social and assert personal aspirations, the individual experiences an inevitable tension between contending but inherent imperatives. The subject, who experiences the tension and the experience of the event, together can be called an awareness event. Through a series of such events wherein the individual is forced to, rather forces himself to interrogate the emergent, the individual starts becoming a *satyarthi*. To illustrate, in a market economy people are encouraged to consume even splurge so as to maintain the resilience of the market. But the consequences are that in the process as individuals they tend to become physically unhealthy if not financially broke. With integrity and discernment a *satyarthi* is able to manoeuvre through such enigma.

Due to the dichotomy between the individual's personal and social and the ever-changing landscape of social relationships, anger and compassion can co-exist. For a *satyarthi* who is in a transition mode this can become a challenging problematic. Either she resolves it or her orientation will get structured into a 'doing good syndrome' or cynicism. Normally anger and compassion should not at the same time become elements of personal or social manoeuvre. While the first seems to belong to the personal and the other to the social, as a matter of fact they belong to both domains. Actually while passion is intrinsic to both, the distinction is akin to that of humility and humbleness; humility as compassion retains anger while humbleness forsakes it.

The problem as Gandhi was to realize is that we tend to reduce anger and compassion into issues of transaction which we then ritualize into modes of behaviour and relationship. His forcing an unprepared Kasturba to take social positions, insisting on not taking gifts, or treating a leper all by himself, all indicate how unprepared Gandhi was about anger and compassion at this stage of his life. Further convictions and intentions are not necessarily alien to each other. *Satyarthi* Gandhi had still to come to terms with the volatile cluster of anger, compassion, intentions, and convictions.

But in these ten years, Gandhi became clear about the distinction between conscious and conscientiousness. He was able to comprehend the role of the reformer as being part and apart from society, and the distinction between such a person's self and social interests as well as the distinction between possession and sharing. Perhaps within this comprehension lay the germ of the nascent concepts of ahimsa and satya as well as the significance of the contradictions within the generic notions of anger and compassion. However, perhaps in all this Gandhi was overlooking the 'me' in the 'I' while making a fetish of a very indistinct 'us'? We all need a peg to picket ourselves; but the peg is not necessarily one of our making. The genesis of the post-independence Gandhian's failure to appeal to large sections of the youth perhaps lies in not recognizing this aspect of Gandhi's personal odyssey. Gandhi too needed to be a *satyarthi* first. In the period of post-independence, before combating the problematic of development and poverty on behalf of the people, Gandhians forgot the necessity of an apprenticeship, i.e. forgot the necessity of them first becoming a *satyarthi*.

England, South Africa: Gandhi as *satyarthi*

By the time Gandhi reached South Africa on 24 May 1893, he had already experienced the realities, illusions, and consequences of living as an immigrant in an unfamiliar society. While on the one hand he was finding his way around the vagaries of an alien milieu, he was slowly albeit surely coming to understand the enormity of human potentialities and the meaning of continuous inner growth. Along with making a living as a lawyer we find him prospecting the significance of an individual's inner dignity, an inner enablement which releases every one of us so as to be able to respond to personal potentialities without trampling upon those of others. In South Africa young Gandhi was acquiring a new persona, that of an interlocutor and a leader: two roles distinct but contingent, forged and tempered first by circumstances and then by choice and personal initiatives.

When he left India for the first time, Gandhi was leaving behind a wife with a little child, who could not read, thereby forefeiting all privacy; a mother to whom he made specific vows of abstaining from sex, alcohol, and meat; a caste leadership which opposed his travelling overseas and ostracised him; and a joint family which was investing on him, hoping for a better future for all of them. Until then he had had a relatively secure life and had no idea about the true nature of society and its discriminations, intolerance, and oppression. In England for the first time he realized and experienced what independent living and personal decision making meant. He slowly started acquiring personal characteristics' and clarity of thinking which in later life would be part of what he was to be. In England he learned a lot.

Back home July 1891 a combination of factors found him struggling to establish himself as a lawyer. While his drafting was reasonably good, he found himself stiff and tongue tied in court. An ill-advised effort on his part to influence the political agent in Rajkot whom he had met in London, seeking to plead for his brother ruined any possibility of diwanship in Porbandar. The prospect of settling in Porbandar had to be given up. Trying to establish a practice in Bombay he found he was going nowhere. Unable to establish himself in Bombay he moved to Rajkot where his income remained meagre. Meanwhile the family was growing with the addition of another son Manilal.

Gandhi was finding himself in an unhappy situation. For a London trained lawyer to have to do freelancing in a small town and not be in a city Like Bombay was trying to say the least. Opportunely an opening beckoned in South Africa. Dada Abdulla and Sons were Muslim traders from Porbandar who were in need of a lawyer who while being conversant in Gujarati and English would also know the language and procedures of the courts to represent them. Gandhi found the offer appealing. In his autobiography he says he 'wanted somehow to leave India', and here was 'a tempting opportunity of seeing a new country, and of having new experience'. Gandhi arrived in the Natal port of Durban on 24 May 1893.

Right from the first week of arrival, Gandhi ran into the blatantly vicious world of racism. "In Durban, a magistrate had him removed from a court session for wearing a turban. He set off by train for the Transvaal, but at Pietermaritzburg, the Natal capital, he was thrown off the train by a policeman and spent the night on a freezing station platform. Proceeding the next day by train, he had to change to the stagecoach at Charlestown, where there was a break in the line. During this trip, he was forced to sit on the outside of the coach and assaulted by a company official. On arrival at Johannesburg, he was refused accommodation in the Grand National Hotel".[5]

Gandhi did not lose his bearing. He was shaken but took things in his stride. He certainly did not allow the issue to fester within himself. While working on Dada Abdulla's case, he had to relate to A.W. Baker who besides being a lawyer in charge of the case was a lay preacher. This brought Gandhi into the world of missionaries and the various facets of Christianity both as a proselytizing religion and a spiritual quest. The interaction made him become interested in religion but in a non-denominational way. His quest at this juncture remained personal.

In the spring of 1894 Gandhi won the case between Dada Abdulla and his cousin. But instead of pushing the cousin into bankruptcy, Gandhi suggested a compromise advising that the cousin make payments through a fresh instalment system to which the parties agreed and were the better off for it. This option of compromise became a characteristic feature of Gandhi's future approach to curb the debilitating impact of litigation. This radical compromise was Gandhi's coming of age. The now 25-year-old would never turn his back to the core sympathy of love and care, and would always insist that these are beyond transactional adjustments.

Since the case was solved Gandhi now had to return. But he stayed back. Later in his autobiography[6] he wrote, "Thus God laid the foundation of my life in South Africa and sowed the seed of the fight for national self-respect". Gandhi had come to South Africa as a lawyer to sort out a commercial dispute. In a perfect synchronisation of chance and necessity, with a conspicuous measure of choice, he now became an activist for a political cause while remaining a lawyer as a legitimate prop.

The *satyarthi* graced with an inner tenacity was rapidly evolving. During this period to try and find answers to the anomalies he found in the milieu, Gandhi kept a sustained dialogue with Raychandbhai.[7] Besides these semi-theological albeit profoundly human discussions, he also sought to broaden his social exposure and information base particularly regarding social intervention strategies. In April 1895, he visited a Trappist monastery in the Natal highlands and was very impressed by what he saw. What really impressed him about the Trappists and their monastery was the lack of racial feeling in the monastery. Whereas elsewhere in Natal, there was 'a very strong prejudice against the Indian population', the Trappists 'believe in no colour distinctions. The Natives are accorded the treatment as the whites. . . . The contrast with other white Christians was stark. 'It proves conclusively', that a religion appears divine or devilish, according as its professors choose to make it appear'.[8]

His growing maturity as a *satyarthi* can be seen in the memorials he drafted for the Indian community vis-à-vis the state and the white community. Each of these was situation and circumstance perfect. "The Natalians were asked why it was necessary 'to make a man pay heavily for being allowed to remain free in the Colony after he has already lived under bondage for ten years'". The Secretary of State for the Colonies "was reminded that it was 'against the spirit of the British Constitution to countenance measures that tend to keep men under perpetual bondage'". The Viceroy was told that the "special, obnoxious poll-tax" was designed to ensure that the Indian in Natal "must for ever remain without freedom, without any prospect of ever bettering his condition".[9]

It is clear he now knew to a great extent what was wrong. However he still had to work out as to what was correct, rather acceptable, and how to bring about these correctives. But for these he still needed some fundamental reorientation regarding the true nature of a social milieu as a whole. He was living in South Africa but was very Indian and India-centric. This becomes clear in the way he sought to explain to an Indian audience as to how Indians were treated in South Africa. Gandhi complained that a law in Durban specified that natives and indentured labourers required passes to go about at night. This for Gandhi "presupposes that the Indian is a barbarian. There is very good reason for requiring registration of a native in that he is yet being taught the dignity and necessity of labour. The Indian knows it and he is imported because he knows it".[10] Again, on 26 September he elaborated on how the authorities,

> desire to degrade us to the level of the raw Kaffir whose occupation is hunting, and whose sole ambition is to collect a certain number of cattle to buy a wife with, and then, pass his life in indolence and nakedness. . . . We are hemmed in on all sides in South Africa'. In Natal they were under the 'yoke of oppression'. 'It is for you, our elder and freer brother, to remove it'.[11]

Gandhi at this stage was looking out for simple straight forward answers. As far as South African society was concerned he was on a narrow bandwidth. Probably this was because he still essentially was a lawyer working on a brief: only that he was now writing a brief for the South African Indian community, and the Indian community generally maintained a distance from the black African Kaffir. That the problem had larger implications was still not a part of his brief. His orientation and world view still had to incorporate the 'raw kaffir', not just as an equal fellow human being, but perhaps as someone who was exploited even more than the Indians.

After a seven-month visit to India, on his return to South Africa in January 1897, Gandhi realized that he could no more continue to just articulate a problem for himself as an individual. Actually, in India, he was already talking from public platforms. Such involvement Gandhi was soon to learn has consequences both for the concerned individual and the community. News had reached the people in South Africa about the distribution in India of the 'Green Pamphlet', which elaborated the living condition of Indians in South Africa. Editorials in the local media argued that Gandhi's statements had "justly roused the resentment of the European colonist".[12] Gandhi had now become a hate-figure among the whites of Natal on account of what he was supposed to have said during his travels in India. It is beside the point that many of these writers took liberties with what they attributed to Gandhi. For Gandhi, the issue was to recognize that solutions are not necessarily sequential to the explication of problems. As an aspiring public figure, he had to move on, which meant that he not only had to suggest solutions but he had to shoulder the consequences also. More crucially he had to move beyond being just a lawyer handling a brief. His briefs henceforth would be from and in the public domain: the people's courts out there in the marketplace, and debates in the marketplace come with built-in norms distinct from those of the sanitized law-courts.

When he landed although accompanied by a white Durban solicitor, he was attacked by a mob and was rescued by the wife of the local Superintendent of Police.[13] Later Gandhi was smuggled out to the security of the local police station dressed in the garb of a government peon by the Superintendent of Police. He now had to accept the complexity and perhaps the humour of the issues involved. As an individual he could look at an issue in isolation as being a unique problem. But viewed from a social perspective the same issue seems to acquire diversity and appear as a cluster of problems which should have a cluster of solutions. The individual is at best a courier. True to his personal progression, *satyarthi* Gandhi refused to prosecute his attackers. However, his dialogues between the personal and the social within himself became sharper.

However, his inner quest continued, and he continued to try to understand the nature of the society he lived in. But he now faced a dilemma. The South Africa where he lived was a cauldron of vitiating contradictions between the British, Boers, native Africans, and coloured emigrants (Indian, Chinese, and Malay), each trying to grab a slice of the wealth being generated by the booming economy. Gandhi as a lawyer-leader of the Indians had to articulate the Indian community's aspirations and self-interest.

But this was not so simple. While some Indians were opposed to helping the British, Gandhi felt this was a 'golden opportunity' to disprove that the Indians were interested only in 'money-grubbing and were merely a deadweight upon the British'. Gandhi's point of view prevailed. Gandhi helped raise an ambulance corps of 1,100 volunteers. While the Gujarati merchants discreetly stayed away, others, particularly the working class, joined; the efforts of the Indian mule-force were appreciated. Gandhi did manage to sustain the community's complex ambiance of desires and illusions.

At a more personal level, the maturing *satyarthi* was going through all kinds of complex issues. His family was growing with the arrival of Ramdas in 1898 and Devdas in 1900. The education of Harilal and Manilal posed a dilemma. Although coloured children were not wanted in European schools, Gandhi with his contacts could have found a place for his children. But he was against this 'favour and exception'. Moreover he was not sure how a Hindu child would be treated in the Christian schools, not to forget that as the only coloureds his children might be at the receiving end of their white peers. He also chose not to send his children to the missionary schools for indentured labourer's children. Education of the kids therefore was left to himself, his wife, and an English governess whom he recruited. The outcome was very inadequate and unsatisfactory because he could not spare even an hour to devote 'to their literary education with strict regularity'. In his preoccupation with himself he overlooked the children's need for peer association.

His relationship with Kasturba remained one-sided with him retaining the right to have the last word. In an episode which he describes in his autobiography he talks about how he was ready to throw her out of the house when she refused to clean the chamber pot of a guest who happened to be a converted Christian born of very low caste parents. While this certainly can be construed as being remiss and inconsistent, he otherwise was becoming more compassionate. Cleaning chamber pots and thereby engaging with the pernicious caste system was no fad or indulgence. It spoke of considerable social enlightenment and a desire to engage with complex intractable issues. But while the episode showed considerable social clarity and commitment, obviously he still had to come to terms with anger. Evidently he was struggling to comprehend the entrenched dimensions of this (not uncommon to human kind) personal proclivity to anger and that this could not be obliterated by social commitments however meritorious these might be. Complicating things further were two other formative issues: that of possession and longing to do social service. In terms of possession and consumption, as a personal persuasion Gandhi was cutting down the family's needs and wants. But he also wanted to assert this as a social conviction. An opportunity arose when he was given gifts when he and the family were returning to India. After some pondering and against stiff opposition from Kasturba, he decided to return all the gifts he and the family were given when they were to leave South Africa. His arguments which he put forth in the autobiography were: "What right had I to accept all these gifts? Accepting them, how could I persuade myself that I was serving the community without remuneration?

All the gifts, excepting a few from my clients, were purely for my service to the community, and I could make no difference between my clients and co-workers; for the clients also helped me in my public work".[14]

The dilemma of this reasoning was indicated by his well-wisher, Parsee Rustomjee, who pointed out that the return might 'lead to the misconstruction of motives in the donor as in the recipient'. For Gandhi the issue was personal in terms of his understanding. That the separate acts of giving and receiving gifts is always a two-way social act, and is more than a personal issue, had still to become obvious because he still was a *satyarthi* trying to comprehend and come to terms with his own personal-centric values.

A paradigm shift

For Gandhi the Anglo-Boer war of 1899 opened a larger vista demanding a more complex world view. On the one hand he recognized that his "personal sympathies were all with the Boers". But he also felt that I had yet no right in such cases to enforce my individual convictions".[15] Moreover he "felt that, if I demanded rights as a British citizen, it was also my duty, as such, to participate in the defence of the British Empire".[16] At the same time, given his struggles against racism, he had no illusions about the intentions of the imperial masters. In effect, as long as he was staying in South Africa, it was not sure as to where he belonged. However, thanks to constant interaction he was becoming clear about the nature of the local Indian community and the associated dilemma of serving such a community. He wrote, "I had some bitter experiences. I saw that I could not so easily count on the help of the community in getting it to do its own duty, as I could in claiming for its rights. At some places I met with insults, at others with polite indifference. . . . It is the reformer who is anxious for the reform, and not society, from which he should expect nothing better than opposition, abhorrence and even moral persecution".[17] Posed with such contradictory responses he then asks a very pertinent and entrenched question: "Why may not society regard as retrogression what the reformer holds dear as life itself?"[18] A professional, where the profession links the individual to society, and the nature of his links with the community depend upon the nature of the community. Contradictions arise from the fact that while the individual accepts the profession, he remains reluctant to incorporate the evolving demands of the community on him as a person into his professional self or vise-versa. This split within the individual due to the demands of the personal and the professional is due to the evolving nature of change and continuity in society. The problem lies in the fact that by himself the individual cannot eliminate this contradiction, more so because he finds himself relishing the benefits of the same. As an upshot, it becomes very difficult for the individual to project a social contradiction-free identity. The Indians in South Africa were there as individuals; for them the focus was the personal and the social was to serve the personal. But Gandhi realizing the underlying contradictions and complexities wanted to reverse this short-sighted view. In his own case he accepts that he had to make choices: choices which would mean becoming a more composite human being and preferably enunciate a new praxis distinct from the prevailing one of reification and alienation.

Sure enough, after six weeks' involvement with the ambulance corps, Gandhi "felt that my work was no longer in South Africa but in India. Not that there was nothing to be done in South Africa, But I was afraid that my main business might become merely money-making".[19] At this juncture Gandhi finds himself in a mixed-up situation. He needed the profession to sustain him as an individual and also sustain the family. His professional involvement was chronicling his social being, and it was becoming increasingly difficult to keep apart the personal and the social. Moreover his social cum professional involvement was becoming a struggle as an Indian, fighting for and on behalf of Indians in an alien milieu against odds which ranged from the racial to the spiritual, all the while looking up to India and to his own Indian-ness for inspiration. And in all this he was also concerned with a growing and disturbing insight: it is the reformer who is anxious for the reform. In effect, he was realizing that "up to now there had been in me a mixed desire. The spirit of self-sacrifice was tempered by the desire to lay by something for the future".[20] It was this spirit which took him back to India and hopefully a broader canvas to work with. In October 1901, Gandhi along with his family returned to India. The *satyarthi* had arrived at a new threshold.

Back in India he went about trying to establish a practice by giving the personal all the opportunity. But within 14 months he gave it up and returned to South Africa. While he reasoned that 'God has never allowed any of my own plans to stand', he also accepted that he was 'brief less'. Gandhi the lawyer had failed to break into the ranks of the lawyers in the High Court. By definition a lawyer's merit is judged by skills and experience pertaining to the local. And Gandhi was now an outsider. The *satyarthi* had to take some hard decisions. The cable from the Natal Indian Congress requesting him to come was a reprieve. Chance, necessity, and, this time, choice once again took him back to South Africa.

Notes

1 Guha (2013, 57); Gandhi, Rajmohan (2006).
2 *CWMG*, Vol. 2 (118–26).
3 Parel (2009, 88).
4 Guha (2013, 506).
5 Hyslop (2011, 35).
6 *An Autobiography* (2004, 130).
7 Guha (2013, 86–87).
8 Ibid. (87); *CWMG*, Vol. 1 (222–28).
9 *CWMG*, Vol. 1 (229–44).
10 Guha (2013, 103)
11 *CWMG.*, Vol. 2 (50–60).
12 Guha (2013, 109).
13 Ibid. (117).

14 *An Autobiography* (2004, 202).
15 Ibid. (197).
16 Ibid. (198).
17 Ibid. (200).
18 Ibid.
19 Ibid. (201).
20 Ibid. (241).

3
GANDHI
A *satyagrahi*

The *satyagrahi* phase

This was a highly nuanced complex multi-faceted phase evolving over stages. Gandhi returned to South Africa in the last week of November 1902. Once again he ran into a malevolent conflation of two distinct texts, racism and imperialism. This was a new state of affairs which reflected some of the realities of India. The whites of South Africa were colonialist and racists who wanted South Africa to be theirs, and if they had to share it with anyone, it had to be on their terms. In social terms they felt threatened by the Asians, particularly Indians, because these races not only brought in a different ethos, but were potential competitors in every sense.

Overall the conditions were not as benign as when he had come the first time. The local bureaucrats, some of whom had worked in the Indian subcontinent recognized his competence and the dependence of the Indian community on his inputs. They decided to cut him out. The Indian community was helpless. At the same time Gandhi had to accept that he was not one of the locals; he was also not an expatriate with similar stakes. As such his role in the processes of change and continuity would remain restricted to advice.

Gandhi decided to call the state's bluff. He decided to stay. He reasoned that otherwise "the community will be hounded out of the country, besides being thoroughly robbed. . . . It will become impossible to put up with the veritable dog's life that we shall be expected to lead". Later he would write that he rejected "the vain fancy of serving on a larger field in India" in favour of dealing with "the great danger which stared the South African Indians in the face".[1] He was now becoming confident of his choice.

By the middle of 1903 Gandhi got enrolled in the Transvaal Supreme court to practice as an attorney. Very soon his practice bloomed. Earlier in Natal he had divided his activities into law practice and public work. His involvement was in the nature of articulating problems. This time he got involved in seeking and implementing solutions to social problems: for instance the case of corruption in the Asiatic Department, response to spread of plague among Indians, setting up of the weekly 'Indian Opinion'. Each of these was an awareness event which gave Gandhi clarity about local processes of social change and continuity. In a way, he was now inclining more towards prioritizing the social over the personal. This meant coming to terms with conscientiousness or scrupulousness as an abiding social ethos.

Voluntary involvements in social activism now become a driving commitment and passion. This conspicuous and conscious import of voluntarism to a profession was a significant decision by Gandhi. A series of events illustrate how he transited thru the *satyagrahi* phase. His skirmishes with the bribe taking in the Asiatic Department helped the Asian community save large amounts in unpaid bribes. What makes Gandhi's thinking *satyagrahi*-like is when on receiving a request, he agreed not to thwart the dismissed officer's application for jobs with the Johannesburg municipality. Consideration and compassion are qualities which need nurturing and these cannot be constrained by insularity. He was now extending his principle of seeking compromise in solving legal issues to social relationships. There need not be a vanquished, although truth should prevail.

The travails of the poor remain tagged to destiny. Gandhi challenged this notion. On learning that twenty three Indians were down with pneumonic or 'Black' plague which they had contracted at a gold mine, Gandhi with the permission of Dr Godfrey personally administered mud packs to three patients. While Gandhi and his team survived, the plague took its toll. All the patients except two of those who had been administered mud packs along with the nurse died. Later, on Gandhi's advice, the residents agreed to move out with all their belongings and permitted the location to be gutted; but not before Gandhi helped in banking their hoarded coins which had been accumulated in holes under the ground. For this the coins which amounted to £60,000 had to be disinfected before the bank would handle them.[2] These awareness events were seminal empirical lessons which became the core stock for clarity of vision and mission regarding satyagraha.

An awareness building event is not a short time bound engagement. Gandhi's involvement with the *Indian Opinion* is illustrative of this. The *Indian Opinion* was to be a journal for and by Indians in South Africa. For Gandhi, this was an engagement and a platform to articulate, i.e. give expression to and bind together, the social within him. In the *Indian Opinion* Gandhi flourished; the interlocutor and the editor emerged with every article and editorial thereby allowing him the stage and also allowing him to be the prompter in the wings. He now started conflating social service with the social aspect of his own self, a narrative which had all the possibility of becoming social-centric albeit a bit one-dimensional. Social service and the social dimension of an individual are distinct texts albeit with commonalities. Gandhi was now in a hurry to dump some aspects of his personality. An awareness event can exaggerate aspects of the experience.

A very significant awareness event which for him was a veritable break event was when Gandhi met Henry Polak. The two shared similarity of views and when

Polak came to see Gandhi off at the Johannesburg Railway station when Gandhi was on his way to Durban, he lent him a book, John Ruskin's *Unto This Last*. Gandhi was fascinated by the book. Hitherto he had been struggling to harmonize to 'serve (self and society)', 'work and earn (honest labour)' and 'live (community)' into a life of social equality, simplicity, and respect for every kind of labour. But he hadn't succeeded; obviously something was missing! In *Unto This Last* he felt he found the principles and the linkages he was searching. The teaching as he understood were: firstly the good of the individual is contained in the good of all; secondly a lawyer's work has the same value as the barber's, in as much as all have the same right of earning their livelihood from their work; lastly a life of labour, i.e., the life of the tiller of the soil and the handicraftsman, is the life worth living. More crucially, while the first of these he knew and the 'second I had dimly realized', the 'third had never occurred to me'. *Unto This Last* made it as clear as daylight that the second and the third were contained in the first. Gandhi now was not only able to put the social in him on par with the personal; he thought he could now seamlessly blend them. He later recalled, 'I determined to change my life in accordance with the ideals of the book'.

Gandhi bought a 100-acre piece of land located 14 miles from Durban and 2.5 miles from phoenix railway station in the 'picturesque valley of the Piezang River'. With Parsi Rustomji helping with money and materials and Indian carpenters and masons whom Gandhi knew from the Boer war days helping erect a shed, the printing press was shifted to the settlement. The 24 December 1904 edition of *Indian Opinion* was printed and dispatched from the Phoenix settlement.

This event truly marks Gandhi's advent into what we can call his *satyagrahi* phase. Henceforth, for him, economic considerations would not necessarily precede awareness building social considerations. As a professional he had to first earn and then spend his earnings as per personal desires. He wanted to resolve this alienation of the professional of first earning and then using the money to gain satisfaction. The hitherto difference between professional involvement and social activism would collapse and both social and personal accountability would develop into acts of self-respect and self-realization. What was a 'chore' for the professional now turned into 'anticipation' for the same person. Initiatives and incentives for the individual would be in tandem where empathy becomes the moral surrogate. But this can be a demanding virtue because while making the social personal is only half the task, the other half necessitates making the personal/private social, which requires transparency of a very high order.

But an awareness event is not the same for everyone. While Gandhi was negotiating a *satyagrahi* phase, his associates were not. The broad objectives of the settlement, its capacity to sustain itself and the nature and role of the members remained vague and open-ended at best. Gandhi's idea of running the press as a community endeavour for which workers were given a basic remuneration, while simultaneously operating respective households and maintaining their particular pieces of land as individual responsibility remained debatable. Initiative, incentive, available resources, and competence cannot be replaced or equated with enthusiasm. An individual and a community's notion of self-sufficiency need not be the same. Millie Polak wrote: "The ideals and theories that had sounded so right and reasonable in the study, or read so well in books, had a chance of being put to the test at phoenix, and as might be expected, were often found impractical when applied to the hard facts of life".[3] The settlement revolved around the press, the settler, and Gandhi. Gandhi dominated the bonding. The unresolved question remained: was Phoenix settlement a place to nurture a *satyarthi* or a *satyagrahi*?

At a more personal level he felt the need for some serious study of Hindu scriptures. Gandhi had been impressed with Annie Besant who argued that, though every human being has the potential to become a saviour, only those who perform "every act as a sacrifice, not for what it will bring to the doer but for what it will bring to other" can do so.[4] This fundamental was not lost on Gandhi; it remained with him all his life.

The lectures that he gave to the theosophists helped Gandhi go beyond the theosophists individual-centric deliberations and helped him reassert his faith in Hinduism particularly the Gita. While he was able to reclaim himself, his bold criticism of the theosophists where he urged them to find purpose in 'real life' was also an audacious step to go beyond the appeal of sects and social groupings.

Before long for him the "Gita became an infallible guide of conduct". "Words like *aparigraha* (*non*-possession) and *samabhava* (equability) gripped me. How to cultivate and preserve that equability was the question. How was one to treat alike insulting, insolent and corrupt officials, co-workers of yesterday raising meaningless opposition, and men who had always been good to one? How was one to divest oneself of all possession? Was not the body itself possession enough? Were not wife and children possession? . . . Was I to give up all I had and follow Him? Straight came the answer: I could not follow Him unless I gave up all I had".[5] This was a direct questioning of his efforts to contain the personal and stress the social within himself. He was realizing that a *satyagrahi's* tryst and transition can be a lonely affair.

All his preoccupations soon got swept away by a major event, the Zulu revolt or the Bambatha rebellion in which Gandhi decided to get involved. Till this time his contacts with the native inhabitants of the country had been minimal. His initial responses were tentative. Writing in the *Indian Opinion* of 28 April 1906, he says, "it is not for me to say whether the revolt of the Kaffirs is justified or not. We are in Natal by virtue of British power. Our very existence depends upon it. It is therefore our duty to render whatever help we can. . . . That is, if the Government so desires, we could raise an ambulance corps". The "nursing of the wounded", said Gandhi, was "just as honourable and necessary as the shouldering of a rifle".[6] Tending to fluctuate between the hermeneutic and the instrumental, Gandhi seems to be ambivalent about the origin and nature of social violence.

The ambulance corps that Gandhi organized was funded by the Gujarati merchants and manned by volunteers from amongst former indentured labourers. For Gandhi it was an eye-opening experience. He started to reorganize the mindlessness of violence, why it was committed and its consequences. He also became aware that the primary intention was to teach the Zulus a lesson and soften them up for the future. It was an opportunity for the state to consolidate the settlers' authority, shades of which he was to find later in Champaran, Bihar. He regonized that revolt and war were the two sides of the same coin representing the coercive nature of both aspiration and authority.

Gandhi tried to remain equivocal. The social in him was not only getting recognition but was on the ascendant. Perhaps he was the first coloured to be a witness in a European marriage. This he followed up with the even more astounding decision to share a common household with the couple. While he made tentative efforts to get to know mixed-race Africans, he remained Indian-centric. In his opinion, "though the hardships suffered by those people and the Indians is almost of the same kind, the remedies are not identical. It is therefore proper that the two should fight out their cases, each in their own appropriate way".[7]

In every one of these awareness events, Gandhi was slowly but surely establishing the prominence and distinction of the social from the personal within his own self. While he still had to come to fully comprehend the larger dimensions of what this meant, he was now clear about his proclivity. To consolidate his inclinations, by the end of the year he took the vow of brahmacharya. This in many ways was a decision waiting to happen. As per this vow he decided "to stop sharing the same bed with my wife or seeking privacy with her".[8] This way he would not only shun lust, he would also get over one more of his personal attachments which he felt distracted him from focusing on the social. In the autobiography he writes, "It became my conviction that procreation and the consequent care of children were inconsistent with public service".[9] While Kasturba herself might not have been a party to the decision, after being pregnant five times, perhaps Kasturba did not want any more children; not to mention her eldest son was already married.

This brings up the question of '*tyaag*', for after all brahmacharya is '*trishna-tyaag*' i.e. renouncing or abjuring longing. This solemn renouncing is a very demanding commitment which is also manifest in satyagraha a new conceptualization triggered by trouble brewing in Transvaal in the form of the Transvaal Government's 'Asiatic Ordinance'.

Satyagraha originated in a mass meeting where it was decided and reiterated that, "this mass meeting of British Indians here assembled solemnly and regretfully resolves that, rather than submit to the galling, tyrannous, and un-British requirements laid down in the above Draft Ordinance, every British Indian in the Transvaal shall submit himself to imprisonment and shall continue to do so until it shall please His Gracious Majesty the King-Emperor to grant relief".[10] This last bit of graciously submitting to imprisonment was crucial because it launched Gandhi on the path of satyagraha *a social manifesto of equanimity in action.*

By 1 July the Asiatic Ordinance of 1906 became law (TARA, Transvaal Asiatic Registration Act or the Black Act as the Indians called it), and with alacrity it received Royal Assent from England. The Indians were presented with a fait accompli. This is when we find Gandhi submitting to ahimsa as *krodh-tyaag* and its significance to satyagraha. He persuaded the British Indian Association "to submit to voluntary registration" in order to "satisfy the government and popular prejudice".[11] The proposal sought to distinguish compulsion from voluntary; a very political caveat wherein voluntary action seeks parity with the hegemonic state. For Gandhi, the procedure of voluntary registration should "be based on mutual understanding" between the Indians and the state. This way, since the contemplated 'gaol - going' comes after the proposal, it would appear more graceful.[12] This gracefulness is the core of ahimsa.

However, this gracefulness has to be tempered on the anvil of a pledge, another ingredient of satyagraha. Gandhi went on to pledge, "[T]hat, should the new law come into force, I will never take out a permit or register under the law but will go to gaol; and even if I am the only one left who has not taken a permit".[13] For Gandhi though it was now time to rewrite the very meaning of struggle, a meaning which would go beyond the simple conflict resolution and fight to win formulae.

The pressure now was on everyone, and cracks started to appear in the solidarity of the community. Broadly the Indian diaspora consisted of rich businessmen, professionals, petty service providers, vendors, and small traders who hawked goods they picked up from white wholesalers and ex-indentured labourers. Among the first to break rank were some rich merchants who tried to convince their customers to do likewise. Gandhi kept on reiterating the issue of 'compulsion as distinct from voluntary'. Moreover the ethos he argued should stress that the state can never have the last word; this has to be with the people. The state however can have legitimate obligations, and registration can be one such compulsion.

In the meantime Gandhi had discovered Henry David Thoreau and the term 'civil disobedience'. Thoreau's teachings were inspiring. Thoreau was a man who 'practiced what he preached'. Gandhi found that his own views about the state resonated with that of Thoreau particularly where Thoreau says that that government is best which governs least. He also accepted that the state and the army are two sides of the same coin and truly speaking, it is we, the subjects, who are responsible for the existence of both the State and the army. Putting the onus firmly on the individual he notes, "But, I do not ask for no government at once, but at once for a better government. This is the duty of every citizen. . . . I would say that we are men first and subjects afterwards. It is not necessary to cultivate a respect for the law so much as for the right. The only obligation which I have a right to assume is to do at any time what I think right. Law never made man a whit more just".[14] This view he retained all his life.

The conflict intensifies

For Gandhi, satyagraha is the unfolding of an approximation making progress through intentional involvement. The approximation relates to both the actual methods employed in the struggles and the expectations. Specific struggles as events are essentially milestones. In the second week of November 1907, Ram Sundar Pandit's case was the first to be prosecuted under the Asiatic Act came up in court. "As a token of support for Ram Sundar, Indian stores throughout the Transvaal were closed for a day. Indian hawkers went off the roads, and Indian newspaper boys did not do the rounds".[15] Gandhi felt that the struggle had yet to begin. To the *satyagrahi*, the gaol he felt would make all the difference. And as it transpired, he was sent to jail on 10 January 1908. He asked for the 'heaviest penalty'. But the judge sentenced him to two months without hard labour.

The Pressure now was on every individual at a personal and also at the community levels. But not all could handle such intense pressure. Ram Sundar Pandit went back to Natal accepting that he could not handle another stint in jail. Gandhi could not accept this and became censorious and prescriptive.[16] Gandhi still had to come to terms with deviancies and people's responses to vicissitudes. Gandhi forgot that not all his colleagues were *satyagrahis*. While some were *satyarthis* others were there because of unavoidable circumstance.

For the various sections of the Indians, retaining a united front was slowly becoming an issue while the state was clear about its expectations. With a series of bills aimed at the individual Indian the state sought to break the solidarity Gandhi had been able to patch up of all Indians irrespective of class, caste, or religion. The long-standing problematic of the tension between self and social interest now became a pertinent issue both for the individual Indian and the Indian community.

1908 was an eventful year. While with the arrest of Gandhi the struggle and passive resistance reached a new level, simultaneously Gandhi recognized that the struggle should not make the state as the 'other'. To the Colonial Secretary he wrote, "We are sincerely anxious to prove to the Government that we are loyal and law-abiding, and that we are willing to adopt any course which will lead out of the present difficulty without violating our consciences, inflicting any indignity or casting any stigma on us".[17]

This statement indicates a hermeneutic shift. Laying out the fundamentals of 'satyagraha action' he was now clarifying to his associates and his opponents the centrality of compromise and reconciliation in a struggle. But there needs to be an element of even-handedness and transparency. Noting that, 'you don't need ten finger-prints for identification' why should only the poor suffer these indignities? "A man who may be perfectly wealthy, I need hardly point out, is not necessarily an honest man, and yet, because he may be known otherwise, his signature alone will be accepted"[18] Gandhi was seeking to bring together the entire Indian community side by side on the same plane, irrespective of wealth. He goes on to suggest that leaders who have a right not to give fingerprints should in solidarity with the poor be the first to waive such rights.

On release from jail he had to go through another wounding though a profoundly distressing event. Gandhi and his companions Thambi Naidoo and Essop Mia were brutally beaten by a group of 'Punjabis and Pathans'. This was a period when Gandhi was using the *Indian Opinion* to reflect upon social relationships, going beyond satyagraha to sarvodaya, and the ethos these stood for. While dialoguing briskly with the Indian community we find him reiterating the distinct import of the personal and social in all of us while simultaneously foregrounding the inclusivity of the community. In the *Indian Opinion* of 18 January he writes, "It must be borne in mind that success in the struggle will depend on what the Transvaal

Indians do while those arrested remain in jail". To all Indians he made an especially perceptive appeal, "Success will never be ours if we do not at all costs keep Hindu-Muslim differences out of matters of common interest. Let everyone accept this as a guiding principle".[19] As for the ethos of the struggle he wrote, "Do not deceive yourself; do not deceive the Government; do not deceive your humble servant".[20]

Along with the earlier clarity about the role of the other in a struggle, we now find him trying to clarify the distinct roles and relationship between 'I', 'we', and 'us'. While the 'I' is the interlocutor and 'we' are *satyarthis* and *satyagrahis*, with 'us' the relationship is still one of tension and impermanence; in this case the Indian community was more like 'us'.

After his release he wrote a series of articles – between 16 May and 18 July, 1908 – on humility, triumph of truth and so on. Through these he hoped to set forth some of the basic ethos and tenet of the ongoing satyagraha. In the first place he contended that victory was not that of the Indian community but of truth. Secondly the community in the process of satyagraha he argued incurred moral obligation in that it was now equally responsible for identifying all Indians entitled to reside in the Transvaal. Thirdly the Indians now have to prove that while they were ready to struggle, they were equally up to the challenge of being constructive. These are onerous responsibilities. While accepting that some might not adhere to truth, or might think of their personal interests, Gandhi felt that they did "fight on behalf of truth" and that the "leaders fought with scrupulous regard for truth. That is why there has been such a wonderful result. *Truth is God or God is nothing but truth*"[21] (italics added). As such he could claim that their "victory is also a victory for satyagraha". While warning "that there are evils to which satyagraha cannot be applied", evaluation of results he felt should mean looking into the context of every specific struggle. However, he argued, "if we are required to do anything which violates our religion or insults our manhood, we can administer the invaluable physic of satyagraha".[22] Perhaps Gandhi was now also trying to prospect beyond the question of struggles between men by concerning himself with the deeper issue of man and God. His seemingly improbable search for truth and God within a background of intense struggles indicates a need to pause and reflect. While talking about victory Gandhi writes, "We do not claim that every Indian adhered to truth in the course of the struggle. Nor do we claim that no one thought of his own interests during the campaign. We do, however, assert that this was a fight on behalf of truth".[23] Thus truth is '*abadhya*' that is unrestrained.

While persuading himself and his associates about the justness of the struggle, Gandhi must have recognized the immense need to relentlessly coax and cajole the personal to stick to the tiring social struggle. Crucial in this was the relationship between the struggles, truth, and God.

Gandhi strove to get beyond the constraints of the threshold by appealing to truth as what was, is, and yet to be. In the din of the struggle and during messy post-struggle analysis, both the personal and the social tend to turn into an erroneous inclusive personal which can be ambiguous. Krishna in the *Anugita* or 'Gita Recapitulated' accepted that Arjun had forgotten all that he had been told on the battle field just before the war and that Arjun was not worthy of re-receiving it. Perhaps Gandhi while contemplating the post-factum scenario was acknowledging the shortcoming and restrictions within himself and his associates. Not surprisingly to continue the struggle, Gandhi had to dig deeper for reasoning, clarity and arguments to sustain it. One such argument was the 'vow'; more specifically, it was the vow that the Indian community had taken on 11 September 1907 with God as witness to continue the struggle even if it meant going to jail. The vow surely is a submission to a power whose will cannot be resisted or thwarted. Gandhi in his efforts to bring in a just social order, was arguing that in 'Truth' he had a conceptual ally which stands for faith as morality, is post-factum perception and comprehensible. Moreover Truth pertains to what we think as *'we know'*, of *'what was'*. This information we then use along with our world view to construct what we call knowledge of 'what is'. This knowledge we then apply to morality and happiness to describe wisdom. For the socially inclined Gandhi it was clear that the information that helped him come to the truth in the first place was not his alone, but included those of others too; this meant his understanding of truth included the world views of others. Besides, the notion of God is essentially knowledge of various authorities: priest, mullah, pundit and so on. Not surprisingly, albeit much latter, he was to explain that he preferred Truth because it was essentially non-sectarian.[24] However the distinction between compulsion and self-interest can be a thin line. Since "every act is motivated by some kind of self-interest. Even in my example, there is an element of self-interest in the service which I render to a friend";[25] the pragmatist, benign Gandhi is very evident.

The struggle escalates

While most Indians accepted the compromise and began registering themselves, a certain section remained inimical. On 5 March, 1908, Gandhi was once again attacked by some Indians when he was addressing a gathering in Durban. The crowd protected him. But the government remained hostile. "In the last week of April, three new bills were introduced in the Natal legislature. The first sought to stop the import of indentured Indian labour after June 1911; the second to suspend the issuing of new trading licences to Indians after 1908; the third to terminate existing Indian licences after ten years, subject to the payment of compensation equivalent to three years' profit. The bills were clearly meant to protect the interests of European traders against their hardworking Indian counterparts".[26] Then in early May, General Smuts decided that the compromise had to have a date tag. Accordingly voluntary registration would be open only for three months i.e. till 9 August. Former residents on coming back had to refer to the still unrepelled Act of 1907. Effectively the compromise collapsed.

The Indian community was now in disarray. On 17 May Essop Mia the president of the BIA was brutally attacked; while a section was ready to resort to violence, the rich were calculating costs because the state had rejected compromise. Gandhi doing some self- contemplation writes, "In Natal, we spend any amount of money to obtain trading licences by underhand means, but we will not observe cleanliness, which is the thing necessary. There are few Indians who deserve trading licences on merit. In the Transvaal everyone thinks only of self-interest. They must have a permit by fair means or foul. As many children as possible must be brought into the colony. This avidity [to have all one wants] is, to be sure, a source of evil".[27] Not everyone it seems was a *satyagrahi* or even a *satyarthi*. He now also has a hard look at the question of 'coloured people'. "We shall know each other better when the mists have rolled away".[28]

Ground conditions were however pushing for another standoff. With the government wanting to make the Asiatic Act applicable, the Indians and the Chinese decided to recall the registration papers which they had voluntarily filled. This was their way of protesting against the 'breach of spirit of compromise'. The state reacted by accusing Gandhi of not just exploiting Indian permit-seekers, but also as a lawyer of charging Muslims more than what he charged Hindus. Communal politics apparently is not a new phenomenon. Smuts was aware that most meetings of the Indians were conducted in the compounds of the Muslim Mosques.

Essentially Smuts had decided to try out a policy of wearing away: wait, watch, and tire out, and if and when necessary use force. The shops of merchants who had courted arrest were boarded up and their goods confiscated and auctioned. Gandhi once again turned to negotiations. But being a pragmatist he sought alternative strategies to sustain the struggle. He now requested some of the more established Natal Indians to travel to Transvaal and canvas for the Indian cause. He also suggested that the Transvaal government should allow six educated Indians to come every year.

In the last week of September he himself courted arrest. This incarceration was a new learning experience for Gandhi, especially about the nature and moral attitudes of human beings, Indians in particular. "I observed with regret that some Indians were happy to sleep in the same room as the Kaffirs, the reason being that they hoped there for a secret supply of tobacco, etc.". For him "This is a matter of shame to us. We may entertain no aversion to Kaffirs, but we cannot ignore the fact that there is no common ground between them and us in the daily affairs of life".[29] Gandhi was still for and of the Indians. He still had to acknowledge that his struggle could remain restricted if it remained confined to just 'by the Indians' and for the Indians.

At a more individual level we find him struggling with the tension between the personal and the social. When Kasturba was suffering from acute haemorrhage, instead of paying a fine and going to help her he stayed in jail. He tried to console her by saying that in case she died he would never marry again! But on being released when he came to know the doctor had given her beef broth for nutrition, he promptly used his right to take her away from the doctor who incidentally was his friend. Similarly he advised Harilal and Chanchal whose marriage he had rejected to sacrifice conjugal relationship and concentrate on the struggle he was leading. We find him struggling to understand the nature of the relationship between 'I' and 'we'.

However Gandhi remained tenacious about the social. Writing to his son Manilal, Gandhi says, "Remember please that henceforth our lot is poverty. The more I think of it, the more I feel that it is more blessed to be poor than to be rich. The uses of poverty are far sweeter than those of riches".[30] He was also trying to keep track of other seemingly trivial but complex fundamental issues. Again writing to Manilal he asks, "You have taken the sacred thread. Want to live up to it. . . . I think that the adoption of the sacred thread by those who have for ages given it up is a mistake. As it is, we have too much of the false division between *shudras* and others".[31]

His relationship with the family remained complex and difficult. Most often he preferred not to differentiate as to whether they were *satyarthis* or *satyagrahis* or just simple folk. He appreciated being part of a family, but remained in two minds about his responsibilities. This being in two minds meant he wanted both detachment and authority, wherein his role would only be to inspire and expect. But to respond to such a complex relationship the family members needed to attain competences which had to be acquired. This meant access to opportunities. To provide this Gandhi neither had the time nor the inclination; he was too pre-occupied, both with his social involvements and principles. When Kasturba lay fatally ill, "Gandhi had 'no doubt' that (yet again) he would choose to go to prison rather than stay with his ailing wife".[32] The whole family relationship was particularly complex and difficult because other than Gandhi himself, no one had a profession. They depended completely on Gandhi for sustenance. The Phoenix farm interregnum just allowed the family members to postpone contending with complex issues. In 'A dialogue on the compromise' Gandhi (perhaps tongue in cheek) argues, "You will agree moreover that those who are accepted as leaders must have a certain freedom [of action] in crisis".[33] Permanent uncertainty is what Kasturba and the children had to live with. Unlike Gandhi they had very little choice. It is to their credit that they tried their best!

Hind Swaraj, Tolstoy Farm, and return to India

In a meeting on 16 June 1909 at the famous Fordsburg Mosque, some 1500 Indians decided to once again send a delegation to petition the Imperial Government in London, and it was decided to send Gandhi and a Pretoria merchant Haji Habib. Gandhi and Habib took ship on 23 June reaching Southampton on 10 July. On arrival they found themselves in a very charged ambiance. An Indian student Madanlal Dhingra had shot and killed Sir Curzon Wyllie. The use of violence and armed struggle as a means of achieving freedom had acquired a following both in India and amongst Indians living in England. With this event, whether as strategy or philosophy, political assassination as integral to resistance efforts against colonial rule had now gone beyond debate. Gandhi sagaciously recognized that Dhingra's violent act "has done India much harm; the deputation's efforts have also received a setback . . . must say that those who believe and argue that such murders may do good to India are ignorant men indeed. No act of treachery can ever profit a nation. Even should the British leave in consequence of such murderous acts, who will rule in their place? The only answer is: the murderers".[34] During the trip Gandhi had to convince well-wishers like Lord Ampthill the erstwhile Governor of Madras Province that he had no connections with any 'party of sedition'.

The journey was disappointing. However it had some very inspiring fallout. He began corresponding with Tolstoy and was able to get permission to print the letter written by Tolstoy to the exile Tarak Nath Das deploring the use of violence in political movements as 'letter to a Hindu' in *Indian Opinion* without the slighting reference to reincarnation, a concept Gandhi believed in. Tolstoy had suggested to the radical Das to desist from violence and instead use methods of non-violence in struggles against the British. This meeting of minds deploring violence in political movements meant a lot for Gandhi.[35] Love instead of violence expressed through self-suffering as a method to resist and get rid of tyranny and accomplish reform is unique indeed; but that it is much more stimulating and sustainable is revolutionary indeed. However, this matter of love is very involved and albeit social is premised deeply on the personal, actually expressed through the personality. Albeit biased towards the social, Gandhi remained perched at the threshold between the personal and the social. While he was respected as a leader of a movement, people were attracted to his personality. Reverend Joseph Doke, Pranjivan Mehta, Lord Ampthill, or Maud remained influenced by Gandhi the person. This dilemma was not lost on him. The personal is never trivial! The other take home for the increasingly social biased Gandhi was another paradox. The liberal British Government by supporting apartheid had instituted an actual 'colour' bar.[36] The exegesis of power cannot be ignored.

Although the trip had little to show by way of success for the struggling South African Indians, the journey on SS *Kildonan Castle* between 13November 1909 and 30 November was profoundly inspirational for Gandhi in terms of helping him consolidate his evolving views and ideas. The act of assassination and its endorsement by other Indians exemplified a reading of violence very different from his; a second albeit more fundamental clarity was regarding the attributes of the inspiration encouraging such acts. As if possessed, Gandhi the Interlocutor in nine days flat wrote his seminal treatise: *Hind Swaraj*. This exposition was not restricted to his South African compatriots; it was addressed to India and all Indians, out there and back home. Denied a dignified transactional social role in his societal home, Gandhi now was articulating the meaning of 'Home' and not just as a 'Residence'. At the core of his thesis were cure, care, necessity, diversity, change, continuity, and of course choice. Boldly polemical, using metaphors in abundance and an Indian style of narrative, interlocutor Gandhi sets forth a 'vision' which he insisted is a 'mission' while elaborating his understanding of society and social. Perhaps in this thesis he underplayed the complex issue of 'chance and necessity'? Maybe this is because this requires a foregrounding of the relationship of 'give and take' which was the essence of his thesis. For Gandhi, the savouring of 'home' would have to be two-fold, that is, in 'the making' and also in the 'wanting of this making'. Further, since swaraj has to nurture and accommodate, it has to provide an ethos too. With this script he now became specifically associating with a homeland which was not South Africa. Perhaps South Africa with its learning, experimenting, and debating was now to be thought of as an apprenticeship for actual home-making. While the allure and the contradictions of looking up to 'swadesh' or 'homeland' remained, the bulwark of his conceptualization which runs through 'Hind Swaraj' nevertheless depended on the ethos he acquired in South Africa.

With this book Gandhi seems to relocate himself. In many ways in the Hind Swaraj, the social in Gandhi it seems is petitioning the personal in him. The 'giver' Gandhi seems to polemic the 'taker', the recipient in him; a process which splits the 'I' and 'me'. He tries to recognize this split within individuals as well as institutions but runs into difficulties when responding to the core issue of power and possession. In the process the issue of give and take remains subdued.

This matrix of 'give' and 'take' is complex. Since Gandhi had relegated the personal, the social alone was expected to do this. What could the social Gandhi give? Satyagraha, vow, brahmacharya, sarvodaya, life in an ashram and so on were all that he had. While the *satyagrahi* would have no problems, the *satyarthi* would not be able to 'take' what Gandhi had to 'give' simply because they were still struggling to recalibrate the personal and the social within themselves. They could either reject or wait till they felt they had evolved, or till they could become followers accepting the profoundness of the 'give' of a *satyagrahi*. Perhaps this is why Andrews had advised Gandhi to return to India. Gandhi's indiscriminate albeit profound 'give' was not only becoming too demanding for the personal in him, but was also impeding the evolution of other *satyarthis* into *satyagrahis*.

However for the Indians, the struggle had to continue. Gandhi's initiative meant gaol for the men. What would the families and particularly the women do without the breadwinner? The *satyagrahis* had to find a new home for their families. With the men in prison, the women and children were finding it difficult to make ends meet. Kallenbach on 30 May 1910 donated a hundred acre farm located about 22 miles from Johannesburg. Passive resisters could live on the farm free of rent or charge for as long as the struggle lasted. Since the farm was in Transvaal, the families found it very convenient.[37] Kallenbach and the Gandhi family moved to the farm.

The ground reality in South Africa was however becoming complex with many of the South African born Indians articulating a different world view with a different set of self-interests. The Indian community was no more a cohesive unit under the leadership of the rich.[38] At a personal level Gandhi's relationship with Harilal was becoming stressful. The young man, now a father of a daughter and a son, was searching for a skill and thus an identity. The skill he hoped would give him a competence and credibility besides that of being his father's son. While Gandhi was concerned more about 'the baser elements' in Harilal's nature, the son was keen to get on in life. He therefore decided to return to India without telling anyone. Gandhi was neither equanimous nor was he able to premise the social over the personal when it came to family. "The more they disagreed with him, the more intense and impatient he became with them".[39] Harilal loved his father. All he wanted was to gain a competence, confidence, and some personal credibility. Gandhi wanted all of these to be determined by himself as per his world view alone. As Harilal put it, "You did not allow me to measure my capabilities; you measured them for me".[40] Gandhi seems to have forgotten that he had to go through a *satyarthi* phase himself. Perhaps in his relationship with his family there was an element of '*satyagrahi* arrogance', which he was not able to comprehend, or was not ready to accept? More importantly it seems he was not ready to accept that *satyagrahi*-ness cannot be thrust upon anyone. If so, then it went against the spirit of satyagraha itself. As far as his family was concerned Gandhi was reluctant to allow them to evolve on their terms. It is also possible that the element of obsession in satyagraha made him impatient and demanding. But satyagraha stretches beyond the individual, and its ethos is minimalism. Does Gandhi's treatment of his family indicate that the family due to its proximity to the *satyagrahi* ends up having to compromise its identity and distinctiveness to minimalism? While to give is one thing, to give up is actually to relinquish. Gandhi found it difficult to surrender perhaps because the personal remains.

Meanwhile the state had opened another front. A court in Cape Town, referring to the Muslim practice of *talak* and polygamy, disallowed the issue of a permit to a Muslim woman married according to Muslim customs to join her husband although she was the only wife. Gandhi recognized this as a part of the state's attrition and skirmish strategy to break the cohesiveness of the Indian community; marriage and religion are volatile but intimate issues. While in this case Muslim practices were being targeted, Hindu men were also known to practice polygamy. The judge in effect was calling into question the validity of all Indian marriages. This judgement which questioned traditions and world views could seriously damage the life of the Indian community in South Africa. Even Kasturba was anxious and wanted to know about her marital status as per the laws of South Africa. If the laws questioned her status, she wanted to either return to India or join the struggle and if necessary be imprisoned.

On June 14 the Bill received Royal Assent. The £3 tax would remain for men and not for women, and marriages would have to be registered to be acceptable. Gandhi recognized that this meant a long-haul struggle. He wrote, "100 men and 13 women will start the struggle. As time goes, we may have more" and also commented that "we are making provisions for an indefinite prolongation".[41]

While Gandhi was preoccupied with all this, the local social milieu was evolving considerably. In July some 20,000 white workers laid down their tools and went on strike in the mines. When police intervened the workers became violent and in the ensuing firing many lost their lives. On the day of the firing, Gandhi and Kallenbach were in downtown Johannesburg. Gandhi wanted to help nurse the wounded, but Kallenbach dissuaded him. Gandhi then proposed that "we should in the face of so much suffering, which we have just witnessed, have only one meal [a day]". Again Kallenbach discouraged him urging him to stick to his austere meals. We find Gandhi mixing up the social and the political and trying to project the personal as social and personally 'take' on himself a hardship so as to 'give' succor to the suffering miners – a very convoluted manoeuvre and positioning.

Meanwhile his son Manilal it seemed had an affair with Jeki the married daughter of his friend Pranjivan Mehta who was staying with the Gandhi family. This violation of brahmacharya before marriage and also with a married woman was a transgression beyond Gandhi's capacity of discernment. Given his commitment to brahmacharya he could find no way to accept, condone, or rationalize the act. But then given his understanding of love and power he was not one for punitive action or punishment. How then was he to reconcile given that he considered brahmacharya to be at the core of all his principles and world view? Gandhi responded with a fast for a week and followed it up with restricting himself to a single meal a day for a year. This vow was a dual atonement: his son's indiscretion and the violence unleashed on the miners. The personal had to become social because the social of one can merge with that of another provided this was a conscious act. Perhaps Gandhi hoped to learn from mistakes done by others. Responding as post factum serendipity is a charming Gandhian method. In the 'fast' he now had a moral surrogate for a coercive weapon. In this while he insisted that the practice cleansed both the personal and the social; the initiator retained the authority of exclusive purview. Perhaps Gandhi the *satyagrahi* had still to accept that satyagraha need not be the last word.

Since 'negotiations had failed' by the second week of September 1913 Gandhi and the Indians decided to revive passive resistance to protest against the £3 tax, racial bar in the immigration law, and the uncertain status of wives and children. But by now the social milieu had altered considerably. As could be expected, various Associations were being organized to reflect the aspirations of these assorted peoples who were connected with India more sentimentally than substantially. This term 'assorted people' should be noted because it reflects the emerging heterogeneity within the Indian diaspora. South Africa was their home and future in every sense of the term. And the younger generation, aspirational and mobile, was not inclined to continue being laborers. This profound shift meant that this new lot would seek encouragement, solace and empathy from local sources. While for this new set South Africa was 'home', for Gandhi South Africa was a temporary location he occupied. His intensity of architecture was not deliberated to pivot around vibrant personal stakes. As he put it, "the real object of our fight must be to kill the monster of racial prejudice in the heart of the Government and the local whites.... There is only one way to kill the monster and that is to offer ourselves as a sacrifice".[42] But for the new South African Indian, such narratives sounded more like that of an opinionated *pracharak*. While they were ready to struggle against racial prejudice which relegated them to an inferior status, they were essentially longing for a non-negotiable inclusiveness as individuals.

With restricted options Gandhi now shifted gear. To push the existing agenda, a group of 12 men and four women left Phoenix to enter the Transvaal on 15 September 1913. This involvement of women was radical and unusual particularly for Indians. Earlier in 1909 the Tamil women had been ready to be arrested with their men. They had been dissuaded. This time the group had 'Ba' with them. The state did not want to allow the Indians a threshold between their home and the habitat.

So the new narrative would be a 'departure' to seek a right to 'stay' because they belonged. Gandhi and the *satyagrahis* sought to emphasize a threshold between the home and the habitat which the state could not wipe out.

Kasturba and the *satyagrahis* were arrested and sentenced to three months in jail with hard labour. But this time, something fundamental was different. Even the leadership of Gandhi himself was under scrutiny. Satyagraha bases itself on the minimal; therefore, its agenda is not open for bargaining. This makes it vulnerable when articulated by a motley group. More than anything, India as the fount of identity and rejuvenation was itself under scrutiny. The question regarding "who needed the satyagraha and how desperately", needed a new narrative. The poor Indian needed to stay because while India remained a living past, it could offer very little. When the poor Indians had opted to become indentured, they knew this. The £3 tax was an enormous burden because at the end of their contract they did not have this kind of surplus. The planters wanted the tax because it would ensure the labourer stayed on. The non-planters could use this tax to send non-indentured labourers back to India in case they wanted to. But the wealthy traders had no such compulsion and would prefer to give up the resistance because they did not see much merit in any kind of solidarity, particularly since they were called to participate and thereby endanger their hard-earned economic status. They could learn to live without access to cheap non-indentured labour. Gandhi was aware of all this and warned.

> For the prejudice in the heart of the whites against us, we are partly responsible. We have several defects. We tell lies and follow wrong courses. We give false evidence. We are dirty in our ways. We can overcome the white's prejudice only if we give up these bad habits. But this is not likely to happen. The Indian who is full of faults will not read writings of this kind. Nor can those who do make him see reason. *Satyagrahis* should die for his sake as well. Their death will be an education for those our brethren, whom ignorance has made blind.[43]

To some this self-criticism might sound trifle rhetorical. Bad personal habits and bad habits of a group are not the same. Gandhi and the Indians were at a crossroad. How many would accept the satyagraha road that Gandhi chose? Gandhi was to find out soon. In a well-attended meeting of the Natal Indian Congress in October, Gandhi was criticized by a very vocal and critical section. While some were questioning the role of 'professional and political agitators', others were losing track of the significance of satyagraha itself.

Upping the ante was another vibrant group, a group which was the creation of the changing milieu, and it had women leading them. In October some 2,000 Indians working in the Natal collieries were on strike and were keen that Gandhi led them. Helping them organize their strike and think about leadership etc. were eleven Tamil speaking women, among them Mrs. Thambi Naidoo wife of a close colleague of Gandhi. For their initiative and helping the strikers, the women were sent to three months in prison with hard labour;⁴⁴ Gandhi obviously could not ignore these momentous initiatives. Through October he addresses scores of striking workers in various towns spread over Natal. Acquiring the skills of an astute politician, in his narrative, he subtly mixed their immediate demands with their fundamental predicament: the £3 tax and the government's reneging on the promises made to Gokhale.

As a consequence of these meetings, the resolve of the workers increased. To avoid being coerced to return to work they moved into the towns of Dundee and Newcastle. But they were still close to the collieries and the management was making every effort to bring them back. "The Council of Action in Newcastle felt that, as long as the laborers continued to live on their masters' estates, the strike would not have its full effect".⁴⁵ It was decided that all of them would move to Charlestown some 35 miles away near the Transvaal border. Carrying their rice and dal, walking all the way, some 1,500 passive workers reached Charlestown on 3 November. At Charlestown they were fed free by the local merchants and quartered in the grounds of the local Mosque. But this was only a temporary halt. The emerging consensus was to cross over into the Transvaal. If not detained they would then keep walking all the way, several hundred kilometers to Johannesburg. Besides, the 1,100-acre Tolstoy farm, another 600-acre farm was also available for the marchers to stay. On 6 November the group left Charlestown to walk towards Volksrust on the other side of the border in Transvaal. This started a series of skirmishes with the authorities. A strike is site specific. But here the government was confronted with a strike where the strikers were absconding not as strikers but as family, as a community. In the place of strikers the government found a group of men, women, and children plodding away calmly as if to seek a destiny but on their terms; a historical precursor of many such short and long marches by the oppressed. This was Gandhi's long march. The situation was tense but marked by a sense of rejuvenating inclusiveness. The state was made to think and make its role explicit; the rich Indians were invited to stand up, be counted, and contribute as per their considerable abilities; and the strikers were made aware that there are no free lunches. Walking mile after mile, sleeping in the open with hope standing in for clarity can be daunting. The bodies took a beating but the will endured. The marchers stuck to the plan till Gandhi, Polak, and Kallenbach were arrested and sent to jail with Gandhi getting nine months with hard labor.⁴⁶ The marchers were sent back to Natal in three trains by the government. But their will and resolve was not broken.

The disposition and sentiments of the striking workers was infectious. Throughout Natal Indians were reacting to the developing scenario. While it was the miners who had gone on strike, it was now the turn of the sugar plantation workers to strike. By the middle of November some 15,000 sugar production-related workers were on strike. Some of the workers moved into the local towns while some went to the Phoenix settlement. The spirit of uprising and revolt spread to every sector of the economy particularly in the urban areas. Brick kilns, city corporations, ports, sugar plantations, coal mines, railways, ships, shops, hotels and even hospitals and sanitation facilities were effected. The strike was so all-encompassing that in a meeting a "speaker asked hospital and sanitary workers to return to duty as an act of courtesy to their fellow citizens".[47] However, for all their pent-up angst, the workers remained responsible towards their civic duties. The thrust of the rising was not lost on the whites. They recognized that the Indians were essentially looking for a better future and this meant becoming educated and not getting stuck as labourers in some plantation or mine, and as an extension, a sense of identity and equality.

But non-violence is a difficult practice. Strikers did resort to violence and in the clashes with the police many were hurt and some died. As could be expected repercussions followed. "In the last week of November, the Government renewed its efforts to break the strike in Natal by force. Contingents of police were dispatched to get labourers back to work. Fleeing the police, many workers swarmed on to the farm at Phoenix.... The workers 'repeatedly stated that they would rather die than go back to their work, and they seemed to be really afraid'".[48]

The detention, bad food, poor living conditions, and hard labour had considerably affected Kasturba's health. Gandhi on his part had decided to henceforth dress like an indentured labourer. He had shaved his head while in jail and now chose to wear white and keep his feet bare. This was his mourning for the strikers killed in police firing and perhaps also for the old *deha* he had discarded. The intrepid itinerant social worker *satyagrahi* had arrived.

The focus now shifted to a three-member Commission set up by the South African government under local and international pressure. Gandhi still had to master the art of negotiation at the end of a skirmish. Gandhi wanted to boycott the Commission. Gokhale dissuaded him because he preferred to view the Commission from a long-term macro perspective particularly because the Viceroy of India had gotten involved. Gandhi reluctantly agreed.

Gokhale now decided to open another channel and mediate. Since he himself could not go to South Africa, he requested his friend C. F. Andrews and W. W. Pearson to go out to South Africa and mediate between the Indians and the Government. With their arrival things started moving fast. While Gandhi on his part kept up the pressure insisting on renewing the struggle, Andrews the astute priest knew when it was time to pull back and negotiate and if necessary reconcile. He urged Gandhi to begin talks with Smuts. Taking a leaf from Gandhi's minimalist philosophy, he focused on two demands: the £3 tax and recognition of Indian marriages.

Gandhi now started to seriously plan about returning to India. Kasturba after her release continued to remain very sick. By March Kasturba's health improved and they could travel to Johannesburg. While waiting for the report of the Commission he had to experience an interesting albeit unhappy development. In the last week of March a group of people representing various sections of Mohammedans in the Transvaal, met in the famous Hamidia Hall.

> The meeting resolved that 'the recommendation of recognizing one wife only and her children ... if carried out, will molest and violate the principle of our sacred religion'. The meeting further made 'it known to whom it may

concern that Messers Gandhi, Polak and their associates have no right or authority whatsoever to represent the Moslem community or any matters concerning them.[49]

This was also a time when he got news of plans to assassinate him.

Once again we find him contemplating about the 'we' particularly the family. He writes,

> Service of the family should come first. This is quite correct from the point of view of our supreme interest. He alone who can render such service will be able to serve the community or the country. What that service consists in is the only point to consider.[50]

But this understanding of the importance of family obligations was not easy. It contradicted his position in an event concerning Jeki Mehta at phoenix. It shows how difficult it is to be a *satyagrahi*. Kasturba suspected Jeki of harbouring romantic notions about Manilal since Gandhi disagreed they had violent disagreements. Commenting on this in a letter to Kallenbach he writes, "My point is that you cannot attach yourself to a particular woman and yet live for humanity. The two do not harmonize".[51]

In the last week of May, a bill in line with the Enquiry Commission recommendations was published. Gandhi accepted that the bill did settle some of the present difficulties. Moreover he accepted that it was now time for some peace from the constant tension of uncertainty.[52] After this it was time to leave. In line with his new orientation for the first time he travelled third class along with Kasturba and Kallenbach.

With his returning to India, Gandhi stopped living on the threshold. Back home he found he had moved to the crossroad. It was no more a question of insider-outsider; it was a question of choosing from alternatives. He could now talk with a sense of belonging; he could now speak for himself without hyphenation as South African Indian. He would not have to defend the need for a personal space in an alien landscape. He now could reengage in a new matrix of ambitions and empathies, a narrative of thinking, being, and purpose where he need not be an adjunct of himself. To articulate this, he now also had a world-view designed and grounded on brahmacharya, satyagraha and swaraj permeated with satya and ahimsa. As for the adjunct, the social worker, latter in his autobiography he explains succinctly, albeit taking some liberties, gratis hindsight.

> If I found myself entirely absorbed in the service of the community, the reason behind it was my desire for self-realization. I had made the religion of service my own, as I felt that God could be realized only through service. And service for me was the service of India, because it came to me without my seeking, because I had an aptitude for it. I had gone to South Africa for

travel, for finding an escape from Kathiawar intrigues and for gaining my livelihood. But as I have said, I found myself in search of God and striving for self-realization.[53]

Gandhi was now a true intrepid itinerant social worker; fearless, homeless and always available to try and solve the contradictions of society.

Satyagrahi and Satyagraha

In India a *satyagrahi* is often considered to be a sanyasi. While many a Gandhian accepted this uncritically, and Vinoba was considered to be a sanyasi, such thinking however benign remains flawed. It exaggerates religious propensities and tends to give uncritical sanctity to its proponents who then tend to become soft communalists. We find such credulous attitude impacting concepts such as Bhoodan. An ingenuous mixture of dharma, daan, and the right of a leader to re-apportion private property not only went against Gandhi's concepts such as trusteeship, but albeit unintentionally gave enormous authority to a leader and his proclivities. Moreover, it allowed its critiques to subtly undermine the thrust of satyagraha itself. Further proponents of western style development and modernization by critiquing satyagraha's seemingly out-worldly ethos were able to render it effete. A sanyasi quits to acquire moksha; a *satyagrahi* quits personal acquisitiveness (both property and social position) to assert the elevating significance of self-in-society. Interestingly while both have to acquire requisite critical and creative competences, and Gandhi had to struggle to acquire these, the method to acquire might have similarities. In the Indian context this remained a problematic for the Gandhian because while for a sanyasi the individual is primary, for a *satyagrahi* it is society.

The Gandhian problematic is one of a transition of a *satyarthi* to a *satyagrahi* i.e. from a good human being to a thoroughly aware self-in-society. The thoroughness reflects the ability to recognize the elemental significance of the social and thereby of social living. The question is how should one articulate such a discourse wherein certain vital principles and minimal aspirations are bound together by a pledge particularly when pitched against prejudiced hegemonic forces?

A *satyagrahi* quests and aspires for self-realization. And like in the *Prasna* Upanishad the problematic of 'lie' holds. Along with openness, humility, commitment, and perseverance, for the *satyagrahi* the mission is not one of idle curiosity. It is rigorously structured around aspirations, belief, and a critical openness to creatively search and re-search. Obviously, a quest emphasizes intentions; these intentions have the potential of a lie. A lie can be a deliberate obfuscation or denial; it can be a partial truth or just plain ignoring of facts. It can also be a manifestation of ignorance; ignorance is not necessarily deliberate. The dilemma a satyagraha movement faces is that a 'lie' can remain undetected, creating its own progenies, unless it is nailed from the beginning by what Gandhi recommends, 'a pledge'. This 'pledge' is the creativity component which goes beyond simple commitment; the group being heterogeneous and therefore unpredictable makes its leadership creative. The *satyagrahi* has to remain scrupulously transparent from the beginning. This means total fidelity to 'integrity' in all relationships. Perhaps this is why satyagraha struggles are akin to 'dharma' like activities and a *satyagrahi* get mixed up with a sanyasi. Dharma incidentally puts a lease on the exuberant exigencies of *artha* and *kama*. This is why in satyagraha an individual must be very careful about the potentiality of the *satyagrahi* adjunct s/he creates. Gandhi at times had to pull up this adjunct, even at the cost of aborting a movement.

Notes

1 Gandhi (2006, 103).
2 Ibid. (107).
3 Ibid. (62).
4 Tidrick (2008, 63).
5 *An Autobiography* (2004, 244).
6 Guha (2013, 194).
7 Ibid. (189).
8 *An Autobiography* (2004, 292).
9 Ibid. (190).
10 Guha (2013, 207).
11 Ibid. (232).
12 *CWMG*, Vol. 6 (352–68).
13 Ibid. (416–17).
14 Ibid. (187–88).
15 Guha (2013, 255).
16 *CWMG*, Vol. 8 (60).
17 Ibid. (41–42).
18 Ibid. (51).
19 Ibid. (32).
20 Ibid. (34).
21 Ibid. (61).
22 Ibid.
23 Ibid.
24 Ibid., Vol. 54 (268).
25 Ibid. (78).
26 Guha (2013, 279).
27 *CWMG*, Vol. 8 (157).
28 Ibid. (246).
29 Ibid., Vol. 9 (149).
30 Ibid. (206).
31 Ibid.
32 Guha (2013, 318).
33 *CWMG*, Vol. 8 (85).
34 Ibid., Vol. 9 (302–3).
35 Ibid. (444–50).
36 Guha (2013, 361).
37 *Indian Opinion*, 18–6–1910.
38 *CWMG*, Vol. 11 (49).
39 Ibid. (417).
40 Ibid. (416).
41 Ibid., Vol. 12 (113–15).
42 Ibid. (187).
43 Ibid. (187–88).

44 Ibid. (471).
45 Ibid., Vol. 12 (513).
46 Ibid. (264).
47 Guha (2013, 485).
48 Ibid. (487).
49 Ibid. (513).
50 *CWMG*, Vol. 12 (380).
51 Guha (2013, 515).
52 *CWMG*, Vol. 12 (436–38).
53 *An Autobiography* (2004, 146).

4
SATYAGRAHI GANDHI RETURNS TO INDIA

A returning *satyagrahi*

For Gandhi, the twenty years in South Africa, the first decade as a *satyarthi* and the next as a *satyagrahi*, were profoundly transformational. After coming back from England with a law degree and high expectations, Gandhi had faced an uncertain future. Chance intervened and he got an opportunity to go to South Africa as a lawyer, and in the process ensured for himself a living and a profession. Over the years that he stayed in South Africa, the content and meaning of both living and profession changed profoundly and in the process so did his complex world view. When he went for the first time, his sojourn was to be a short assignment. But he stayed on for twenty years. However, ironically he 'went away' only to 'stay back'; albeit in a foreign country he retained his habits and with some adjustments his habitat, his habitations. In a way 'Gandhi the Indian' went away only to come back as 'Indian Gandhi'; Indian as a suffix and a prefix tells a lot about what happened to Mohandas Karamchand Gandhi in the twenty years that he spent in South Africa.

On his return, while he might not have had much to show materially, he, however, came back an accomplished being, full of ideas, experiences, and wisdom, most of which was acquired in the thick of finely tuned struggles conducted simultaneously against both the self and the South African state. Besides the money which he earned, everything else, including his fads, was personally acquired. Every aspect of his being evolved through processes of diligent and hard work, learning, reading, rejecting, and consolidating an identity through challenges waged at both the personal and social levels. As a shy young barrister he went to South Africa dressed in suits and shoes, only to be thrown out of a train for insisting that he too was a human being. When he came back he had given up his shoes and had taken to dress like an Indian indentured labourer: a practice he had struggled to eradicate.[1]

Why did he change his attire? More specifically, why did he decide to dress like an indentured labourer, a practice which when he was returning was already fading? Perhaps this was a rhetorical political statement knowing that something was missing in what he himself was trying to do, while also indicating possible patterns of engagement to resolve various anomalies. It could also be an assertion, particularly at the personal level, that the engagement with society, henceforth, had to have a distinct form and content. Perhaps it was a muse which contoured the mystic into what he became: an 'intrepid itinerant mystic social worker', a very complex personification of all his praxis. The attire added the timelessness of a mystic to the intrepid itinerant Gandhi. In many ways it was a measure of genuine empathy Gandhi felt for a labourer, particularly one who had to indenture to be able to live.

Besides this sartorial predilection towards the end, the twenty years of stay had been to use his terminology the journey of a 'seeker' or '*mumukshu*'. But a *mumukshu*'s journey is a lifelong affair. Andrews, a priest and a fellow seeker, who in many ways was a professional social worker himself, with his trained and highly sensitive mind could discern some disjunction which Gandhi had not noticed. Andrews felt Gandhi was monopolizing a position and a space which was progressively being contested, albeit in a restrained fashion. Andrews recognized that either Gandhi was too big for the job or that he was working with concepts which were too radical for the South African milieu. A core problem was racism. Gandhi as a leader of Indians, drawing inspiration as an Indian from India had been responding to this utterly degrading issue, only partially; partially because the Indians knowing that the British tacitly supported apartheid, considered themselves British Indians and distinct from the kafir. Moreover the Indians were not sure as to whether South Africa was their 'home'. Gandhi had no real organic contact with the original native African people. Moreover, some of the emerging problems, such as those of the miners, were not Indian specific. These included the white and the black working classes. If he had to relate to these larger working-class constituencies, then he would have had to make South Africa his *karmabhoomi* and give up India as the primary source of inspiration. Moreover, the cluster of leaders with whom he associated as a leader to lead the struggles against the South African state were uninclined, perhaps even incompetent, to handle and lead complex class-based movements? The South African socio-economy was systemically moving from a colonial imperial pattern to a monetary-finance system with the South African leadership seeking to instil apartheid as integral to the milieu. Individuals from the Indian community were being inexorably drawn into various levels of the emerging South African socio-economic mosaic. As a consequence they were acquiring new and distinct patterns of self and social interests. The struggles had to correspondingly relate to these new clusters of aspirations. Gandhi and the old leadership recognized this, but were not equipped to deal with its dialogical nature. The Indian community was at a crossroad. While some of the tenets and ethos of the old struggles continued to hold meaning, the manoeuvre now needed to be based on a sharper and more multifactorial world view which could respond to the local processes of transformation. But who would initiate this? Given that the skirmishes with the state were becoming increasingly frequent, was Gandhi capable, ready, and inclined to respond to the demands of the 'moment' with alacrity? Was he ready to design and then mentor a platform in tune with emerging demands of the transforming Indian diaspora? And above all, what would all this mean to the 'Indian' in the 'South African Indian'? If the nature of the strikes in the mines was anything to go by, then his ideas and involvement might have to be adapted.

But Gandhi the seeker was returning a conformed campaigner. At the conceptual level, with a rather innovative reading of the Gita, he came back with a decidedly innovative understanding of brahmacharya, satyagraha, and swaraj, each with a strong grounding in satya and ahimsa. At an individual level he had been systematically working on the distinct aspects of the personal and the social within individuals. He himself had evolved through a series of awareness building events, from a *satyarthi* to a *satyagrahi*. In the process he reworked the concepts of tyaag as distinct from daan. Thirdly in his *satyagrahi* phase, he was keenly involved in his ashram experiments. These ashrams were spaces with a two-fold intent. At one level, they helped sustain efforts to distinguish and understand the personal and the social within us, and at another level, they provided aid to nurture the ongoing satyagraha.

During the last ten years of his stay in South Africa which can be called the *satyagrahi* phase, in the course of his social involvements, he worked with and developed a number of seminal and persuasive concepts: brahmacharya, ahimsa, satyagraha, swaraj, sarvodaya, the personal social tension, and ashrams as a *satyagrahi* institution. Viewing humanity as a whole he started developing a world view of essential and radical change and continuity connecting the individual and society to various concerns and the interconnectivity of these concerns. In South Africa his efforts were more in the nature of conceptualizing and experimenting. Moreover these were conducted in a comparatively small scale, were relatively less volatile and less complex, and were also conducted against a rather immature state which itself was in the making. Confronted with a political theology which not only advocated religious inclusiveness, but also a total lack of bitterness towards the rival, the race and Bible-wielding Boer leadership found itself at a loss about how to respond. The South African leadership might have been similar, but it was certainly not as nuanced as the imperial British who ruled India. Consequently, between the British and the Boer, at least initially, Gandhi had the space to learn, conceptualize, and try alternatives.

After his return Gandhi substantially elaborated his concepts. While in the next chapters we will elaborate the significance of each concept using both the South African experience and his subsequent involvements in India, here we will just draw lessons with an analysis of the South African experience. The import of this is in the fact that the core elements of the narrative he was to articulate during his subsequent three decades of involvement in the Indian independence movement were all conceptualized by the time he left South Africa.

The interlocutor and his discourse

Andrews' missive poses some fundamental questions. Firstly, does an interlocutor have a shelf life and if so why? Secondly an interlocutor actually helps express the aspirations of a heterogeneous group which embraces diverse interests with each nurturing distinct fundamental interests and leadership ambitions. This diversity means the group can be internally susceptible to conflicting interests. Thirdly the inner tension within the group which is due to its being contingent on various elements, can lead to the leadership taking imprecise and fuzzy decisions, often to their own and the group's detriment. The problematic is in the interlocutor's perception or understanding and also her capacity to be equanimous while deciding from amongst alternatives. Gandhi's social involvement throughout his stay in South African is a history of coming to terms with such complexities. For the first ten years *satyarthi* Gandhi tried to live a decent honest personal life while simultaneously becoming socially conscious. Being thrown out of a train because he was coloured rudely brought to him the raw reality of racial prejudice; by convincing his first client to be conciliatory he brought forth the humane in the human; involving in spiritual discussion alerted him to the distinction between the transactional and the transcendental; as an Indian in South Africa he had to prominently engage with geographical and human frontiers. Above all, this was also a period of coming to terms with his likes or attachments and dislikes or aversions, some of which he elaborated in the Hind Swaraj and latter in his autobiography. In all this, he came to take a very critical and creative look at the personal and the social within his own individual self. He for instance recognized that while we prefer to think that it is the 'I' which decides our likes and dislikes, actually in our complex societies, it is the 'me', a heavily encumbered social construct, which dominates our decisions although it can never do so without the collaboration of the 'I'. This collaboration however is beset with enormous tensions particularly if the individual is aware and conscientious. Agency or intervention can lag or even breakdown because the actual nature of the 'moment' or the immediate present is kind of hazy if not obscure to the individual in the discursive narrative of the 'I' and 'me'. Moreover the 'moment' is imperious, tending to gain impulsiveness when decisions can easily become susceptible. To illustrate Gandhi was ready to throw Kasturba out of his house because she was reluctant to clean the chamber pot of a guest who happened to be a low-caste convert, even when he knew that in South Africa going away was not possible for Kasturba. He, it seems, settled for soft-authoritarianism. He would discuss, but would like to retain the right to have the last word. The 'I' and 'me' contradiction is not just a simple academic manifestation!

Problematically in our so-called developed societies, the 'I' seems to be an eternal latecomer. Not surprisingly this brings forth the significance of 'me' and its inspiration, the community, as a mentor. Incidentally, perhaps unfairly, the family remains stranded between the individual and the community creating distinctions between 'I' 'we' (I and family) and 'us' (I, we and associates, excluding the 'other'). Communities depend enormously on the quality of face-to-face dialogue amongst its members. But when this dialogue is moderated and mediated by an adjunct of any member, perhaps in the form of a *satyagrahi*/social worker/seer, we can have a difficult situation, particularly because of the adjunct's urge to appropriate the moment/present and, in the process, usurp the same. This can lead to enormous differences between the 'I', we, and us leaving everyone floundering particularly with issues such as immediate and fundamental interests. In the course of all this, the adjunct, assuming a status of aloofness and objectivity, can appropriate the community's agenda to create models of knowledge both about the local and the world, an understanding through which it then appropriates the individual-home-community relationship. This it seems is evident in the case of Gandhi, particularly in his relationship with Kasturba and Harilal. Perhaps '*satyagrahi* Gandhi' was an adjunct about whom Andrews was warning?

To elaborate, the *satyarthi* turned *satyagrahi* Gandhi progressively started talking about living a simple life. But 'why' did he want to live a simple life? Complicating this was his contention that his simplicity was not that of a recluse, but that of an active social participant. Incidentally and problematically this was a personal choice in which Gandhi did not consult the family. A simple but active life when lived with others can be a 'selfish' concept vis-à-vis others because simple can be a very relative, albeit intimidating ethos. Simple living is a complex discursive narrative which enjoins restructuring of existing living patterns, putting enormous physical and emotional pressure on others. Gandhi's apportioning such a role for himself meant adjustment by family members who might not have been equipped for the same. Harilal's essential complaint was against such fait accompli that his father tended to propose and impose on him.

The Zulu rebellion was an eye opener for Gandhi. Ostensibly it was a war, rather a brutal action to subdue a revolt. Gandhi recognized the essential contradictions, the hidden agenda of the white rulers, and the enormous brutality of human beings. This involvement, in which his association was that of a social worker, who did not, or was not allowed to bear arms, also made him aware of his keenness for social service. His involvement, besides making him contemplative about the nature of human relationships, put him firmly on the path to become an 'intrepid itinerant social worker', intrepid because he started becoming fearless and confident, and itinerant because while he did not necessarily create the situation, he did make himself available to respond and address whenever and wherever a situation needing succour arose. Even so, Gandhi's experience did teach him the limitations of the itinerant. A social worker has to recognize his/her competence, ground realities and the nature of existing or emerging opportunities to influence the on-going social narrative. It can be argued that this is when the mystic in him started to emerge. As an ordinary man he recognized his limits although he did try to stretch them. But by choosing to become involved in the war he now sought to move beyond such restrictions. Could he then overcome both social limitations and personal proclivities and become truly liberated from the restrictions imposed by time and place?

Contemplating on his involvement in social service led him to recognize the 'mystic' in 'serving others'; for him this also became a way to serve God as a tangible, spiritual, and secular act. It became a faith. The mystic is in the way Gandhi separates 'lok-seva' that is selflessly serving people from 'lok-kalyan' the domain of Truth and God, a project way beyond an individual. The transformational efficacy of brahmacharya, satya, and ahimsa were the consequent spill-overs of this transition of the 'intrepid itinerant mystic social worker', a personality who did not have to have any false modesty about his own being. As he evolved and grew into himself, everything personal took a back seat.

Gandhi: knowing the 'I', 'me' and 'us'

Interacting with the Boers, the British, and in a limited way with the local native Africans, Gandhi was able to prospect beyond his personal space. For him his association with the Boer war was a break-event. Unlike in the Pietermaritzburg event, this time he was aware of the situation. It is also around this time that he starts becoming clearer about the import of the very subjective desire to *'serve society'* as something significantly distinct. But then *'serving'* can be awkward because it can be inundated by issues that are secular, spiritual, and moral in addition to the ever-present avarice. The importance of service is that it questions the relation between 'I' and 'mine', thereby clarifying for us our personal potentialities through an underlining of the ambiguity between our individuality and social proclivities. Service with the aid of 'choice' helps us interrogate the notion of freedom.

Gandhi aspires to translate such ambiguities into strength by unequivocally serving others. Since life would have no meaning if one is not able to attain perfect love on earth, the only alternative is to strive for it. For him, to be able to gain perfect joy and peace and thereby love, an individual has to completely subjugate his or her own personality to that of society. Gandhi thus was redefining belongingness as an attribute which does not radiate only from the individual because it is like a mapping of give and take, and a terrain of comprehensive *aparigraha*, i.e. non-possession. Further, for him it meant a prioritizing of the social within us. But this comes with a dilemma. Being virtuous and practicing virtue are not the same because the act can cover up the motivation behind the practice. *Satyagrahi* Gandhi had to resolve such potential contradictions.

By 1904, influenced by Ruskin's *Unto This Last*, Gandhi purchased a farm where we find him pushing his individual transition by prioritizing the social over the personal. The purpose of life for Gandhi is to know oneself and the instrument for this knowing is selfless service, and efforts have to be made to push the personal further behind into the rear. But, the social cannot accept loneliness; it needs a mate. For Gandhi, the *satyagrahi* therefore becomes a necessary and sufficient adjunct. To elaborate, just like love, kindness, and generosity, morality too involves social relations and is apparent only in relation with others. A man Gandhi argues becomes human when he recognizes the family and then is able to include in this family his community and the human race. The idea is to feel the similar as same for every human being and thereby humble the 'I' while accepting the necessity of its presence. However, in the process an element of possessiveness can emerge.

The individual is a part of the family and very often the threshold from where the individual dialogues with society is the family home. Such a dialogue can become demanding if not contingent when family members are taken for granted. Gandhi thinks this occurs, "because love of family is based on selfishness and the family members are worshippers of selfishness".[2] This is a very arbitrary and non-democratic opinion since it seeks to arbitrate very primordial relationships where the individuals concerned are related not by choice, and who might not be equipped and competent to respond on a par. Perhaps this was a reason why Gandhi fluctuated between being patriarchal and being a democrat while dealing with his family. Gandhi apparently was not always sympathetic to the needs of a *satyarthi*.

Possession and social service

The Boer War while exposing the futility of war had made Gandhi aware of the practical implications of *himsa*, ahimsa, love, and hatred. He was progressively becoming convinced that self-control and living a simple life alone could ensure a meaningful life of ahimsa, love, and satya. But this self-control has to be acquired through action where action has to be selfless service that is suffused with the spirit of '*anasakti*' – nonattachment. His reading of the Gita had made it clear that while fundamental principles are immutable, practices and modes of conduct are amenable to reason and are mutable. Analyzing the message of Krishna to Arjuna, Gandhi comprehends a profound principle. Arjun's protest was not about killing, but about killing kinsmen. The problem lay in possession and possessiveness regarding 'my kinsmen'. This distinction and insight frees Gandhi from the fetters of '*mama*'; possession and possessiveness which can make the best of people not only ignorant, but indecisive too. The path to equanimity lies in non-possession, *aparigraha*. Talking about voluntary poverty, social service, and the paradoxical necessity of having to be in politics to be able to do social service, he asserted, "I came definitely to the conclusion that, if I had to serve people in whose midst my life was cast and of whose difficulties I was witness from day to day, I must discard all wealth, all possession".[3] Since there is always a paucity of things and abundance of unsatisfied wants, possession and possessiveness will always lead to strife and violence. Therefore, he concludes that the only thing that can be possessed by all is non-possession that is not to have anything whatsoever: in other words, a willing renunciation. It must be noted that while 'me' is always in the present because it is constantly evolving, 'I' and 'mine' transcend time and coexist in the past, present, and the future. For Gandhi this created a lifelong tension because social service is partial to the 'me'.

Gandhi accepts that to give up possessions and dedicate oneself to the service of one's fellow beings is a demanding undertaking. It can leave "ample room for hypocrisy and humbug, because a man or a woman may easily deceive himself or herself and deceive his or her neighbour also, by saying: 'In spirit I have given up possessions, and yet externally I am possessing these things; you must not examine my deed, you must examine my intention; and of my intention only I must remain the sole witness', That is a trap and a death trap".[4] Conviction and intentionality remain a complex constraint of the 'I' and 'me', where the 'I', taking succour from the 'mine' undermines the 'me'. Renunciation too in a way is a possession because you acquire a competence. And over time the renunciant can become an adjunct of 'I'; the 'I' through capability as a possession (God-men come to mind) can make provisions for the future to secure it. This urge, invariably leads to appropriating more than what we need because we are never sure as to how much will secure the future. In the process we allow the ubiquitous and capricious 'want' to dominate our ongoing existential discourse vis-à-vis needs. This want, the personification of possessiveness, undermines the seekers quest for truth and equanimity. Therefore Gandhi suggests a deliberate and voluntary reduction of wants. For him "a seed must disintegrate under earth and perish before it can grow into grain".

Owing and owning

For Gandhi social involvement is the cultivation of a spirit of yajna. For him, "Yajna means an act directed to the welfare of others, done without desiring any return for it, whether of a temporal or spiritual nature, 'Act' here must be taken in its widest sense, and includes thought and word, as well as deed. Others embrace not only humanity, but all life".[5] The issue therefore is one of a spirit of renunciation; that is how to erase the 'I's and 'mine's' from religion, politics, economics and so on.

This brings up the problematic of the word '*sva*' (as in swaraj, swadeshi and so on), which in Sanskrit stands for self and possession or wealth. Can we have a sense of self without a sense of possession; an 'I' and 'me' without a 'mine'? And can we also segregate the more complex, '*ahankara*' ego from the '*mamakara*' possessiveness?[6] And while at it, can we respond to the question as to why these questions emerge in the first place? Gandhi took a rather uncluttered stand. To live we consume, and to consume we need to produce things which we can consume. All such products by definition are social because production processes, by which we produce consumables, are never exclusively an individual's prerogative. The relationship of man and nature, resulting in consumables is a sum-total of hand-me-downs stretching back to prehistory. Everything produced depends upon an unrestricted access to this corpus of social knowhow which is a social endowment and common heritage. If such is the situation where every product is a product of universal give and take, then everything we consume should legitimately be everybody's to have or not have. Anybody can claim and or authorize possession itself. Thus possession itself becomes an engagement with give and take which is neither exchange nor reciprocation but happenstance.

Since by birth human beings are dependent and indebted creatures, for Gandhi, we and our society are essentially a product of the spontaneous sacrifices rather yajnas of our ancestors over millennium. Essentially human history is a collective ongoing yajna to which individuals bring their offerings. In short, every individual is a beneficiary of a world to the creation of which his contribution is very, very modest. Having partaken of the remnants of the oblations offered by our ancestors in the ongoing yajna, it is incumbent on us that we don't shirk from contributing to the continuity of the yajna and thereby ensuring the future of society. However, since historically accumulated debts can never be 'repaid', all we can do is accept them with grace and gratitude, and on our part continue the ongoing universal yajna by accepting our personal and collective responsibilities. The '*sva*' in effect is an abiding and enabling dilemma of give and take.

Gandhi considers this dilemma to be one of conflicting claims of owning and owing: of the simultaneity of owning and being indebted. To resolve this inherent contradiction Gandhi decided to bypass the generally hegemonic 'I' and 'mine' and make the 'me' explicitly central to his social discourse. The 'me' he felt is more sympathetic towards the yajna. From this given embodiment of contradictions and aspirations, Gandhi derives three fundamentals: tyaag, tapas, and ashram. Firstly, for him, an individual needs to prioritize the social within so as to minimize the acquisitive, while simultaneously acclaiming the indebtedness. This is tapas. Incidentally Gandhi remained a firm believer in rebirth, and as such was not particularly bothered about the need to estimate an individual's contribution-returns balance-sheet. Secondly to consolidate the benefit of tapas it has to be preceded and escorted by tyaag. Lastly this relationship is an expression of the more mundane 'give and take'. Gandhi sought to institutionalize these as an ethos in his ashrams.

Tyaag and tapas

Engagement between the 'I' and the 'me' is generally articulated around the notions of endowment and entitlement. Endowment refers to natural abilities and talents by birth, while entitlement refers to personalized claims which we think we have a right to. Both depend on the efficacy of the social. Even to a genius rare talent has no meaning unless it is recognized by society. By recognizing it, the individual only informs the personal within of a distinct endowment.

Tapa is a practice of austerity which aids in restraining us from wrong tendencies and indulgences. Indulgence is an expression of not being able to contain and contend with one's own self. Through tapas we seek to come to terms with our sense of discontent, an attribute which is a product of our contradictory capacity of being able to go beyond the restrictive instinctual, and a habit of trying to rectify everything else before rectifying oneself. Tapas by actively discouraging attachment, puts our proclivities into perspective by critically and creatively looking at aspirations, responses, and longings. Consequently tapas become a yajna that is a prayer and also a tyaag or giving up of both discontent and attachment.

For Gandhi tyaag is a very crucial concept. But does it become a 'giving up' only 'to acquire'? The tyaagi or renouncer is a symbol of authority within society.[7] At the core of Gandhi's notion of tyaag is his urge for equanimity which was influenced by the Gita, "[But] work alone is your proper business, never the fruits [it may produce]: let not your motive be the fruit of works not your attachment to [mere] worklessness" (Bhagwat Gita, 2:47). Work when done with a spirit of detachment is yagna. In other words the guiding principle has to be one of '*phala-tyaag*' that is renouncing the rights to the benefits of involvement. This renouncing includes access to the benefits per se and also the rights to conceptualize what these benefits should be. But it precludes any exclusive right to arrogate the benefits. Thus for Gandhi renouncing does not mean abandoning or quitting the creation of benefits. It is also not an act of charity. It certainly is not abandoning the world and retiring into a forest. For him it is the spirit of renunciation which should 'rule all activities of life'. By forestalling appropriation and its inherent conflicts, renunciation can ensure a better 'today' and also a better 'tomorrow'.

This spirit of renunciation has '*phala-tyaag*' at its core which combines simultaneity of involvement (in duty) and detachment (from benefits). This tyaag reflects the inherent essential qualities (nature) of Nature which harmonizes give and take. The best way to understand this could be by understanding the so-called 'monkey behaviour'. A monkey on a tree with fruits tends to pluck one, take a bite or two, drop the fruit, only to pluck another one and repeat the process. As a consequence it drops a lot of partially eaten fruits to the ground. A man observing this is severally censorious pointing to the enormous wastage the monkey's eating habits indicate. For him a monkey should first eat the whole fruit and only then pluck another one. The monkey's behaviour is destructive, wanton, and capricious – 'monkey behaviour'. But does the tree which bears the fruits think so?

The tree yields beyond its reproductive needs. Only a few seeds will ultimately become trees. So how does the tree perceive the antics of the monkey? After all, the monkeys do tend to drop a lot. Actually these partially eaten fruits are eaten by others who otherwise would have no access to them and have to wait till the fruits ripen. But by then they might not survive. Many other animals, insects, microorganisms not only consume and survive on the fruits dropped by the monkeys, but their rich dung enriches the soil. This guano in turn is acquired by the tree and other vegetation around the tree as their food. The tree thus has sacrificed to acquire its survival while also ensuring reproduction. The tree remains involved and detached, serving others to serve it. This non-antagonistic give and take is the true significance of tyāg. Gandhi employs this non-antagonism to explicate ahimsa and brahmacharya. Ahimsa for him is '*krodha-tyaag*' that is giving up of anger. The question is why do we get angry? Anger arises because we think we are being denied legitimate: possession and possessiveness. By giving up anger, Gandhi hoped to get over the clinginess of possession and possessiveness and thereby acquire self-reliance and self-control. You don't give up control; you re-negotiate the whole notion of possession and possessiveness between 'I' and 'me' taking mine out of the narrative. Compromise, compassion, nurturing and so on become part of this innovative discourse. In the same way through brahmacharya he hoped to renounce longing. Brahmacharya for him refers to '*trishna tyaag*', renouncing or abjuring of longing. Essentially brahmacharya means 'walking in knowledge or wisdom'. In Gandhi's case the stress was on abjuring sex to be able to do so. Sex presupposes a partner for satiation or fulfilment. This primordial and indispensable duality was an anachronism for Gandhi because he felt it brought in the 'I' via deception. Through the renouncing of longing, he hoped to acquire a sense of equanimity. Tyāg however is not possible without the inspiration of satya and ahimsa. A more detailed discussion of these issues will be done in the following chapters.

However, in Gandhi there is another dimension to this issue of give up to acquire. This is implicit in his refusal to associate renunciation with going to the forest. Within renunciation is a subtle element of acquisition owing to achievement which is inherent in all renouncing. The problematic of tyaag is in the fact that the act becomes an end in itself. Gandhi recognizing this suggests that tyaag is an event and as such remains encumbered with inherent expectations. Since this negotiation is with the self, perhaps the negative fallout of expectation can be mitigated by cultivating a sense of unsolicited compassion and transparency, traits Gandhi cultivated and propagated. In his own way he sought to restrict the personal so as to acquire the capacity to deny a role to self-deception through expectations.

To sum up, given his understanding of owing and owning for Gandhi tyaag in a sense is modified steadiness; a person gives up an avenue of expression only to acquire another permanency, suitably modified to suit emerging proclivities. Tyaag can only be an awareness event readjusting the existing to make it more meaningful. Gandhi preferring awareness or as he put it, 'evolving revolution', chose to remain a renouncer, a tyaagi and not become an ascetic. "Ascetics were figures of loneliness working out their salvation each for himself, the renouncer was concerned about other people and this concern was expressed in his desire to lead others along the path which he had found".[8]

Gandhi as a renouncer had not dissociated from his family. Consequently, all his life he had to deal with the bipolarity of the householder and the renouncer; the urge to be assimilative and well-established against seeking exclusive salvation. Not surprisingly to sustain his activities we find him relying a lot on daan and tapas; he relied on daan to sustain the material particularly after he gave up his profession and on tapas as austerity to sustain the seeker. But a renouncer in an ashram is in another mode. He remains apart from society. Considering that his objective is salvation and in an ashram he is not necessarily burdened with acquiring daan, his concern for society becomes tenuous. Moreover, the ashram-resident can easily develop attachment to the ashram as a necessity for tapas. Perhaps this is why Gandhi chose to remain an itinerant. He gave up every ashram he established!

The Ashram

The ashrams for Gandhi were significant platforms to articulate his strategies to transform contemporary civilization. Since only the individual exercises conscience and therefore becomes the acquirer of legitimate moral power, the individual himself becomes an end. But unlike the individual an institution which cannot acquire conscious remains only a conceivable means to an end. In an institution interests become responsibilities and rights become duties thereby making or creating a commonality of interests. This commonality is what Gandhi hoped would give his ashrams legitimate moral authority to influence social transformation processes.

An ashram emerges to accommodate a renouncer who in his dedicated search for alternatives attracts others, both as associates and as followers. Here an inmate, whether a renouncer or *sanyasi*, liberated from the mundane labours of daily existence is able to focus on the quest of true knowledge or salvation. An ashram promotes enquiry and is thus also a place for a *mumukshu*, i.e. a seeker of *moksha*. An ashram prioritizes simple living by restricting needs and wants. While an ashram might involve in income generation activities, normally it survives on daan or charity. Organizationally its operations are governed by explicit rules, and these rules determine the nature of the ashram and the quality of its outreach.

Gandhi hoped to modify the concept of ashram to solve the *satyagrahi*'s bipolarity of being a renouncer and a householder. In his view an ashram should reflect a lifestyle which would be midway between a home and an institution, free from family restraints and institutional containment. He maintained that an ashram should indicate paths for people to realize their innate potentialities through experiencing oneness with nature and fellow humans. The phoenix, Tolstoy, and the latter Sabarmati, and Sewagram ashrams, were his efforts towards engaging with meaningful ennoblement. For him an ashram meant, "a community of men of religions where religion was total faith in the principles of truth and ahimsa". As such, while the objective of the ashram remains self-realization by the individual, social service has to be the means for this quest. Social service for Gandhi has to be the link between society, the resident-renunciant and the ashram. For Gandhi salvation was not in smothering the resident's lifestyle but in adapting the humdrumness of living by giving scope to the dormant or morality within. Since morality conspicuously and consciously encompasses the 'other', the householder-turned-ashram renunciate's existential agenda can be transformed into a quest of communal welfare by harmonizing the person's habits, habitat, and habitation.

Based on a process of withdrawal, renewal, and rededication, the essential ethos of the Gandhian ashrams were an adaptation of the stricter ascetic traditions. The principles Gandhi associates with the ashram at Phoenix, his first endeavour, were 'rigid simplicity', 'perpetual continence', 'detachment from the world', and formation of character with a view to self-realization'. By the time he established the satyagraha Ashram in Ahmedabad these were converted to strict vows: truth-telling, non-violence, celibacy, control of the palate, non-stealing, non-possession, refusal to use foreign cloth, fearlessness, and acceptance of untouchables. These vows were expected to aid moral and spiritual growth. Individuals were encouraged to come and benefit from interacting with like-minded people, while well directed interactions with the larger community through service would keep them abreast regarding the travails of the larger world. The idea was not to defend tradition, but to live and make it. In practice the ashrams were a hybrid of an extended family and a small Community. They were both an experiment and a site for experimentation and training of *satyagrahis*. His endeavour was to establish, "a new caste or a new code of conduct suitable to the present age and in conformity with Hinduism".

To incorporate the best qualities of an institution, make it function like an extended family, and be a learning platform to train *satyagrahis*, Gandhi changed the traditional practice of locating ashrams away from human habitations. He established his ashram amongst people, thereby ensuring that the *satyagrahis* never became dissociated from the people. For him the *satyagrahi* has to be a socially involved renunciate. As such for him the ashrams had to be windows and workshops for interaction at three levels: within the ashram, with the local community, and with the larger world. He sought to establish an organic link between the ashram and the larger community. The ashram nurtured an idea and its practitioner before an event and then post-event facilitated in sustaining it. To aid praxis, the rules governing the ashrams evolved from the flexibility of the Phoenix and Tolstoy farms, to stricter vows at Sabarmati. But the 'stricter' led to a dilemma. The ashram attracted many uncritical followers than *satyarthis* which forced it had to spend too much time and effort to sustain itself.

In terms of social praxis, ideally the ashrams were to aid the *satyagrahi* through a process of withdrawal, renewal, and re- involvement. It would begin with a pause at the ashram to reflect about the nature of social alienation, fragmentation, individualism, etc. This would be followed by a process of reflecting on the intentionality behind being a *satyagrahi*. Reinvigorated by a reconfirmation of faith in the principles of the truth and ahimsa, and oneness and harmony with fellow human and nature through participation in the ashram activities, the *satyagrahi* could then go back to her calling i.e. serving the people.

While Gandhi had put in a lot of thought regarding the ashram and its objectives and ethos, as a living space two aspects remained nebulous: the criteria to choose an ashram inmate and the problematic of the ashram became an end in itself. As has been said, when Gandhi stayed in Sevagram it became "the de facto capital of India since service of the country is the function of a capital city". But then without Gandhi, it lost its dynamism! The ashram it seems demands a driving force and ethos is not enough. An inmate has to be initiated into tapas austerity and meditation all of which need mentoring. This becomes particularly difficult when the inmates are a mixture of householders (*satyarthis* and followers) and renunciants (*satyagrahis*). Gandhi had no clear explanation. Paradoxically while Gandhi went away from Sabarmati ashram the institution survived and survives!

To sum up, an ashram is a place where hope, prayer, and resolute commitment discovers succour, comradery, and peer-guidance. It is a place of sojourn for the *satyagrahi* to contemplate, reorient, and go on with the mission. Gandhi's ashrams were not a stopover of a recluse. They were meant to be an ante-room for consultation. The question is whose hegemony should prevail in this site/space: that of those who have arrived willingly with or without ideas in their heads and prayers in their lips and possibly without an invitation; or perhaps that of dispensations that have their own ideas and might be apprehensive about the intentions of the new arrivals. The core issue was with the ashram's capacity and intention to mentor and sustain free debate within itself and with the society outside. This becomes problematic because ashrams have a discursive relationship with society. Social transformation, transition, and mobility, when mediated by ashrams, tend to become estranged experiments and rather antithetical to the local people's experiences. For the individual ashram resident, this is a difficult predicament. S/he can find that her capacity to debate with the 'outside' is straitened, constrained, tentative even provisional, while that with a co-ashram resident relatively more conducive. A new 'we' could very well emerge and take a life, all its own. This is a veritable handicap: creating self-centeredness and then living it.

Chance and choice

In South Africa Gandhi could have gone with the flow and benefited enormously. This is evident from his access to monetary resources. When he started from India he faced an uncertain future and of course hopes; in South Africa he chose to pause, think, ask questions and not allow the system to harangue and hurry him. He sought to know and understand the road humps conspicuously embodied by for instance apartheid. He paused at the roadside next to the hump, but unlike most of the Indian diaspora, he chose to not take the well-trodden path alongside the road hump. He recognized that he was on the threshold and wanted to take charge of his life; as an honest person, he took the first step to become a conscious *satyarthi*. Taking the Pietermaritzburg event in his stride, insisting that Dada Abdulla compromise with his nephew even after winning the case, and sticking to the vows he had made to his late mother are all indications of this choice.

The issue therefore is this question of making a choice. In the case of Gandhi this follows a more elemental problematic, that of chance. Chance had brought him to South Africa even though the subsequent necessity of what kind of life to make was more relative and open. He had the choice to build on the chance and adopt any lifestyle. It was this choice offered by chance which subsequently made him intrepid. However, chance is not some eureka moment. While it certainly is an opening, to optimize it requires well-reasoned choices. What stands out is that in spite of considerable monetary success, Gandhi chose to restrict his law practice, first to become a *satyarthi*, and then to give up completely to become a *satyagrahi*. He chose not to walk away, preferring to become a humble 'interpreter between two communities'. It was his personal convictions and the will to live by them which converted chance into a vigorous opportunity. Over twenty years he chose to convert the opportunity chance provided into a unique lifestyle. In terms of the struggles of the South African Indian he not only convinced others but convinced himself that he was the right man in the correct place. While it was not a preplanned design, it certainly was one of being receptive and of having the sagacity to blend chance and choice. *The import of all this is that choice, and not necessity, followed chance.* Perhaps necessity which does ensure stability and continuity is not necessarily a motivator of creativity and originality? Gandhi shows how.

Historically social transformation narratives are expressed as reforms or revolts and are generally articulated by the elite. Transformation will not take its own course; mankind has travelled way beyond hunting and gathering. The elite a very tenacious group, whether as rulers, reformists, or revolutionaries, will retain hegemony and articulate a sense of duty on behalf of society. Of course, these will reflect the internal contradictions of specific societies; there is no avoiding that. But we can have alternatives and chance can play a role. Through science and technology, the hegemonic elite, reformists, and revolutionaries seek to eliminate such dependencies. Chance for them is anathema. They know what they want and are also convinced about how to get it. For them social transformation is a neat matrix of change and continuity called development with change in charge. Accordingly all choices have to encourage change. In the process an individual is converted into a professional. The professional serves the system, is an itinerant and evolves acquiring solitary self-contained concerns pertaining to the sustenance of the system. Breaking the individual-family-neighbourhood assemblage, not equipped with the wherewithal to acquire alternatives, the professional is left nursing one hope: a benevolent *parivar*. And history also tells us that this hope is generally fulfilled but usually with a twist. The *parivar* first emerges as a virtual and then as a demanding outfit which sheds all vestigial qualities of benevolence.

In all this Gandhi stands out. Never giving up on his awareness of the role of chance and choice, he expressed it through his reliance on 'a small, still voice'.[9] Actually, he seems to accept the fuzziness of chance. To fully understand Gandhi's involvement in South Africa and even latter, we will have to decipher and interpret the significance of this dilemma of the import of chance and choice in the narrative of conscious involvement in social transformation processes.

Notes

1 See Kishor (1999).
2 *MPWMG*, Vol. II (1986, 72).
3 Tendulkar, Vol. 3 (1951–4, 155).
4 *MPWMG*, Vol. I (1986, 384).
5 Ibid., Vol. III (1987, 463).
6 Chakravarti (2013, 56).
7 Thapar (1984, 56–93).
8 Ibid. (57).
9 *CWMG*, Vol. 55 (255).

5
MORALITY AND WISDOM
Brahmacharya, satya, ahimsa, satyagraha

Back in India as per the advice of Gokhale, Gandhi took a sabbatical from activism. He travelled to both acclimatize himself with the reality of the Indian milieu, and also in a way, test the waters. Although an internationally known leader he had not really stayed in India for any length of time. He now needed a role for himself. This phase did not last long. The anticolonial movement had started gaining eminence among the people and very soon Gandhi was swept into the ongoing national movement. As such he was able to seamlessly transit from one struggle to another. Every concept and strategy which he had elaborated in South Africa now became a vibrant domain of conceptual innovativeness to establish his relevance in the new milieu. While the national movement gave him space and a context, his South African experience provided the broad outlines and parameters for intervention and involvement.

While the generic satya was an important concern, it was non-possession and equanimity which had drawn him critically and creatively towards a narrative of satyagraha. And as the engagement unfolded he had decided to embrace brahmacharya and eschew sex. These he had felt have to be the first step towards the articulation of 'morality and wisdom' particularly because he was seeking the resonance of the voice of the people and therefore had to be alert. The individual and the system needed to be in sync. This meant strengthening the intellectual while being constantly alert to the intuitional, which for him meant listening to 'the little voice'. "Again and again he had found that the powerful combination of faith and experience, pure reason and daily application, was both self-transforming and infectious, and he felt that his own life vindicated its strength".[1] The question however was to get over self-centric preconceptions and overcome false basis of thought and action, a product of misplaced appreciation of what we do or don't do. The social within us has to become not only dominant, but the personal has to become quiescent. This might rouse the divine human within us, but it had left many of his associates, particularly the *satyarthis*, gasping to retain a sense of equanimity. It is in this context that the twin notions of satya and ahimsa, along with the more anthropocentric brahmacharya gains credibility. Satya and ahimsa are not given. They have to be claimed through discernment and practice. Like insight, they to develop because while human perfection is a given, individual perfection has to be achieved. For Gandhi this revelation is an enquiry wherein, "Life to me would lose all its interest if I felt that I could not attain perfect love on earth".[2] Accordingly his first major concern was to continue his engagement with morality and wisdom.

Familiar milieu, new orientation, old concerns

When Sarvapalli Radhakrishnan invited Gandhi to contribute to a volume on contemporary Indian philosophy, Gandhi was reluctant. His reasoning was simple. And his reply was precise. "The fact that I have affected the thought and practice of our times does not make me fit to give expression to the philosophy that may lie behind it. To give a philosophical interpretation of the phenomenon must be reserved for men like you".[3] And Radhakrishnan wrote; "In placing the interests of universal truth before those of national politics, Gandhi had lit a candle that would not easily be put off".[4] For Gandhi the essential question was the quality and nature of life, and what to do about it if it was not what it could be.

> The more I observe, the greater is the dissatisfaction with the modern life. I see nothing good in it. Men are good. But they are poor victims making themselves miserable under the false belief that they are doing good. I am aware that there is a fallacy underneath this. I who claim to examine what is around me may be a deluded fool. This risk all of us have to take. The fact is that we are all bound to do what we feel is right. And with me I feel that the modern life is *not* right.[5]

For the post-*satyarthi* Gandhi, the quest becomes an engagement with 'sat' – to exist, encompasses satya – truth, ahimsa the hallmark of compassion, and brahmacharya, an attainment to become truly competent as a human being. Around this core he then designed the concept of satyagraha. In this transition, the role of the moral order and equity in every social engagement remains seminal. The import of what Gandhi stood for is very distinct from the normal acceptance of 'things-as-they-are'. Our attitude of giving precedence to ends, wants, and rights over means, needs, and duties respectively leads to exclusiveness, be it in economics, politics or culture. Moreover, in our pre-occupation with incentive and competition, necessary collaterals of exclusiveness, we seem to be encouraging violence at every level of society. And in this preoccupation we tend to overlook that at the root of all this is our lust for power and its corollary fear of the powerful. Gandhi as if compulsively sought to resist and debunk this.

Gandhi's engagement implicitly draws our attention to the amorphous, albeit persuasive problematic of 'lust for power', its consequences, and the various debates which have tried to explicate this problematic. Accepting the notion of the 'other' being within our own selves, a case can be made that where power is the capacity to be able to consciously create and re-create one's life, the powerful will be offset only when those not powerful understand what power which is otherwise latent within them, means to them separately as individuals, and as a collective. Our capacity of thought-reflection and discrimination-discernment help us engage with truth in all its complexity. These also allow us to access basic moral insights about what is right and what is wrong, and thereby caution us about the temporality of certitudes. Not surprisingly for Gandhi, "dharma is the means by which we can know ourselves",[6] more in the sense of *purusartha* and not rituals.[7] Dharma here is the mode of right living i.e. "knowing our duties towards society" which is characterized by mutuality of means and ends. This mutuality i.e. where the terms are relational and not oppositional, is what informs ethics. Swami Vivekananda had explained the significance of this in his address in Los Angeles on 4 January 1900. "Our great defect in life is that we are so much drawn to the ideal, the goal is so much more enchanting, so much more alluring and so much bigger in our mental horizon that we lose sight of the details altogether".[8] Gandhi sought to find the details.

Actions are valued not just for their rewards but for their inherent intentionality and intrinsic value. Not surprisingly while talking about economics the most conspicuous and determining of human practices, Gandhi says, "I must confess that I do not draw a sharp or any distinction between economics and ethics".[9] Just like dharma goes beyond revelations and traditions, ethics too goes beyond codification of do's and don'ts. Morality is an engagement with a perpetually emerging tableau, and it also means a constant attention to the controversial notions of incentive, initiative, and reward. A further problem is that these notions remain embedded in the even more complex, albeit very casually articulated ideas of equality, globalization, and development. As a result, it is quite possible that when we discuss, for instance, the notion of development, we deliberately or otherwise exaggerate the significance of initiative or for that matter incentive, which can be detrimental to the social good. Environmental degradation comes readily to mind. Gandhi by stressing ethics, tried to rectify this vulnerability by bringing a large dose of participation and transparency, particularly through the ideas of satya, ahimsa, brahmacharya, and satyagraha. He rarely spoke of development or modernization as arbitrators of civilization. This does not mean he was against change. He wanted to ensure that the last human was conspicuously present in the process of change. Swaraj for him thus became moral self-rule, and for this, it simultaneously became imperative that we discern moral modes of action. Consequently competition, incentive and initiative have to have moral or ethical underpinnings. The normative and the axiomatic have to be in harmony, perhaps even homogeneous. Competition must not become antagonistic and incentive an excuse for self-aggrandizement with initiative becoming a camouflage for vested interest. Obviously, the issue is one of motive, and the question is what makes motives moral or immoral. While self-interest and a desire for security might drive motives, sooner or later it has to face up to interrogation by those who remain at the receiving end of this self-centric urge.

The problem is 'does ethics become purposive while mediating between self-seeking and justice'? Social justice being relational is engaged with what 'we' (includes I and us) owe 'others', where others includes everybody. Obviously social justice incorporates obligations. Therefore, for Gandhi the question of social justice involves 'others' and 'owing to others'. "We", writes Gandhi, "are born debtors in the world to which we owe a debt and we are dependent on others right from birth. Man becomes man only by recognizing his dependence on others".[10] In effect, we are part of a world that is interdependent spread over time and space. This also means that equality is conterminous to social justice. However the question remains, 'justice and equality for what'? Consequently Gandhi remained deeply vigilant regarding equality and justice. He preferred the more elemental satya and ahimsa. Equality comes with proviso such as responsibility, accountability, and authority, which are very temporal and contingent.

Presided by human agency, justice often is transitory! Truth is indifferent to social justice and social justice because it is ephemeral often contradicts truth. Every so often, naturalized explanations of inequality tend to legitimize inequalities based on assumed truths, for instance caste and the idea of development. And this holds for development and its embedded violence. The cunning of development lies in its capacity to alternate between the rhetorical and the substantive. Between endowments and entitlements and between progress and decay, the development rhetoric is able to keep us firmly engaged with 'what we apparently don't want' while surreptitiously pushing 'what we should want'. By focusing on ethics Gandhi kept 'what we want' firmly demarcated and recognizable. His approach to intervention in social transformation and restricting the lure of economism had two fundamental parameters. The first exposes policy and strategy to three fundamental norms: wants and needs, ends and means, and rights and duties. The second refers to an eternal vigil regarding the lure of technology, science and unbridled consumption. Perhaps we should critically but creatively look as to why Gandhi, "rejected modern innovations such as the nation-state systems, modern science and technology, urban–industrialism and evolutionism without rejecting the traditional ideas of the state, science and technology, civic living and social transformation".[11] It is not a question of validating traditions; it is one of appreciating the potential within us while living with traditions. And paradoxically why does this often become an exercise in tolerance? Equality is not sameness. For Gandhi it was similarity of involvement and access. He abjured violence because it curbed participation, which in turn meant restricted access. The issue is one of dharma not homogenization. But the question of authority remains mixed up. So the only authority Gandhi is ready to accept is that of the 'moral'. But then is this enough? If equality and justice are not to become instruments then the quest has to confront authority, and in particular the relationship of authority to wisdom which is grounded in happiness and morality. Wisdom is when we not only know i.e. are aware, we also know that we know i.e. are alert. But this vigilance comes with a tag: more morality reduces happiness while more happiness reduces morality. Morality is about consciousness and conscientiousness and not just principles. The problem regarding authority is not about principles but its self-proclaimed prerogatives. As such, no reform, wrote Gandhi, "has ever been brought about except through intrepid individuals breaking down inhuman customs or usages".[12] Gandhi while not necessarily debunking tradition took it to task.

The issue of ethics is a concern for the living. For Gandhi the significance of wisdom lies in its pragmatic utility. A wise and ethical man accordingly is good, judicious, resourceful, and able to evaluate personal intentions. Ethical suggests a commitment to social transactions. After all happiness is a desire. Welfare is a dialogue; utility is a necessity. The conflict between the personal and the social emerges because happiness, welfare, and utility tend to put one against the other; therefore, the wise while questioning desires and intentions, will critic an individual according to her self-ability as an individual and aptitude as a social being. The import can be found in what Krishna tells Arjun, "May one lift oneself by oneself"[13]; and "Knowledge is covered by this insatiable fire of desire, the constant enemy of the wise".[14]

A paradigm shift

It is only normal to try and be able to stand up for ourselves; most of us also feel that we should be able to stand up for others too. The first can be rationalized as self-interest. The second is rather complicated given that we know that wanting to help others might gainsay our own self-interest because self-interest is a complex and relative discernment regarding our relationship with others. Moreover this relationship in society is also one of power and empowerment, wherein the very idea of freedom itself is contingent and often under threat. For Gandhi freedom and the threat to it emanates not just from the milieu but also independently from the individuals who constitute the milieu. Empowerment can become an unreliable initiative of the social within the individual, concealing the subjective aspirations of the individual. For Gandhi the causal relationship between expectations and involvement remained a profound concern all his life, beginning perhaps from the Pietermaritzburg episode.

Gandhi had a taste of the raw flavor and significance of the consequence of being un-empowered when he was thrown out of the train because of the color of his skin. And he could do nothing. However he did not give in either to despondence or cynicism. He sought a path of moral autonomy for the individual, commencing with himself. After he won the case for Dada Abdulla, he suggested a compromise and reconciliation. Subsequently during the Zulu rebellion when he had to remain contended with nursing the wounded, he had the time to contemplate upon the paradoxical relationship of power, helplessness, and brutality, all in the name of 'being just'. In the process he ended by asking himself some very significant questions. What does moral autonomy mean? Why were the otherwise physically powerful Zulus finding themselves powerless? Was it possible that feeling powerless was not just a question of physical strength and guns? Perhaps, power is an enablement which has to be sought, acquired, and nurtured mainly by the social?

Of course does enablement stand for a social or a personal attribute of the self? Above all, is this power, self or socially generated?

After the Boer War, Gandhi sought to interrogate such issues beginning with the personal, the tangible, and then reaching out to the social. In the highly brutal war, where he had to dress the lacerated bodies of the Zulus who had been mercilessly flogged, he perceived deliberate cruelty. That the Zulus had truth on their side was also not lost on him. Gandhi now had an option. The problem as it had manifested was certainly social, with groups arrayed against each other. However, he chose to find explanation to this problematic in the personal 'being' of the individual; and he began with himself. Since enablement as an acquisition can potentially change the individualism of the individual in many subtle and gross ways, it has to be accompanied with a degree of consciousness and transparency. It has to ultimately manifest as critical and creative competence. For Gandhi, the enormous brutality of the war brought forth the overwhelming social significance of satya and ahimsa. To conspicuously bring the personal into the discourse he adopted a radical shift opting for goodness and harmony; in other words a strong advocacy for morality and happiness which by the way is a project of harmonious 'give and take'. Since morality consists of doing what we ought to do, for Gandhi a moral act must spring from our own will. Moreover, it is not enough that an act done by us is in itself good, "it should have been done without compulsion". "For an act to be moral it has to be free from fear and compulsion".[15]

Beyond and besides all this is the issue of Gandhi considering himself to be a searcher after Truth, and like a scientist, making experiments. Most, particularly academics prefer to consider Gandhi to be an idealist who at best had some rudimentary theory or system in his interventions and involvements strategies. After all, Gandhi was a sublime strategist! But Gandhi would beg to differ. While he was involved in experiments with satya, brahmacharya and so on, his most unique experiment was his proposal of ahimsa as a means of truth. "I maintain that far more undreamt of and seemingly impossible discoveries will be made in the field of non-violence".[16] And in the process he of course hoped to present an alternative to the development and modernity world view of industrial-capitalist civilization. With Gandhi skepticism regarding modernity was not just an anxiety. While he did remain wary if 'isms', he systematically sought clarity which required rigorous method. He worked systemically with methods of inquiry and experiments to test theories. Regarding his experiments with ahimsa he writes, "I have been practicing with scientific precision non-violence and its possibilities for an unbroken period of over 50 years. I have applied it in every walk of life, domestic, institutional, economic and political".[17] In all this his approach was on 'how', i.e. policy, method, and theory, all to lay down praxis. The means it seems is premised over credo and procedure. But Gandhi was not just a mahatma; he was a very practical man. For all his love of wisdom, he never lost sight of policies which sustained the structure of what he stood for. For him, satya and ahimsa were not part of some larger statecraft. When Gandhi changed 'sad' of '*sadagraha*' to 'satya' of 'satyagraha', the relative distinction of good as real and satya as real is momentous.[18] The relative and the absolute are thus recognized and the theory of ahimsa can now link satya with *agraha*, overcoming the restriction and temporal preoccupations of 'good'.

Gandhi's experiments sought to distinguish between science and technology. A technology is a choice and this choice is not necessarily that of the scientist. The right choice is made by the hegemony that pervades a social order, and therefore you have the issue of conflict of interest. His experiments with truth were to understand the nature of this choice and seek a possibly correct method to make a choice. Ahimsa is the means to sort out the conflict of interest problematic of society. This it does by rejecting the notion of appropriation by the social as necessary to sustain the personal.

A couple of points regarding sadagraha and technology can be made. Perhaps in hindsight it can be argued that Gandhi was correct in preferring satyagraha over sadagraha. 'Splitting up' is the meaning of the root *sad* in Sanskrit. For a *satyagrahi* this would have made the process more complex, albeit precise. While facilitating the individual progress towards liberation manifest as self-realization, *sad* enjoins consciously splitting up or separating from the old. Satyagraha as praxis on the other hand is restricted to initiating and understanding the urge for self-realization as self-knowledge. Satyagraha is not self-knowledge; it is only a prelude to the process of *sad* which only a harmony of the individual's personal and social can ensure. Paradoxically satyagraha encourages living for the other, thereby stressing the social which in turn restricts the individual's propensity to split from the existential angst of the personal. Essentially satyagraha is for the *satyarthi* and not for the *satyagrahi*. Satyagraha while hailing the itinerant lessens the individual's predilection towards security. However, to consolidate the initiative of satyagraha the emerging *satyagrahi* has to appreciate the demanding '*sad*'; *satyagraha for the satyagrahi has to evolve into sadagraha*. Post-Gandhi, the leading Gandhians while in many ways recognizing this dilemma, preferred to pander to some notion of all aspiring Gandhians as being equal as *satyagrahis*. Obviously this could not be sustained. Hierarchies emerged but the consequences of this was neither appreciated nor apprehended. The quest of say Vinoba was not of a *satyagrahi* but of a sadagrahi. The post assassination conference is very illustrative of this. As for technology it is essentially vicarious. It is a surrogate for wants. In its relentless urge to deliver, it sanctions the building of more and more complex machines, the practicalities of which cannot transform the person from within. Machines remain confined to the transactional social. Gandhi therefore felt that technology cannot help human beings reach the enormity of the universe as a personal experiential affair. Actually by encouraging want, they become fetters.

Brahmacharya, sexuality, and gender

Brahmacharya: celibacy

Gandhi had been conscious and conspicuously aware of the issue of sex, abstinence, and chastity from the time he went to England as a married student who was leaving his wife behind. He had pledged to his mother to abstain from any sexual relationship while in England, and he had maintained his vow. Subsequently, during what we have called his *satyarthi* phase, he had occasion to discuss and think about sex, sexuality, and related issues such as women, marriage etc. For him his religious studies and appreciation of concepts such as *avatar, sanyasi, aparigraha*, equanimity, *sthitapragna*, the role of prophets, and the writings of Tolstoy and so on, had if anything made these critical elements in human life. In a discussion with Raychandbhai when he praised the conjugal love of the British prime minister Gladstone and his wife, Raychandbhai had asked as to which was more esteemed, "the service of Mrs. Gladstone as a wife or if she had been a sister or servant?" The problem was the question of lust. Love is tainted with lust. "It would become morally praiseworthy only when it became free of that taint, as in celibacy".[19]

While Gandhi was impressed with Raychandbhai's reasoning, he had not been able to follow the injunctions of celibacy. He still sought comfort in his sexual relationship with Kasturba. Consequently his family grew, as did his domestic responsibilities. By 1903 when he decided to set up the Phoenix establishment these responsibilities restricted his freedom and his urge to serve had to be circumscribed by his private responsibilities. His liberty was regulated by the demands of a growing family.

His involvement with the ambulance corps in the Zulu rebellion of 1906 provided an enormously poignant and contemplative environment, albeit gruesome. The Zulu rebellion came as both a revelation and an engagement. The work of the ambulance corps entailed long hours of marching from one skirmish to another. This meant long periods of silent walking which encouraged contemplation. Gandhi now was becoming clearer about the 'why' of social events. If anything, it was becoming clear what power meant, what possession and possessiveness can render, and the enormous brutality that the urge to possess and control can unleash. While the cause and impact of the rebellion did point to the apparently quiescent issues of satya and ahimsa, it also brought forth the question of response to such conflicts, not only at the social but at the personal level too. The rapidly evolving *satyagrahi* concluded that the response should not only focus on the social within him but that it should merge with the larger social through social service. But this is easy thought than realized. Power has a mesmerizing way of projecting the personal over the social by appropriating the social entirety through personalization of institutions. It obfuscates the 'take' of the powerful by projecting it as a 'give'. The whites by cleverly projecting civilization and development as inevitable quietly foisted their self-interest and the necessity to have to subjugate the blacks in the social transformation processes. Their 'take' thus became a 'give'. Realizing it, Gandhi wanted such manoeuvres to become evident to all.

For the *satyagrahi* Gandhi the path was obvious and clear. As a response he started by engaging with himself by asking as to how he could become competent to remove social anomalies through personal service. Towards this he felt brahmacharya could be one of the foundational strategies. Accordingly when he returned from the Zulu war, he took a vow to practice brahmacharya in form and spirit. While he did discuss this with his colleague's he did not do so with Kasturba.

Ostensibly she had no issues, probably because one of the consequences would be that she would not have to bear any more children and thus restrict and contain the family's responsibilities. After all she was older than Gandhi and in her late thirties. She must have thought that early forties is no time to get pregnant; particularly when around this time she might have been contemplating about her son's marriage. However, a decision which requires mutuality should be explicitly mutual in every sense; perhaps Gandhi overlooked this.

Over time Gandhi's views about brahmacharya evolved, although the core view, that attachment is detachment, persisted. For him! By rejecting attachment, he sought to bring forth and appropriate the potential of detachment. Dispassion, renunciation, non-possession were to be the driving attitude. Sex is both a pantomime and an act of reality. The strutting, the courting, the convincing, and the act are all part of a primordial requisite of sexuality, belongingness, and independence, and perhaps also of necessity, chance, and choice, all of which encourage a disposition of longing. Gandhi sought to call the bluff of this longing by reducing sex to a carnal compulsion. For him the issue was of becoming clear about the limited role of sex and to not allow choice to cover an indulgence as necessity in the name of autonomy of being. "I think it is the height of ignorance to believe that the sexual act is an independent function necessary like sleeping or eating".[20] Gandhi therefore sought to deglamorize and restrict the obligatory to the bare necessity of procreation. As far as he was concerned all the so-called labor and pleasure of love was a domain of the self-indulgent philanderer. But the male and the *satyagrahi* adjunct duo within him apparently remained unconvinced. A difference of opinion persisted between these two. Throughout his life, till the very end, he continued to experiment, debunk himself, go through phases of self-guilt, and at times feel lost. But he never gave in and strove to reconcile the apparently contradictory thought processes of the male and the *satyagrahi*. His driving reasoning was clear, "All power comes from the preservation and sublimation of the vitality that is responsible for the creation of life".[21] Since his core concern was to tap and mobilize the higher impulses of his fellow men, a precondition of which is mastering of the senses and purification of the spirit, he held the desire for sex "as unnatural in the human species and its satisfaction detrimental to the spiritual progress of the human family".[22] Primarily concerned with the *satyagrahi* adjunct, Gandhi it seems was leaving other struggling *satyarthis* as well as the male within him, struggling with the mass of insights he generated. The problem is that sexuality is not enigmatic and moreover it can be created spontaneously; it is a double bind between necessity and choice. But Gandhi was not convinced. "According to me, it is desirable for a man and a woman to avoid being alone together at all times and in all places, in order to safeguard their Purity".[23] What then is this perplexing 'brahmacharya' all about? Is it something exclusive to the *satyagrahi* where such a person according to Gandhi is one "who has resolved to practice nothing but truth and such a one will know the right way every time"?[24] Perhaps Gandhi while debunking individualism, sought to preserve 'love' and purity exclusively for the social?

Essentially brahmacharya refers to *trishna-tyaaga* or renouncing of longing, particularly the abnegation of sex and lust. *Trishna* refers to longing, hankering, a craving for what is unattained; it is the Sanskrit root of the word is '*trish*', meaning to be thirsty or to thirst for. Renouncing or getting over longing is the cessation of desires and attaining serenity. However renouncing is the act of giving up something or restraining oneself so as to acquire something else. For Gandhi, "willfulness is not conscience; conscience is the ripe fruit of strictest discipline".[25] And for him discipline is "a conscious practice of self-restraint and an ever-increasing effort implicitly to obey the will of God speaking within and then known as the inner voice".[26] Perhaps Gandhi was seeking to discipline himself so as to be able to hear his own conscience?

In the Hindu ashram system, a brahmachari is a student questing brahmacharya, the path of Brahman, who to facilitate the quest temporarily renounces everything including relationships and even authority over his yesterday and tomorrow, to acquire knowledge of Godhood. Gandhi applied renouncement, an underpinning of brahmacharya, to the issue of sexuality. For him restrain is a core human attribute crucial to the self. Restrain as resistance enables us to transcendent existential limitations. His usage of the term brahmacharya suggests both an aspiration and a process of restrain so as to activate the path of self-illumination apropos the true meaning of life. But unlike that for a student, for the truth-seeker or *satyagrahi*, brahmacharya is a life-long commitment; it is not just a means but an end in its self. He writes, "In brahmacharya lies the protection of the body, the mind and the soul". And he describes the need for brahmacharya in various ways. In a comprehensive way, "brahmacharya means control of the senses in thought, words and deeds".[27] Further it is "a course of conduct . . . adapted to the search of Brahman, i.e. truth".[28] Even in his seventies, justifying his experiments to not only overcome the least vestiges of lust but also to benefit from brahmacharya, he clarifies, "My meaning of brahmacharya is this: one who never has any lustful intention, who by constant attendance upon God has become proof against conscious or unconscious emissions, who is capable of lying naked with naked women, however beautiful they may be, without being in any manner whatsoever sexually excited. Such a person should be incapable of lying, incapable of intending or doing harm to a single man or woman in the whole world, is free from anger and malice and detached in the sense of the Bhagavad Gita. Such a person is a full Brahmachari";[29] in effect one is absolutely free of longing!

Coming back to the issue of renouncing, to make his resolve practicable and resolute, Gandhi added a couple of stipulations. The first is the need to initiate this as a 'vow'. A vow is a pledge which enjoins and honors a decision already made. Since a vow is made in the name of being truthful, ignoring it is tantamount to being untruthful to one's own self. The second is the problematic that such renunciation without an element of aversion is not lasting.[30] This aversion gives the vow a discrete world view. Brahmacharya for Gandhi thus becomes a perspective, a responsibility, and an aspiration extending beyond the individual. This engagement of Gandhi perhaps overstretches the point. How for instance did an urge to restrict having children so as to be able to serve, become an *agraha*? Fasting, restricting food habits, nature cure, and so on can be understood; but as a seventy-seven-year-old, conducting an experiment to gain divine strength remains unique to Gandhi and his world view. The problems emerge when he draws conclusions as consequences. For instance he insists that in the case of Kasturba, "what developed the self-abnegation in her to the highest level was *our* brahmacharya".[31]

In human beings while the sexual urge in essence is instinctual, evolution and conscience has alleviated hormonal and biological fetters. Generally it is expressed sustained and gratified through various social norms. Behaviors and norms meant to sustain and satiate this urge is sexuality. In human beings the male is inclined to be sexually active for most of his life. While the desire to reproduce is primeval, in the social human sexual activeness can become an indulgence, even becoming a preoccupation with sex reduced to a service as a commodity. Such activeness besides being physically demanding can lead to gender abuse because women have to pander to this deviance. For Gandhi the problem lies in our thinking wherein we separate our own selves into male and the female aspects, and valorize the male. Therefore for him nature is not the culprit, our thinking is. Gandhi thinks chastity and celibacy are necessary to reorient this recalcitrant thinking and help the mind attain requisite firmness.[32] He went one step further and demanded that sexuality should be a public concern and that celibacy be central to national reform. "The conquest of lust is the highest endeavor of a man's or a woman's existence. And without overcoming lust, man cannot hope to rule over self; without rule over self, there can be no Swaraj".[33] For Gandhi the social being must have the last word.

But the social can never ignore the personal. Gandhi desired to seamlessly merge the personal and the social. This needed the recognition and cultivation of patience.

> Thus brahmacharya was the cultivation of patience along with the entire spectrum of the inner life where desperation surfaced. It was by no means training into merely physical abstinence. But Gandhi, true to many familiar traditions in India, knew that the body and its training was the technical path to the achievement of higher ideals, in this case the deeper forms of a *cultivated patience* needed for ahimsa.[34]

Since the sexual urge with its focus on the individual's personal, seems to be in conflict with this, he undertook to explain it. For him sexual activity is not only enervating, it is energy wasting. He maintained that expending semen was like throwing the human physical and mental system out of gear. It also meant a loss of psychic energy. He therefore considered the sexual act to be profoundly selfish, exploitative, and a form of self-inflicted violence. He separated love from sexual cohabitation and did not accept that intercourse could ever be an integral aspect of any profound man–woman relationship. For him just like sex separated two halves of the human being, similarly conjugal love separated the pair from society into self-serving beings. Further he felt that sexuality divides the human race with each sex remaining only half a human being. Sexuality implicates a subtle process of overpowering and subjugating the whole of otherness by exaggerating the sexual otherness of the other's sex. Thus by necessity sex remains aggressive and self-serving. As such it went against the very basis of ahimsa.

But this logic and world view does not solve the problem of the need to procreate. To resolve this, Gandhi preferred to reduce sex to the bare minimum and only within marriage. Separating mind and body, he sought to premise the mind over body. Drawing from Hindu lore he equated the eternal soul with the mind; on the contrary the body being ephemeral merited lesser attention. Therefore, while Gandhi did nurture and take care of his body, conjugal love which is body-centered remains inferior to the love of humanity; in the ultimate analysis humanity manifests as the eternal self. Perhaps Gandhi was apprehensive of the raw emotional energy that sex unleashes. As such, instead of engaging with it, he preferred to try and minimize it by first discrediting and then minimizing its potential. Actually Gandhi felt that the call of sex and its fetish for the individual is detrimental to seamless universalization of compassion and love.

Sex for Gandhi remains a very 'mannish' pre-occupation. He never seems to think that sexuality could engage and influence women too. This attitude led Gandhi to some uncharacteristic opinions. Commenting about orphanages that admitted 'foundlings', infants abandoned because they were born out of wedlock, he said, "I am not convinced that providing for such admissions is ethically sound. I have a kind of feeling that such facilities lead to increase in indulgence".[35] Overall for Gandhi, "there should be a clear line between the life of a brahmachari and one who is not".[36] For him every brahmachari should be able to, "rise to the height of universal love", and give undivided attention to national regeneration. This became confusing when Gandhi extended this logic to his relationship with adult women. Perhaps Sarla Devi Chaudhurani[37] had a different opinion about linking personal relationship and national regeneration?

For Gandhi the division of the sexes provided a dilemma. He was ready to accept the personal and the social division and sort it out by prioritizing the social. But this does not work in the case of the sexual division. It is too fundamental and primordial a division to be epistemologically transcended and reasoned off without leaving a lingering trauma. Each sex is as if doomed to be half a hominid. For Gandhi the only way out was by "internally appropriating the other, sex and the qualities associated with it".[38] But this is more easily said than done. It is not a question of 'I' and 'me'; nor is it possible to avoid reality and hence the problem. It is immanent and transactional. The only way to elucidate it is by *krodh* tyaag i.e. ahimsa and *trishna tyaag* i.e. brahmacharya wherein ahimsa is the necessary condition while brahmacharya is the sufficient cause.

For Gandhi, the problem however acquired additional complexity and perhaps became a dilemma because the sexual act underscores a duality; this is a reality which meant that to be whole, he not only had to contend with the personal social duality but also with another, a male-female duality which while enjoying a more elemental legitimacy, enjoined a dependency. Surprisingly, the otherwise astute Gandhi overlooked the fact that mediating the personal and the social is the maverick individual, a '*jiva*' who ignorantly or otherwise aspires to appropriate and 'become' that which is the transcendental truth of the human being.

Not surprisingly Gandhi accepts that self-restraint can easily become self-indulgence. Accordingly he warns, "Those who believe in self-restraint must not become hypochondriacs. . . . there must be no brooding. There should be no conscious effort to drive away evil thoughts. That process is itself a kind of indulgence".[39] This is a very telling comment and rejoinder to all his followers interested in knowing about self-restraint and self-indulgence the very core of his concept of brahmacharya. Restraint is related to the understanding and position that sex essentially is 'animal passion'; and as such it is to be avoided. Since it is necessary to procreate, intercourse must be restricted to reproduction. About birth control Gandhi is categorical. "There can be no two opinions about the necessity of birth control. But the only method handed down from ages past is self-control or brahmacharya".[40] Perhaps he applied the simplistic logic of 'we eat to live and not live to eat' to sex and copulation. For him, "Artificial methods are like putting a premium on vice".[41] "The reasoning underlying the use of artificial methods is that indulgence is a necessity of life".[42] "Procreation is a natural phenomenon indeed, but within limits. A transgression of these limits imperils womankind, emasculates the race, induces diseases, puts a premium on vice, and makes the world ungodly"; and for him "Moral results can only be produced by moral restraints".[43] He was convinced that sex was essentially a moral concern and a problematic to be resolved by the conscience.

> What, then, is brahmacharya? It means that men and women should refrain from carnal knowledge of each other. That is to say they should not touch each other with a carnal thought, they should not think of it even in their dreams. Their mutual glances should be free from all suggestions of carnality. The hidden strength that God has given us should be conserved by rigid self-discipline and transmitted into energy and power, – not merely of body, but also of mind and soul.[44]

Further, "We hardly realize the fact that incontinence is the root cause of most of the vanity, anger, fear and jealousy in the world" (ibid). For him observing brahmacharya is a duty, and the consequences are not for us to judge. As he put it, "If the observation of brahmacharya should mean the end of the world, that is none of our business. Are we God that we should be so anxious about its future?".[45] This is surprising for one who claimed to be a scientist. How could he push out aspects of his hypothesis and leave it to God?

The problem that he recognizes cannot be restricted only to sex and self-control of this urge. Brahmacharya cannot be practiced without control of all the senses which includes food habits, cure, and care of the body and so on. Our problem begins with our being a slave to our palate and consumption inclinations. Gandhi does not think that the palate is compliant to the consumption mode set by society; it is the individual who is complicit. Perhaps by setting up the individual against the vicissitude and hegemony of society and its consumption mode, Gandhi hoped to bring in the significance of brahmacharya into the discourse of national regeneration.

"Brahmacharya properly and fully understood means search after Brahma. As Brahma is present in every one of us, we must seek it within with the help of meditation and consequent realization. Realization is impossible without complete control of all the senses. Therefore brahmacharya signifies control of all the senses at all times and at all places in thought, word and deed".[46] This was his aim, a goal he wanted to achieve. For Gandhi, the way to attain brahmacharya is by first accepting it as a necessity and then going on to control one's senses, give up associating with people who do not subscribe to such efforts and pray that divine grace leads us in our efforts. "Human society is a ceaseless growth, an unfoldment in terms of spirituality".[47] For him this meant a pursuit of truth. But such a pursuit "requires utter selflessness". This in turn leaves no time for begetting children and running a household. Moreover exclusive and demanding sexual relationships warp the consequences of the ever dynamic problematic of social change and choice.

For Gandhi the body is a temple with the deity playing truant. As a pujari he was supremely tuned to his body. Hygiene, nutrition, bowel movements, enema, massaging, and above all brahmacharya were guidelines he conscientiously followed. As a *pujari* he suffered no false modesty. For a *pujari*, faith and discipline were integral to *saadhana*. Gandhi therefore, "viewed celibacy as something intrinsically good, contributing to inner freedom".[48]

For the social-minded Gandhi, while chastity remained a personal act, celibacy presumes a social position. For brahmacharya to be meaningful, even imperative, its import has to become a social quest. Since the underpinning is God as self-realization, it can never be taken out of context and alienated within the individual. Moreover, the context stubbornly remains life and the mode of living. For Gandhi, the objective is not some balancing of ethics, instinct, and logic, but it is transcending all these. The transactional is only to indicate the transcendental and thus Dharma. No doubt for him brahmacharya becomes a yajna, a sacrifice. Obviously *trishna tyaag* has nothing to do with escaping to the forest. He observes, "That *brahmacharya* which can be observed only by living in a forest is neither *brahmacharya* nor self-control".[49]

Understandably Gandhi's thinking about brahmacharya not only influenced, but to an extent anticipated his understanding of gender and related issues. The transactional complications of brahmacharya spilled on to the vital gender issue and social practices such as marriage, prostitution, etc.

Women – gender

Gandhi's understanding of the gender issue permits no misreading. "The ancient laws were made by seers who were men. The women's experience, therefore, is not represented in them. Strictly speaking, as between men and women, neither should be regarded as superior or inferior".[50] He had earlier clarified, "I passionately desire the utmost freedom for our women. I detest child marriages. I shudder to see a child widow, and shiver with rage when a husband just widowed contracts with brutal indifference another marriage. I deplore the criminal indifference of parents who keep their daughters utterly ignorant and illiterate and bring them up only for the purpose of marrying them off to some young man of means. Notwithstanding all this grief and rage, I realize the difficulty of the problem".[51]

Gandhi sought to live up to the ideal of an androgynous person who is 'both a man and a woman'.[52] For him, "My ideal is this: A man should remain man and yet should become woman; similarly a woman should remain woman and yet become man".[53] Predictably he soon ran into the deep-rooted contradictions and convictions articulating man-woman relationships. He accepted the strength of the male and its misuse; but he was impatient with the consequences of women in this lopsided power equation and the historical baggage that women carry. It is as if he wanted them to forget, forgive, and carry on with some course correctives. Additionally he expected them to be the repositories of virtue. The normally tolerant Gandhi was rather impatient with sex in relation to women! Broadly his thoughts about women and gender issues can be assembled under four clusters: as individuals, and within marriage, household, and society.

"As Nature has made men and women different, it is necessary to maintain a difference between the educations of the two. True, they are equal in the life but their functions differ"[54] is how he felt. He remained an essentialist who uncovered scope for adjustments. While he expected men to "Liberate their women from the evil customs and conventions",[55] he also cautioned that "ultimately woman will have to determine with authority what she needs". For him, "a daughter's share must be equal to that of a son. The husband's earnings are the joint property of husband and wife . . . if a husband is unjust to his wife she has the right to live separately. Both have equal rights to the children. Each would forfeit these rights after they have grown up".[56] Gandhi accepted "the separate spheres" thesis. "Men and women are of equal rank, but they are not identical".[57]

In terms of occupation, work and the social sphere Gandhi extended the qualities distinguishing the two genders into "natural division of the spheres of work".[58] However, he remained ambivalent about the autonomy of women vis-à-vis economic status. "Women in the new order will be part-time workers, their primary function being to look after the home".[59]

But then Gandhi was also against women taking up outside work. He never accepted the capitalist notion of 'employment and wages'. Gandhi was not ready to surrender 'employability' to the market system. To the problems of discrimination and exploitation he did not want to add the even more complex reification and alienation. Perhaps he felt that the ingress of market forces is containable and can be contained. This gives the feeling that Gandhi refused to look at the reality of the creeping capitalist market dominated economic milieu. His formulations can be perplexing. At one point he insists that, "the wife is not a slave of her husband, but a comrade, his better half, colleague and friend. She is co-sharer with him of equal rights and duties. Their obligation towards each other and towards the world must therefore be the same and reciprocal".[60] And then he goes and restricts her domain of economic involvement to the household ignoring the fact that many women earned their livelihood as agricultural laborers and factory workers besides being responsible for all household work. Gandhi tends to be biased towards making work and labor gender specific and not gender neutral. But then why should women alone be responsible to sustain the individual-family-community link?

However for all his arguments about equality, when it came to the issue of prostitution Gandhi remained adamant. Even his usual compassion deserted him. He refused to recognize that prostitution could be due to utterly coercive and alienating circumstances. He totally rejected that social conditions could and did make sex a commodity. He insisted that women had it within them to opt out. Prostitution for him manifested the worst form of opportunism. As far as he was concerned circumstances don't condone this. For him sex remained a debilitating human attribute, and the response should either be total celibacy or chastity within marriage with sex restricted to procreation. Accordingly he also refused to accept the notion of contraception, which he considered to be violence perpetrated by the market. For him, "the difference between a prostitute and a woman using contraceptives is only this – that the former sells her body to several men, while the latter sells it to one man".[61]

But then Gandhi had no clear idea as to how to remove this evil practice other than expecting the women to give up their "unworthy profession" and "become the true *sannyasinis* of India. Having no care of life but of service, they can spin and weave to their hearts content".[62] He however was humble enough to accept that "once a prostitute, always a prostitute- is not a sound proposition".[63]

However, marriage as a basic indispensable bonding of two individuals remained a unique and awkward social obligation for the individual-centric Gandhi. For Gandhi while marriage is a coming together of the two aspects of the human being, and the role and function of the two might differ, neither was superior or inferior. Marriage should aid in the spiritual development of the couple and love should become an "intense affection without lust". The personal and the social thus converge in harmony via a social institution i.e. marriage which then "becomes a means of service". Ideally marriage therefore becomes a coming together of two distinct personalities with their distinct personal and social becoming involved in an intimate and intense discourse to sustain the primacy of the social; it is a very tall order indeed. Not surprisingly Gandhi suggests that perhaps marriage is not such an ideal condition. Gandhi writes, "ahimsa is impossible without utter selflessness. Ahimsa means Universal Love. If a man gives his love to one woman, or a woman to one man, what is there left for the besides? It simply means, 'We two first, and the devil take all the rest of them ... it's clear that such persons cannot rise to the height of Universal Love, or look upon all mankind as kith and kin. For they have created a boundary wall around their love".[64] Characteristically he offered a solution; "They (the couple) can behave as if they were not married.... If a married couple can think of each other as brother and sister, they are freed for universal service".

Gandhi sustained a fundamental question. "What is the object generally understood of marriage, except a repetition of one's own kind?"[65] Gandhi remained skeptical about the role of marriage in creating a purposeful social milieu. In terms of the man-woman-society link, a moot issue remains: social service will produce society, but how will it reproduce the women and men? Gandhi of course would prefer to leave that to God! For women this is a twofold hurdle. Perhaps had he not forgotten how he had dragged Kasturba to oust her from 'his home', he might have tried to go that extra mile and theorize about this most elemental problematic?

Satya

Satya is '*abadhya*' unrestrained, unchecked. It is something that stands unaffected by our knowing or not knowing; it is that which is not contradictable by experience. You don't engage with satya to acquire it! For Gandhi, "It is that which alone is which constitutes the stuff of which all things are made, which subsists by virtue of its own power, which is not supported by anything else but supports everything that exists. Truth alone is eternal, everything else is momentary. It need not assume shape or form".[66] For him satya remains both cognitive and experiential, as long as we are not infatuated by the dualism of mind and the world, the subject and the object, a very mesmerizing condition of modernism and its epistemology, satya is not a choice between either and or;[67] it is always 'also there'.

To understand the true significance of satya one has to recognize that 'mankind' is possibly the only morality driven creature who can aspire to go beyond the dependency on intuition. This capacity also means that he can be delusional, or he can be plain stupid and stubbornly unreasonable. He can aspire in abstract terms and thereby get carried away by the very process of aspiring, completely forgetting the intentions of the aspiration. Form and essence, subject and object can become discrete and thus create a binary: truth and untruth. As a consequence, anthropomorphic man, caught between the contradictory pulls of truth and untruth creates the Anthropocene age. We find ourselves stranded like an Owl on a dry branch of a dying tree awaiting nightfall.

Self-realization and Moksha were Gandhi's abiding life-long quest. For him these were a transactional initiative as well as a transcendental inspiration. However, since it is always the transactional which by tending towards the transcendental leads the way, it is the transactional which has to have everyday commonplace meaning and comprehensibility because the eternal is not bound by ephemeral meanings. For him this whole trajectory is mediated by satya and ahimsa. "Truth is the same thing as moksha" and "I often feel that ahimsa is in truth, not vice versa".[68] To understand this process however becomes difficult because Gandhi remained an interlocutor all his life, and as an interlocutor he grew from clarity to clarity. He remained an editor for a host of narratives: brahmacharya, religion, national movement and so on. While as an editor his comments reflected the collective narrative of the text (national movement) his individual contributions retained his personal opinions. To his followers particularly the *satyarthis*, this was not easy to follow. His innumerable letters find him helping them. However, in all these communications, interventions, and so on, two core sympathies never changed the significance of satya and ahimsa. He puts it thus; "ahimsa is my God, and Truth is my God. When I look for ahimsa, Truth says 'Find it out through me'. When I look for Truth, ahimsa says 'Find it out through me'".[69] Even here his thinking remained heuristic in that it sought to enable a person to discover or learn for themselves. The emphatic declaration is manifest in conscious intervention and social work, wherein the context of every event is truth, while the content circumscribed by ahimsa. In everyday life it means, "You may decline to make any statement if you wish to, but you may not tell an untruth".[70]

Darkness is caused by something eclipsing and thus obscuring. Effort should be made to remove the cause. The consequence is illumination. This is the way to grasp truth or replace untruth. To remove darkness by bringing light as superimposition is counterproductive. This will be the subject's version and vision of truth; such a truth will be an epistemic imposition. As such it will never be sustainable. When Gandhi seeks to equate love with truth he is trying to decipher the cause of hatred, the untruth. Just like when the water drains away after a flood and leaves behind the silt which in turn ensures a bounty, so does the removal of the cause of untruth. But just like encountering the flood is difficult, so is facing truth. This is because the path to truth begins with *nityakarma*, an activity which has to be performed daily. This is an activity which by itself gives no merit to the performer, yet gives negative merit if ignored. But the problem is with *nityakarma*, rather with what is the *nityakarma* of 'I' and 'me' and how this impacts the personal and the social. Are they distinct? Truth is not just the tenth man counting himself in, but also a construal for an inclusiveness which is a necessary binding of belonging without qualification. But then as Gandhi realized, truth has a wide range of subtexts. Writing in the *Indian Opinion*, 1 April 1905, he translates Bhishma's description of truth as: "Truthfulness, equability, self-control, absence of self-display, forgiveness, modesty, endurance, absence of envy, charity, a noble well-wishing towards others, self-possession, compassion, and harmlessness – surely these are the 13 forms of Truth".[71] Above all, for Gandhi truth and religion are inseparable. He says, "One of the axioms of religion is, there is no religion other than truth. Another is, religion is love. And as there can be only one religion, it follows that truth is love and love is truth".[72]

Given the nature of our society, perhaps Gandhi's restraint is to indicate an element of contingency and that you can't have the best of both worlds. One has to choose, and the onus of this choice is on the individual. How you do it, what preparations are necessary and why, are questions Gandhi sought to answer through satya, ahimsa, and brahmacharya. But choice comes with an inherent potential of coercion. This is because choice is attended by attachments, self-interest, and dualism. Satya and ahimsa seek to mitigate the potential antagonism inherent in personal self-interest. Satya by asking 'why' seeks to clarify the nature of the foundation of self-interest while ahimsa, the test of which is compassion, eases this by focusing on 'how' to seek. For Gandhi, satya ensures conviction and credibility while ahimsa enables acceptability and commitment. They clarify the ontological (being, becoming) and the teleological (explaining goals), expecting the epistemic (knowledge, inquiry) to present the case. Very often epistemic considerations dominate and make the ontological and teleological fall inline; they are a very deliberately cultivated feature of the modern man. In *Hind Swaraj* and *Anasakti yoga* Gandhi questions this.[73]

For Gandhi, satya became God while ahimsa became love that is humaneness and total transparency of intentions. While satya emerged as conscious claim of entitlements, ahimsa developed as conscious claim for endowments. Satya is not just self-evident, it is also self-sufficient. For Gandhi truth has to be acknowledged. He sought to be present during the event. While satya comes from the word *sat: to be, to exist*, only that which exists for ever can be satya. However to arrive at satya is a complex process. One's experiences and observations help; we become informed and thus create knowledge. But this knowledge comes with a world view i.e. a method which helps us comprehend the information and glean the knowledge. This world view incidentally is a social endowment available to us as social creatures. Moreover this world view has a way of expressing 'what was' and 'what should or could be'. Effectively this world view enables the social in us, creating a tension between the social and the personal within the individual. This becomes significant when the personal is constantly pressurized to accept and agree. As a consequence, frequently our knowledge becomes conditional. One way of coming to terms is by creating a handshaking distance between knowledge and ourselves, and this is possible only when we take a critical look at the world views influencing and creating it. And the way to this is via wisdom which is a harmony of happiness and morality wherein the individual can never have too much of either. Truth is this relationship of knowledge vis-à-vis wisdom, and wisdom is true-knowledge. A major constraint faced by the individual is the ingress of 'what was' i.e. the past. Is the past just a memory helping assemble the present? Is it compassionate or does it act as agency for the social to assert? The world view in which the individual is just a speck in the assemblage does have an agenda. It can also have a contingent opinion regarding truth. Gandhi "found that the nearest approach to truth is through love".[74] But love has a weakness for the personal within the individual, thus setting up a polemic with the social. This polemic itself becomes a preoccupation which seeks to become a world view; we then are back where we started.

But then a world view is also a belief. For instance, "Truth and untruth often coexist; Good and evil are often found together".[75] It can easily give rise to faith. While the world view can encourage creativity, as faith it becomes conservative because of its weakness for the expedient and an exaggerated appraisal regarding its legacy. Gandhi tried to sort this out by discoursing 'what we should do' and 'what we ought to become'. In this, while he was a firm believer in the import of the individual, he was also understanding about autonomy. While he affirmed that "the individual is the one supreme consideration",[76] he also maintained that "perfection is attained through service".[77]

A question can be asked: what is the morality upholding satya and ahimsa? Gandhi suggests a determined commitment to the 'moment', i.e. just when change confronts us. To quote him, "One step enough for me, says the voice of wisdom"; "Sorrow springs from dreaming of the future and from lamenting the past".[78] Ultimately the quest of satya is to be found in the way we live. "My experience tells me that, instead of bothering about how the world may live in the right manner, we should think how we ourselves may do so. We do not even know whether the world lives in the right manner or in a wrong manner".[79] Moreover it must be understood that "The truth that we see is relative, many-sided, plural and is the whole truth for a *given time*".[80] As such understanding of satya is not a question of faith. Gandhi explicates, "Faith has no place in a matter which can be grasped by reason".[81]

Explaining that 'truth is not as simple as it appears' Gandhi explains the challenge by using the example of seven blind men who touched an elephant at different parts. "Their descriptions therefore differed from one another. They were all true from their own points of view and yet each appeared to be untrue from the points of view of the rest. The truth was beyond all the seven. We are all, you will perhaps agree, in the position of these seven sincere observers. *And we are as blind as they are blind*. We must therefore be content with believing the truth as it appears to us".[82] However this "need not worry the seeker.... It will be realized that what appear to be different truths are like the countless and apparently different leaves of the same tree".[83] Answering the question 'what is Truth'? Gandhi suggests that since people evolve through innumerable ways, they can very well come to superficially dissimilar conclusions. Therefore experiments to arrive at truth have to be first exposed to vows: "speaking and thinking of truth, the vow of *brahmacharya*, of non-violence, poverty and non-possession".[84] In a way aspiring truth is a *sadhana*. After all, "Truth is not a material quality but is pure consciousness".[85] For him the path to Truth is via extinction of ego. Along with the elimination of ego, the individual is able to discard the restrictive aspects of personhood, a liberation which is the manifestation of God. For Gandhi, "The body exists because of our ego. The utter extinction of the body is *moksha*. He who has achieved such extinction of the ego becomes the very image of Truth; he may well be called the *Brahman*. Hence it is that a loving name of God is *Dasanudasa*".[86]

The question is not whether Truth is cognitive, experiential, or a proposition. It is a disposition and not some last word. It is an ethos linking the individual to the community. Since this linkage is constantly rocked by change, continuity, chance, and necessity of social transformation, it is always fresh albeit anticipated. When Gandhi says, "As I proceed in my quest for Truth, it grows upon me that Truth comprehends everything", and concludes with "The wonderful implication of the great truth *Brahma satyam jaganmithya* (God is truth, the world a myth) grows on me from day to day", he is indicating the distinction of 'being and 'becoming' and of truth as recognition of one's being as eternal.[87] Not surprisingly "where there is Truth, there also is knowledge which is true". Therefore, "There should be Truth in thought, Truth in speech and Truth in action". And when this process is articulated "By *abhyasa*, single-minded devotion, and *vairagya*, indifference to all other interests in life" the quest for Truth becomes *tapascharya*, a cognitive learning process,[88] and the quest becomes an awareness event.

While satya is the 'substance of all morality', it is revealed only by praxis at the critical conjunction of theory and practice; satya encourages, ensures, and endures. As a moral link between actions, it ensures a continuum and rootedness. By ensuring harmony in purpose as reflected in thought, speech, and action, it upholds creativity in satya-agraha. Satya by not depending on reciprocity reconfigures the association of the personal and the social. In the process it defines the fundamental discourse of 'give' and 'take'. Give and take manifest 'change and 'continuity': give is the change, while take is the continuity. Both are governed and influenced by choice, chance, and necessity. The social and the personal reflect this, with the social being more accommodative of chance and the personal favouring necessity. An individual's choice of habits, habitat, and habitation are a manifestation of this give and take relationship with the larger milieu. The give ensures the relevance of the individual's essential vibrancy, while the take delimits because it impinges on the person's self-acclaim by having to proclaim an inadequateness regarding self-sufficiency of the individual being.

For Gandhi 'give and take' was a problematic. The personal within him would have no problems to choose as an individual. But the social has to respond to parameters which are usually changing and ambiguous, particularly since the notion of give and take also comes with the notion of ownership; ownership means possession and this in turn means power, the harbinger of untruth. Gandhi tried to sort this out through the notion of truth and the morality of social service. But then between whom is the social service? Moreover the one who is served also has an opinion; she is also a giver. It can be argued that effectively Nachiketa gave more to Yama than what was given to him as boons.[89] Yama shared an insight while Nachiketa gave him back his harmony of being, which had been dented by making Nachiketa wait. Here we also have a question of what is more humble – to give or take. Harilal had no trouble in his relationship with his father. All he wanted was space and liberty to learn by making his own genuine mistakes. He gave his father all his love and genuine respect but was not ready to be subsumed under some compassionate notion of social of which Gandhi was an affiliate and insisted Harilal was too. Harilal continued to disapprove Gandhi's inability to trust his own personal. Harilal could never convey his feeling that, when the personal is made to serve the social within oneself, ahimsa gets humbled; this can take the form of humiliation, a brooding elusiveness. Harilal wanted the give to come from the personal of Gandhi, not from the social.

Ahimsa

Ahimsa, or non-violence, unlike satya is for all intents and purpose a social phenomenon. It can emerge only from existing personal and social relationships both within the individual's personal and social and within that of the community. Since these relationships impact society in that social responses are dependent on the nature of these relationships, they become crucial to the individual's and community's well-being. However, for Gandhi every social response originates and exists due to individual responses. These responses might be mediated by a social institution, but it emanates and carries on from the individual. Obviously the individual therefore has to become competent to initiate appropriate responses which would in turn configure significant social relationships. For him this becoming competent is satyagraha. For Gandhi, ahimsa which is the 'law of one's being' is the pause between satya as freedom and *agraha* as insistence. To rephrase, ahimsa as the law of one's being is the individual's hope and will to tread the path of satya. However, the conjunction of freedom and insisting for it can be very stressful.

Gandhi had personally faced up to violence from the time he landed in South Africa. Thrown out of a train, nearly lynched by a white mob, brutally attacked by fellow Indians, Gandhi had no illusion regarding *himsa*. Yet instead of retorting in kind, he preferred to try and understand the underlying ethos which stimulated violence and how it contorts both the perpetrator and the victim. This led him to the anti-thesis, non-violence or ahimsa, a term highly revered in the Indian tradition. However, he soon realized that ahimsa is inextricably yoked to satya. Actually ahimsa is the means while satya is the end. Moreover when you want satya you realize you have to accept ahimsa its adjunct. In effect you can never want more of ahimsa is how Gandhi summed it. This clarity became one of Gandhi's core perceptions.

As early as 1896, Gandhi in his 'Grievances of British Indians in South Africa' wrote how his method in South Africa is to conquer hatred by love. For him therefore the hope is "To see the universal and all-pervading Spirit of Truth face to face one must be able to love the meanest of creation as oneself".[90] The issue therefore is to be able to locate the locus of power which creates meanness as well as love. Presumably in society it should be with the people. But people are ignorant of this. Obviously the task then is to make people aware of their responsibilities and available authority. The only caveat and this is crucial, don't misuse authority. Incidentally this clarity foregrounds Gandhi's understanding of the nature of politics. Thus for him while ahimsa became the binding link between satyagraha and swaraj, it is also meant renunciation of the will and capacity to do *himsa*. "Gandhi's appeal to *ahimsa* was ultimately an appeal to the conscience and reason of the individual, an affirmation of purity of means in the pursuit of any social or political goal".[91]

Ahimsa enjoins giving scope to compassion and dispassion. This requires *krodh-tyaag* or renunciation of anger an offspring of passion and possession. It is not a non-response, in that it does not encourage avoidance. It is a cultivated quality of the conscious and a product of such a person's constant dialogue with personal likes and dislikes. It leads to satya while simultaneously encouraging critical analysis of trust and transparency. But dispassion by itself begs the question. It is only half the decision. The other is dedicated commitment to aspire something. Gandhi sought equanimity and self-control through *krodh-tyaag*. Controlling and managing anger are not the same as renouncing anger. While controlling or managing anger seeks to restrict responses to gain necessary competences, the objective is to replace the sources of anger, the '*other*' and not necessarily the reasons why such sources create anger. Gandhi in ahimsa stresses renouncing. As such there is no other.

Obviously the first question is what Gandhi expected from ahimsa. Ahimsa reveals but does not eliminate ignorance; that is a task only satya can accomplish. Ahimsa focuses on the contradictions behind conflicts within society. Contradictions indicate the homing quality of conflicts, and ahimsa by returning back to the individual indicates sustainable solutions. This is the abiding distinctiveness of ahimsa linking the individual to morality. Illustrating this are Gandhi's experiments, accepting the necessity of politics and not accepting the paramountcy of any one religion. This needs elaboration.

Restraint and abjuring violence are concomitant to ahimsa. Expounding from the Gita, Gandhi writes, "Violence is simply not possible unless one is driven by anger, by ignorant love and by just hatred. The *Gita* wants us to be incapable of anger and attain to a state unaffected by the three *gunas* (sattva purity, rajas restlessness, and *tamas* torpidity).[92] While ahimsa or non-cruelty is an acquirable human quality, himsa or taking of life is integral to nature's law of living. In the give take and regeneration of nature, death and birth are akin, actually in harmony and in tandem. The ideological separation of himsa and ahimsa is an exclusive articulation of human beings. It is in abjuring himsa and its association with anger stemming from being denied legitimate expectations that humanity detects an exemplary humane potential. To understand the significance of the himsa-ahimsa polarity, Gandhi suggests recourse to *krodh-tyaag* the renouncing of anger and thereby the desire for position and possession. Tyaag or consciously giving up the lure of position and possession is ahimsa, a moral calling and a calling of the wise. Backing position is power and authority, while supporting possession is the right and might of '*mama*' or mine/I; I being our most precious possession. Tyaag of 'mine' facilitates the awareness of ahimsa. But tyaag proposes to give up something to acquire something else. What can *krodh-tyaag* give in return? For Gandhi the renouncer acquires equanimity and self-control.

Social entitlements and endowments are at the root of possession and possessiveness, which in turn are the cause of all anger. Even the so-called learned are prone to anger because of the non-actualization of expectations their world-view and knowledge warranted. Ahimsa is a cognitive course which creates a certain wellbeing by cautioning and reminding us of the coercive qualities of possessiveness. It however expects discretion discrimination and an analytical disposition. Since it is an attitude, it remains subject to an individual's reading of personal and social events. For Gandhi ahimsa is essential to social insight because it looks up to satya with which it has a mutual relation to verify '*samatwa*' equality. But in our day to day existence we might find elements of conflict between the two. Why? As per satya, we know that killing or taking life for food is a part of nature's practice of living; himsa or killing is a link between birth and death and thereby of regeneration and continuity. But for human beings it is not that simple. We conflate killing and dying. When we lament when somebody dies, it is not just a question of somebody passing away. It is actually a recognition that something has been taken away and hence forth will not be available. Killing is a deliberate act while dying is matter-of-fact. It is the socially constructed ethos of intention and intentionality of hurting and killing which ahimsa eschews. Ahimsa indicates and encourages reflective and voluntary practices to help us set up meaningful rules of conduct to help us transform ourselves along more propitious ways. It thus becomes an aid to morality which helps us distinguish and understand processes of how discernment and reflection helps us go beyond instinctive nature ordained parameter of himsa. Thus Gandhi would neither allow religion to influence his decision about a dying calf nor did he have problems with accepting euthanasia. Ahimsa by questioning our orientation influences our attitudes particularly those which seem to be benign.

In nature himsa emanates from necessity and is a systemic quality. Humanity has re-designated this systemic quality into killing as death, thereby warping and falsifying it through conflating the dissimilar compulsions of nature and society. Ahimsa is a social construct. And while it is accessible to everybody, ahimsa remains an anthropomorphic means of selection and exclusion. What then is this distinctness of ahimsa?

For Gandhi ahimsa is the necessity of finding that which is hidden. Giving up anger (preferably along with longing) is a way to access systems of alternative possibilities which otherwise remain obscured due to our given natural competitiveness with each other. Conscious non-competiveness helps search the potential behind the apparent. In a way ahimsa is a radical perhaps disorderly position which dodges vertical relations of domination by permitting entry at all levels of relationship; ahimsa avoids elitism. In our normal discourse truth, potentiality, immanence and transcendence remain in an absurd pantomime of hard to decipher gestures. But this need not be so; the narrative of living can become systems of expression and perception. Ahimsa helps establish such systems. And to its merit does not threaten regimes. This it does because it offers alternative links to the plausible via choice; a new system of possibilities is thus created which does not necessarily need to abolish the present. Himsa and ahimsa in a way are contingent and ahimsa while enlightening is not necessarily a project of deliverance; it is not necessarily concerned with historical destinies. But Gandhi by making ahimsa an adjunct of the social within makes *samatwa* equality functional and since this equality refers also to power, he makes the individual think politics. After all, social equality is a question of power. He in his own way avers that he took part in politics 'because politics encircles us today like the coils of a snake'. And "My devotion to Truth has drawn me into the field of politics".[93] Equality is where purpose and agency, ethos and principles merge. It applies to all and is deemed to hold for all. For Gandhi, equality is the spiritual and moral surrogate of manual labor.

Gandhi's politics presupposes ahimsa. While he recognizes the astutely rhetorical distinctness of 'saying' and 'meaning' in politics, the transparency ahimsa ensures clarity. Not surprisingly ahimsa can make more sense when it is guaranteed by the state; but then that would be an oxymoron! Therefore for Gandhi, ahimsa can play the role himsa does for nature; cull to sustain balance. Further, ahimsa brings forth the concealed contradictions in the separation of the social and the personal within us. Events, thoughts and speaking in lieu of others can be an act of himsa. In ahimsa Gandhi sought inclusivity by forestalling the authority of uniqueness. Actually the equality characteristic of ahimsa neutralizes the rhetoric between the 'I' and 'me'. Ahimsa is not a goal; it is a belief and needs constant verification. Its objective is not to eliminate, but to help the subject recognize inherent social inequalities and personal disabilities through satya. Ahimsa while seeking to correct a wrong can initiate a discourse by and for itself over and beyond the 'subject'. In the process it can become a narrative without a script, albeit involved in acts of liberation. In short it can become a heuristic indulgence. Therefore for Gandhi while satya can become a debate between multiple interests, ahimsa has to be the refrain of a legitimate partner; it has to remain an adjunct just like silence is of sound.

This brings us back to *krodhatyaag* which is at the core of ahimsa. Krodha-tyaag for an individual, in many ways is a paradigm shift. In a social setting anger emanates from denial of an ostensibly legitimate entitlement. While this legitimacy remains a debatable issue for the social, for the personal the claim is apparent. Anger emerges from such normative and subjective claims. Gandhi suggests we exorcise the claims of anger and thereby make a sympathetic linkage between the knower and the known (legitimizer and legitimacy), the giver and the given (legitimizer and claim), the taker and the attained (claimer and the claim). Further when ahimsa mediates between the debatable and the grounded i.e. the social and the personal, for the individual the narrative becomes one of a very matter-of-fact 'give and take'. Ahimsa a moral concept of the 'wise' thus becomes a method to transform oneself in order to access truth which is self-evident and self-sufficient. Incidentally this truth is noticeably discernable in the context of its relationship with power, knowledge and the subject. In this, tyaag becomes an effort to stay involved in truth. Not surprisingly for Gandhi, "Ahimsa means the largest love, the greatest charity. If I am a follower of ahimsa, I must love my enemy. I must apply the same rule to the wrong-doer who is my enemy or a stranger to me, as I would to my wrong-doing father or son".[94] Ahimsa is a two-way process. While what I think is good for me, I think the same is also good for you. Simultaneously I accept that what you think is good for you, is good for me too. This anticipating the other as non-antagonistic is integral to and a promise of satyagraha.

For Gandhi the 'Me' is a blend of the 'I' and the 'thou' (the second person pronoun referred by the other). Further this 'Me' shares with 'I' an integrity regarding subject, knowledge and power. For the elite, *krodhatyaag* means them withholding, even abjuring their power. It is a 'non-violence of the strong'. As an 'active force' it has no room for cowardice or even weakness. But it has to be acquired with due personal humility and not social morality. Even Gandhi had to struggle. He nearly threw his wife out for refusing to clean the chamber-pot of a guest.

Over the years, Gandhi came to the conclusion that while the end is satya, ahimsa is the means; while duty is satya, rights belong to ahimsa; while give is satya, take is ahimsa. In the individual, ahimsa encourages a feeling of being one's own agent. While ahimsa encourages the presence of good will and the absence of ill will (Tolstoy's criteria), it also encourages the people to be discerning and decide for themselves. Gandhi does recognize the laws of nature vis-à-vis killing; but he is careful when figuring out when and where human beings have blurred the lines of these laws. For him killing if at all can only be for the sake of the killed. This is recognition of the contradiction of the '*swa*' within swadharma, swadesh, swatantra, swaraj and so on. Since the 'swa' belongs both to the personal and the social, it is always struggling against efforts seeking to straightjacket it within universal rules of appropriation. When internal contradictions consolidate and the social dominates, the '*swa*' gets smothered under rituals such as nationalism, sectarianism, communalism, secularism and so on. Gandhi would, "be readier to insist on the right attitude towards non-violence or truthfulness than to dictate specific conduct that would require unalike cases. But even with the *attitude* of non-violence, which alone he thought right, he did not wish to impose it on those with opposite convictions, much as he might hope to convert them".[95]

Ahimsa evolves through discussions, experiments and commitment. In Gandhi it started with goodwill and friendliness, incorporated fearlessness, abstention from harming others, and consolidated as an attitude of non-enmity towards all. Effectively it meant absence of malice and hostility and a total abjuring of violence. As agency it necessitates non-separation from the victim because most violence in society is systemic and therefore intentional. As such, "The use of violence necessarily involved strong passions, especially anger and hatred, and disturbed the equanimity and moral harmony of the agent. For yet others, it corrupted his consciousness, defiled his soul and hindered his spiritual progress".[96] Thus for Gandhi, "Non-violence is not a cloistered virtue to be practiced by the individual for his peace and final salvation, but a rule of conduct for society if it is to live consistently with human dignity".[97] Interestingly he also insists, "Yours should not be a *passive* spirituality that spends itself in *idle* meditation, but it should be an *active* thing which will carry *war* into the enemy's camp";[98] "ahimsa ruled out all forms of selfishness, including blind attachment to life".[99] Not surprisingly, "Gandhi was not and did not see himself as a private individual living his life as he pleased. He was a moral 'scientist' engaged in conducting moral 'experiments'".[100]

A question can be asked: 'does ahimsa mean empowerment?' The problematic of empowerment must be recognized as distinct from enablement; it is an acquisition. Gandhi might find it difficult to explain either ahimsa or satya in Rama's attitude towards Sambhuka the *Sudra tapaswi* who was condemned to die to sustain an institution. Perhaps ahimsa as the creativity within criticism can only indicate and not create vis-à-vis power. Ahimsa as we have noted is not necessarily a debate only between equals. Nor does it intend to make unequal equal. Ahimsa engages with and interrogates inequality.

Social transformation is a process of change and continuity. Change in this process is always accompanied by violence because it selectively reorders and eliminates existing features and essentials. Continuity on the other hand speaks of birth, regeneration, construction, sustenance and non-violent adaptations. For most analysts and leaders the focus has been on change. Why this focus on change? Perhaps this is because of the eternal contradiction between the motivating thrust of the personal and the social; sustaining the personal is continuity while sustaining the social is change. When Gandhi talks of suffering; "Suffering is the law of human beings, war is the law of the jungle", he is only asking for the personal and the social to suffer each other.[101] This for Gandhi is the most encouraging way, "for converting the opponent and opening his ears, which are otherwise shut to the voice of reason";[102] of course beginning with oneself.

Gandhi argues that if human beings were violent by nature, then humans would be extinct by now. While the instinct of self-preservation sustains violence as aid to continuity, ultimately the quest for truth Gandhi argues can be seen in the relentless transition from the transactional to the transcendental. Gandhi's conception of non-violence as universal love is essentially an effort to harmonize the social and individual processes of change and continuity. This incidentally requires compassion and humility. Often as far as ahimsa is concerned Gandhi took the middle path between theory and practice. As he puts it, "The theory is there; our practice will have to approach it as much as possible. Living in the midst of rush, we may not be able to shake ourselves free from all taint . . . but the chief thing is to put our theory right".[103] While ahimsa does respond to immediate and fundamental interests, for Gandhi the question is to understand the law of one's being. In effect, albeit in a subdued way, ahimsa warns us that freedom can be very intimidating. Gandhi's relation with his family illustrates this. Freedom is intimidating because it uncompromisingly aspires for satya even from the inept.

Thus for Gandhi ahimsa is a philosophy, a method, a hope, a desire and a commitment. Above all it is a characteristic which makes human beings humane. When we aspire for satya we have to prepare for it. This preparation is impossible without the benign influence of ahimsa which insists in 'all' as nothing. It gives us the capacity to say no to the apparent so as to acquire the more thought-provoking essential. For Gandhi every social response is an individual's response. The response might be mediated by an institution, but the onus is always on the individual. These decisions are in turn based on the person's competence backed means, and have an expectation. Further these decisions structure human relations. For Gandhi these relations are what pave the way to '*moksha*'. Gandhi nevertheless accepted that we do make mistakes. He however chose to follow conscience rather than prevaricate and wait to become perfect. He recognized the fact that while to err is human, to learn from mistakes is acquiring wisdom. Conviction, faith and reason remain evolving qualifications of all individuals. Within this the creative emerges when all ideas, convictions, faith, and reason are put to incessant criticism. This is the forte of ahimsa.

Satyagraha

During his stay in South Africa, Gandhi had matured from a dedicated young lawyer and a *satyarthi* to a leader of a varied group of expat Indians. As a leader he found himself involved in a protracted struggle with the local authorities. In this resistance against injustice the basic question was 'what should be the nature of the struggle'? Should it be one where one section is pitched against another, with rebuilding alternatives left to the winners for the future? Or should it be a movement which keeps suggesting an ethos wherein there are no victors and vanquished, where both sides learn to live with each other and actually start course correctives during the struggle itself? Gandhi opted for the second and thus emerged satyagraha.

Satyagraha is Gandhi's profound conceptual contribution to political philosophy. In terms of praxis it is complex, demanding, and highly nuanced. After using it in South Africa for the first time, discussing its scope Gandhi writes, "The government has now promised not to apply the law to Indians on the condition that the objective of the law should be secured by the Indians themselves acting of their free will, that is, without the compulsion of that law".[104] Continuing he writes, "We consider this a victory for truth". This 'for truth' which remains firm against any form of social or individual vicissitudes and coercion, remains the essential promise of satyagraha, which grew in clarity as Gandhi and his companions refined it through practice. By 1916, eight years after its conception and now back in India, Gandhi reminisces, "In brief, the significance of *satyagraha* consists in the quest for a principle of life".[105] In practice satyagraha for Gandhi stretched from a practice to a principle and a world view. Satyagraha venerates the individual's search for truth but does not necessarily extend this to an institutional obligation. Moreover, just like Gandhi's own problematic of the interdependence of the social and the personal, this concept too embodies a similar tense connection between individual and an institution. Furthermore, since it is premised and grounded on satya, it claims to know what it wants, but is not as sure about what it does not want, and would be willing to abjure; consequently it remains an eternally pregnant expectation. Does this mean that satyagraha is fated to remain tentative? Satyagraha in a way remains a unique event, a distinct political narrative of reconciliations, agreements, and differences. At its core satyagraha retains an abiding faith in the principle of unity and diversity, where unity is an on-going dialogue of human association including especially the political, an essential link between 'thought, word and deed', while diversity indicates the importance of every individual's distinctive contribution to this dialogue.

Satyagraha is a combination of satya and *agraha*. Satya stands for truth while *agraha* insistence. Obsession stands for giving expression to and binding together the significance of this truth. Its complexity arises from the eternal social tension between the individual and societies' obligations; while an individual can express truth as an individual being, to bind this together as a moral and ethical code she has to ensure that it becomes a social endeavor. It is thus that satyagraha can range from being an obsession to an opportunistic involvement. Every individual perceives truth differently, but for the sake of social harmony is obliged to take a conciliatory stand. This can be a challenging demand complicated by selfishness, ethics, and sectarianism. In this sense, satyagraha while being epistemic and political is also philosophical. Essentially the import of satyagraha results from its operation. Satyagraha therefore emerges as the narrative of a mutual project of the *satyarthi* and the *satyagrahi* under the leadership of the *satyagrahi*. Inherent within this narrative is the mutuality of suffering and love, similar to 'give' and 'take'.

For Gandhi, active involvement and intervention in social transformation processes was not to just seek justice as some post-factum homily. While he aspired for freedom from bondage his intention was also to make people conscious of their inalienable moral autonomy which is based on satya and ahimsa. Satyagraha seeks to hail the moment of collective social consciousness with sarvodaya and swaraj to follow. In this, while satya is the goal, ahimsa remains the means. Satyagraha as a political doctrine is non-violent resistance, and as praxis it avoids differentiation between intentions and conduct. Therefore, for the *satyagrahi* it is a call to 'master the details of morality'.[106] Satyagraha seeks simultaneity in resisting evil while encouraging equanimity. As truth-force it serves as agency for sustainable non-coercive participatory processes of social transformation. This is the import of Gandhi's stress on constructive programme being integral to satyagraha. "Thirty-four years of continuous experience in experimenting in truth and non-violence have convinced me that non-violence cannot be sustained unless it is linked to body-labour and finds expression in our daily contacts with our neighbours. This is the Constructive Programme".[107] We find Gandhi doing just this in Champaran, the first satyagraha he initiated in India. "It is, he thought, the judicious combination of constructive work and effective resistance that makes satyagraha radically subversive of all forms of elitist politics. He urged volunteers in the constructive programme to occupy themselves with that neglected work which brings neither fame nor power".[108]

Struggles can make or mar an individual. For Gandhi the efficacy of resistance has to be evaluated in the emerging personality of the resisters or *satyagrahis*. If the *satyarthi* emerges as a compassionate thinking person, the system will respond accordingly. Satyagraha is like 'walking on the edge of a sword" and Gandhi argued, "If, on any occasion, we fail, we shall discover that the failure was due to some deficiency in the *satyagrahi* and did not argue the inefficacy of *satyagraha* as such".[109] "That being so", Gandhi argues, "it is necessary to inquire as to who can offer so admirable a battle – one which admits of no defeat – which can have only one result".[110]

A fundamental concern of satyagraha is the issue of 'means' employed in a struggle. In any situation where there is a conflict of interest between differing claimants, you have a situation of distrust. Besides plain coercion, the powerful can resort to manipulation by way of personification, puritanism, and retributive requitals. The *satyagrahi* too can in a similar manner resort to exemplification, dogmatism, and simple distrust ostensibly for a larger cause. Appealing to traditions, morality, and so forth both obfuscate the import of emerging issues; all in the service of a larger cause. Thus we can have a situation where in both the contenders can create a perfectly self-centred and chauvinistic dominance because both can resort to the 'fall in line syndrome'. Consequently personification can be used to justify roles in strategies during struggles, puritanism can lead to an intractable 'we-they' syndrome, and a disciplinary mindset can lead to cultures of authoritarianism. Consequently for Gandhi means became as important as the ends, particularly when questioning hegemony. He contends, "It is a matter of common observation that what we have won can be retained only by the same means through which it was got. What is won by force can be retained by force alone".[111] It is this conceptualization which distinguishes for a *satyagrahi* the distinction between the approaches of the state and that of civil society. While satya is beyond resistance, to imbibe it requires commitment. "A *satyagrahi* is ever his master. . . . Once a person had become a *satyagrahi*, he will always find ways for offering satyagraha".[112] Obviously this necessitates an element of insistence. While this persistence is based on an urge for truth which has to be acquired, the beauty of truth is that it adjudicates force; "Truth-force then is love-force. We cannot remedy evil by harboring ill will against the evil-doer".[113] Truth can assume an ideological appeal of its own. Perhaps this is why Gandhi was particular about religion and its impact on the practice of satyagraha. "Those who take part in it must have equal respect and regard for the religious convictions and susceptibilities of those who profess a different faith from theirs. The slightest narrowness in their outlook is likely to be reflected magnified multifold in the opponent".[114] After all, he reasoned, "A *satyagrahi* has nothing to conceal in his heart because he intends to serve everyone";[115] including obviously the enemy. Gandhi accepts that satyagraha would mean an individual having to submit her personal liberty to society which by nature is hierarchic. But according to him it is an immensely transformational barter with redeeming qualities: "civil resistance is a most powerful expression of a soul's anguish and an eloquent protest against the continuance of an evil state".[116]

When does a resistance become a satyagraha? Gandhi applied himself to this question when incarcerated in the Yerwada prison and wrote about the birth and subsequent spread of satyagraha in South Africa.[117] Satyagraha as a political philosophy of resistance emerged from an appreciation that all oppressed people and every oppressed individual can adopt passive resistance or satyagraha "as being a more reliable and more honorable instrument for securing the redress of wrongs than any which has heretofore been adopted".

Satyagraha was conceived and birthed in South Africa. Gandhi's orientation was rapidly evolving beyond the call of a *satyarthi*. This personal transformation and its narrative started when Gandhi sought a more nuanced and humane approach to social involvement in resistance initiatives. He was not ready to accept compromises which did not change fundamental anomalies. For him, while resistance had to be initiated, the process had to be rejuvenating, perhaps even cathartic. Further solving the problem itself should suggest processes of rebuilding a more self-fulfilling milieu. Accordingly, Gandhi and his companions in the British Indian Association decided to resist but with distinctly innovative criteria when the ruling South African regime passed the Asiatic Act and the Transvaal Immigration Act. Since the Indians accepted that resistance had to go beyond the petition and negotiation drill, the ensuing passion and the humane urge drew Gandhi to look closely into the linkage between satya, ahimsa, and resistance against injustice. Consequently, his alternative non-violent resistance satyagraha shed its restrictive nomenclature of passive resistance to emerge as a more nuanced, demanding, and constructive form of resistance. Satyagraha soon became a development on the earlier passive resistance.

Satyagraha as a practice started when a pledge was taken in a resolution passed at a meeting on 11 September, 1906 attended by almost all sections of the expatriate

Indian community living in South Africa. At this meeting it was decided that, "the Indians solemnly determined not to submit to the ordinance in the event of its becoming law in the teeth of their opposition and to suffer all the penalties attaching to such non-submission".[118] For Gandhi the most intriguing part was the speech of Sheth Haji Habib; Gandhi reminiscences that Habib wanted the gathering to "pass this resolution with God as witness and must never yield a cowardly submission to such a degrading legislation".[119] Of course the struggles continued because the problem for the authorities stemmed from the problematic of Indian qua Indian. By 24 November when the Indians converged once again at the Forbes mosque at Johannesburg to discuss their future course of action Gandhi claimed their "petition no longer lay with an earthly ruler; it was to be addressed to the Creator".[120] For Gandhi the pledge therefore became a solemn commitment with the Creator. This thus was akin to a vow, a personal commitment with the Creator as witness. This vow thus emerges as an adjunct of satya during struggles. "To pledge ourselves or to take an oath in the name of that God or with Him as witness is not something to be trifled with".[121] For him while "there is wisdom in taking serious steps with great caution and hesitation", caution and hesitation have their limits. "Personally I hold that a man, who deliberately and intelligently takes a pledge and then breaks it, forfeits his manhood".[122] With this perspective Gandhi could now go beyond the restrictive notion of passive resistance.

Most find it difficult to associate and comprehend the usage of the term non-violence or ahimsa in the practice of active resistance. The contemporary term 'empowerment' is often preffered. But this term does injustice both to ahimsa and the grim notion of power. This insightful shift in Gandhi's own philosophy occurred when during a mass meeting a European sympathizer alluded to the fact that Indians took to passive resistance "which is a weapon of the weak". This weakness of course indicated to the weak Indian. Seeking to dispel any such inherent flaw Gandhi explained, "If we continue to believe ourselves and let others believe, that we are weak and helpless and therefore offer passive resistance, our resistance would never make us strong, and at the earliest opportunity we would give up passive resistance as a weapon of the weak".[123]

The issue therefore is one of 'apparentness' of 'strength' and 'force' and the import of this to non-violent resistance. Satyagraha is akin to the supple root which brooking no resistance grows to even break through grim concrete. Drawing from experience and history, Gandhi was apprehensive that passive resistance could very well become the convenient first step to a later usage of force, if and when the resistance became stronger. Ahimsa would then become just a tactical provisional palliative. This is not what satyagraha should be. Learning from subsequent struggles with General Smuts and the South African authorities, Gandhi recalibrated the essential thrust of the struggles. The first step was to recognize the distinction between vision and mission. Ahimsa and satya were not only to be integral to satyagraha but also be its essential ethos. There are formal philosophies which while discussing, elaborate and present just the epistemology of a concept. Then we have Gandhi, Vivekananda, and others who are pro-active philosophers for whom epistemology, ontology, and teleology are inseparable. Therefore, keeping the evolving *satyarthi* in mind, Gandhi discarded passive resistance although accepting that it can have an element of harassment to achieve something. His reasoning was uncluttered. In satyagraha the minimum is the maximum, i.e. there is no bargaining around a set of demands. A specific satyagraha stops with the realization of the goals it has set for itself. Satyagraha can only have minimal demands and will not flog success. As Gandhi puts it, "the community was not bound as to when and regarding what subjects they should offer satyagraha, in deciding which question they must only not transgress the limits prescribed by wisdom and appreciation of their own capacity. Satyagraha offered on every occasion seasonal or otherwise would be corrupted into *Duragraha*".[124] In the same vein Gandhi was clear that cunning had no place in satyagraha because it "is not only morally wrong but politically inexpedient".[125] Satyagraha cannot be reduced to a political skirmish.

In satyagraha the law of progression amounts to an axiom.

> As a satyagraha struggle progresses onward, many another element helps to swell its current, and there is a constant growth in the results to which it leads.... For in satyagraha the minimum is also the maximum, there is no question of retreat, and the only movement possible is an advance.[126]

Thus, although the *satyagrahi*'s path "is sharp as the sword's edge", like with the river tributaries constantly join it swelling it to a broad water-way. But while the river can swell and become large, to amplify satyagraha other streams cannot be deliberately cut into it. Starting from the self where without trivializing, satyagraha "may be offered to one's nearest and dearest",[127] as a 'force containing within itself seeds of progressive self-restraint, satyagraha exudes firmness, wisdom, charity, and deliberation, progresses resolutely to merge into the ocean of liberation'. However, in all this there is no place for violence. "Satyagraha postulates the conquest of the adversary by suffering in one's own person".[128] It appeals to the good (perhaps latent) in the adversary because no one can be only evil. The hope is to reveal the togetherness of the good and the being even struggles. The vow sanctifies this involvement and because it has God as witness it cannot be a deal between leaders. In 1908 Gandhi wanted the Indian community to "give up its anger against the whites. We are often thoughtless enough to say that the whites can have nothing good in them. But this is patent folly. Mankind is one, and even if a few whites make the mistake of considering themselves different from us, we must not follow them in that error".[129] For the individual thus it becomes a twofold engagement of attentively serving oneself and the community. Much latter he was to write, "Liberty cannot be secured merely by proclaiming it. An atmosphere of liberty must be created within us. Liberty is one thing, license another. Many a time we confuse license for liberty and lose the latter. License leads one to selfishness whereas liberty guides one to supreme good. License destroys society, liberty gives it life. In license property is sacrificed; in liberty it is fully cherished. Under slavery we practice several virtues out of fear; when liberated we practice them of our own free will".[130]

This interrogation questions the competence of fear and freedom to be the agency of virtue. Resistance, like knowledge can be interpreted as a social relationship and a process of negation to either assert or disassemble power. Satyagraha is a mission not a vision. Perhaps it can create the necessary conditions but not all of the sufficient conditions.

Satyagraha for Gandhi cannot be restricted to tactical necessities. While it is a struggle against exploitation, it has to concurrently mitigate the cause of such oppression. And this simultaneity is more fundamental than solving a particular problem. Satyagraha has to create sustainable alternatives not just solve temporary problems. This needs courage, personal, and community self-respect, willingness to recognize the social within us vis-à-vis the personal, a capacity to want to rebel against that which is not true within us, and clarity that authority has to be generated not snatched as a trophy. Above all as an associate of satya it has to accost the problem of brutalization which is a product of oppression, a brutalization which alienates self from the being, thereby undermining an individual's capacity for sagacity. Perhaps Gandhi was foregrounding the fact that we can lie to ourselves because all of us don't have the same conception of truth. "We see truth in fragments and from different angles of vision". Above all antagonism and violence generates feelings of insecurity, anger and hatred, perfectly avoidable passions. Satyagraha is an exercise in creating alternative social vision.

Satyagraha however is also to try and help an individual maintain an identity and not become a number or statistics. For all of Gandhi's premising of the social, he never lost track of the individual. The mutuality of 'I, me, thou, they' remains, but in mutuality, resistance and coercion, concord and oppositional, strength and weakness, self-criticality and intentionality, trust and transparency become substantial issues. Satyagraha incorporates ethical opposition to immoralities, 'a programme of transformation of relationships'. Being in equal measures compromise and confrontation, it is a learning process for all participants. In a way satyagraha is a profound process of the unfolding of a person's personhood under the benign influence of truth. For Gandhi while it is a call against subjugation, it is not one of swapping the role of the dramatis personae with the tenets remaining unchanged. As praxis satyagraha is a social criticism in which the victim, the oppressor, and the *satyagrahi* are morally linked with none being absolved of being responsible for the predicament of subjugation. Since action alone can resolve a predicament, satyagraha seeks to bring all the three into the narrative. While the method has to be non-violent, it has to liberate all the parties. Since it entails perseverance, transparency in the face of antagonism and inclusiveness, it has to be a 'weapon of the strongest': strength coming from conviction. It can never lose sight of the mutuality and affinity of means and ends, rights and duties, and wants and needs. For Gandhi humanity remains a shared legacy which satyagraha seeks to make explicit. But this independence and interdependency remains contested because of the proclivities of the acquisitive '*mama*'. Satyagraha as a conscious engagement becomes an edifying narrative wherein intentionality of all concerned is brought forth with trust and transparency. Since the goodness of the consequent is contingent and contributory, responsibility in satyagraha is never one-sided. To ensure this, for Gandhi, satyagraha becomes a two-fold programme: firstly, to express and struggle against what we don't want, and secondly to offer creative alternatives about what we want.

While truth itself is *abadhya* for the individual it often appears as a constrained, obligated, and confused perception. Since all individuals are unique, the nature of this perception is unique too. However, every individual constantly seeks to examine this perception by understanding how this relates to sincerely held personal beliefs of thought, word, and deed. In the process the person also recognizes that in situations of conflict this perception of truth becomes clearer and comes to the forefront. A rational discussion about this perception vis-à-vis that of others, in turn, helps us comprehend the 'problematic of conflict of interest'. Basically there is no just conflict resolution; it is always a conflict of interest resolution. When the interest becomes an issue of dialog, we recognize the potential and relativity of our perceptions. For Gandhi, satyagraha makes understanding of perceptions central and transparent in any conflict resolution process. This resolution however has to be inclusive and accommodative in that no one perception is even first among equals. Obviously this requires humility in not only recognizing the significance of other perceptions, but also those holding dissimilar perceptions. Satyagraha in this sense becomes an agency for sincere conflict of interest resolution, by opposing insincerity, prejudice, and self-interest. In turn this brings in the notion of give and take in Gandhi's terminology head and heart. "I have come to the fundamental conclusion that if you want something really important to be done, you must not merely satisfy the reason, you must move the heart also. The appeal of reason is more to the head".[131] In effect satyagraha neither fetishizes reason, nor does it reify mutuality. To ensure this Gandhi banks on ahimsa to sustain his thesis of 'maximum as minimum' as 'the law of progression'.

The import of an ethos however has to rest on its usability. "Although often presented as a simple-minded moral method relying on the power of the soul, Gandhi's *satyagraha* involved an ingenious and complex tripartite strategy based on a fascinating blend of rational discussion, self-imposed suffering and political pressure. The first appealed to the head, the second to the heart, and the third activated both by influencing the structure of power sustaining the relationship between the parties involved".[132] Satyagraha and the *satyagrahi* then undertake to bring together the various perceptions of truth and show that the core is *abadhya*. Morality and happiness, humanity, and the individual cannot be at cross-purpose.

Basically, satyagraha seeks to resolve the oppressive give and take linking the oppressed and the oppressor. Gandhi has a decidedly different stand as to why such a situation develops. According to him, we tend to overlook the fact that it is the oppressed who by tacit acceptance, even if reluctantly, give authority and credibility to the oppressor. This warps critical and creative self-examination by the oppressor who accept their *take* as legitimate, ignoring that it has to have a mutual balancing *give* to sustain it. Obviously the oppressed learn the consequences of such tacit acceptance. Tactically a way out for the ruling authority is to concede and pass a law. But such laws retain fundamentals of privilege wherein the prevailing hegemony continues. This is where satyagraha stands out. Satyagraha does not merge, debunk, or hierarchize perceptions of truth. It shows the distinctness of every perception vis-à-vis satya. Since it is the path and not the destiny, it can run into obstructions, but it cannot be appropriated by any one *Pathik*, any one ideology or any one protagonist. The problem is most of the time societies are in a state of transition when traditional knowledge and modern knowledge are in opposition. In such a milieu, hybrid knowledge takes over. Gandhi was constantly mindful of the potential for mischief by this 'hybrid'. In many ways Gandhi conceptualizes the role of the *satyagrahi* as 'agency' to mediate transition by cross-examining both the protagonists. Satyagraha provides the site and prepares the individual *satyagrahi*.

Satyagraha Gandhi hoped would create the necessary circumstances for the community to make their own history. Obviously for this the *satyagrahi* will have to provide the sufficiency criteria and re-work economic, political, and social relations.

The *satyagrahi*

From the above it is clear that satyagraha retains one unresolved, perhaps unresolvable, problematic. It splits the *satyagrahi* from the event because while the event ends with fulfilment or failure of its temporal expectations, the *satyagrahi* goes on since for her there is no success or failure. Satyagraha remains a 'quest for a principle of life'. Implicit is the fact that although the project of the *satyagrahi* remains life long, every single event sustains her very being; the *satyagrahi* progresses through a succession of satyagraha events. The problematic lies in what should be the emphasis: the nature of the sequence or a particular event. A sequence oversees the ethos and the nature of linkages, while every event is a cluster of specifics. Of particular importance is the sustaining and adapting of memories and sentiments to inspire and monitor ensuing events. The congress party in some ways became the institutional repository of the memories of the concatenation of various satyagrahas which aided and gave a distinct identity to the freedom struggle. But Gandhi was reluctant to give such a role to an institution because he feared misuse of such memory. He wanted the congress party to be disbanded once freedom was acquired. For him satyagraha was too sacred a practice and the heritors can only be the people. Perhaps he felt that an institution could never be expected to be sensitive to 'that little voice' listening to which is important because satyagraha is not a political strategy. He was also aware of the various offshoots such as boycott, non-cooperation, fasting, and so on. He was also mindful that all the satyagraha that he initiated, supported or mentored, or even withdrew, were unalike in terms of mass support. Consequently the role of the *satyagrahi* becomes critical and even vital. Memory of satyagraha is to aid the *satyagrahi* and not become some heuristic folklore to encourage political manipulation.

The above becomes evident when we see how Gandhi explains various facets of satyagraha particularly the role of the *satyagrahi*. Summing up while 'looking back on the Indian struggle in South Africa', he explains, satyagraha as a praxis, carried out to its utmost limit is independent of pecuniary or other material assistance;

violence is the negation of this great spiritual force; it can be cultivated or wielded by those who will entirely eschew violence; it can be used by individuals as well as by communities; it may be used as well in political as in domestic affairs; its universal applicability is a demonstration of its permanence and invincibility; it can be used alike by men, women, and children; it is impossible for those who consider themselves to be weak to apply this force; and this requires the adoption of poverty.[133] Explaining 'The essential law of *satyagraha*' in 1919 he writes, "It is only where a conflict of interest arises, then arise the progeny of untruth, viz.; anger, ill-will, etc., and then we see nothing but poison in our midst. A little hard thinking will show us that the standard we apply to the regulation of domestic relations is the standard that should be applied to regulate the relations between rulers and the ruled, and between man and man".[134] Elaborating on 'who can offer' satyagraha he detailed five prerequisites: pursuit of truth and faith in truth; indifference to wealth; obligation to break away from family attachments; being loyal to truth and never becoming a tyrant; leaving everything ultimately to God, thus never knowing defeat in this world.[135] These take a *satyagrahi* way beyond the calling of an ordinary activist because such a person is one who derives 'strength from truth'. In effect a *satyagrahi* is committed for life and this she does as an individual. Gandhi the *mumukshu* could never allow an institution to mediate his quest. It is in this sense that before concluding it becomes imperative to analyze the notions of vow and fast which remains central to Gandhi's thinking about satyagraha.

Vow or a solemn pledge as practiced by Gandhi is a concept that derives a lot from the Hindu concept of '*vrata*' and the *yama niyama*, self-restraints and fixed observances scheme of Patanjali yoga-sutras meant particularly for a sadhaka.[136] However Gandhi reworked it because "the word 'vow' is not necessarily a suitable equivalent of *vrata*". For Gandhi, "if we resolve to do a thing, and are ready even to sacrifice our lives in the process, we are said to have taken a vow".[137] A vow is an undertaking albeit to one's own self. Here undertaking is an intended choice meant to accomplish a particular goal. It enjoins self-discipline and self-purification. It thus becomes a self-imposed constraint and its import lies in that "constraints are a parameter of decisive living".[138] As such, "a vow applies to only good deeds". Moreover, "moderation and sobriety are of the very essence of vow-taking".[139] Effectively a vow is a pledge and a self-committal.

For Gandhi the meaning of life lies in the quest for Truth i.e. self-realization. But self-realization is not possible without conscious or deliberated self-discipline. However, like all human endeavours it is also subservient despite being deliberate and premeditated to the larger ends of human destiny which incidentally is in the agenda of a very few. As such the seeker of truth recognizes that the search is not only intense tapas, it is also a lonely affair. Very often such a quest reflects a commitment and might require having to take a solitary stand against the arbitrary and unjust nature of society, like ploughing a lonely furrow. A vow, the first-born sibling of involvement and achievement evinces a commitment to conscious engagement. It indicates the necessity of morality as a benchmark. For Gandhi a vow is something more than being a precursor of an act. In its relationship with the social, the vow reinstalls the personal in its true nature. In effect a vow by strengthening the body, mind, and soul, through true involvement in yoga, assists in the individual's progress to the authenticity of self-realization. It thus is the swadharma of action because it necessitates a critical reappraisal of the role of the individual's free-will. A vow is in a sense a constructive albeit voluntary compliance of conscious action towards self-realization. Thus as import, "a vow imparts stability, ballast and firmness to one's character".[140]

In more practical terms the vow gains importance by ensuring commitments at two levels: the focus of the search and the pitfalls of dogma. The idealism of the individual and that of society might not match. It need not. The vow makes you aware of this fundamental contradiction. "The 'vow I am thinking of is a promise made by one to oneself. We have to deal with two dwellers within: Rama and Ravana.... The one binds us to make us really free, the other only appears to free us so as to bind us tight within his grip. A 'vow' is a promise made to Rama to do or not to do a certain thing which, if good, we want to do, but have not the strength unless we are tied down, and which, if bad, we would avoid, but have not the strength to avoid unless similarly tied down".[141]

The vow is a pause, which you require to come to terms with a simple tenet: "There is generally no difficulty in determining a principle. This difficulty, comes when one proceeds to put it into practice".[142] As a pause, vow helps the *satyagrahi* to come to terms with emotions and prepares her for stayagraha. In many ways vow is training through resistance and constructive actions: resistance amplifies the conflicting demands our aspirations make, and constructive actions retains our continuous resolve to re-assert the focus. In a way a vow is a means to acquire equanimity. A vow encourages us to recognize the contradictory nature of all our endeavors. While our actions on the one hand are ensuring and sustaining, on the other hand they are limiting, restricting, and restraining. Thus for Gandhi, "God is very image of vow".[143]

When a person seeks to undertake a task which inherently has conflict or resistance ingrained within it, the person should accept it and prepare through undertaking "a vow of resistance", i.e. accept involvement as "an obligation that must be fulfilled come what may". Resistance then becomes a duty and the obligation is not contingent on the cooperation of anyone. Vow thus accepts that others might be inadequately conscientious or might lack the will. Here Gandhi warns against the "as far as possible" mindset. It "betrays either pride or weakness" is how he inferred. Vows illustrate how while during an event, effort is necessary, it might not be sufficient. A vow gives strength to ensure commitment and attainment irrespective of experiences regarding the other. It is an aid in the method of a seeker to accomplish a mission.

In effect a vow links the seeker to what is being sought in a very conscious and committed fashion. However, a vow is meaningful only when there are options and not as an upshot of helpless. When you have an option and as a sentient person take a conscious decision to get over the restrictions of the senses, you accept the austerity mode so as to strengthen the will. It is a bitter decision because it makes you give up some of your much treasured likes and dislikes. For Gandhi a vow has to be undertaken with devotion. The attitude is important. A sanyasi and a soldier both undertake disciplining of the senses but for different reasons: for one it is a choice while for the other it is a necessity. While it perseveres with the end, a vow is always a means, never an end. A *satyagrahi* is never prejudiced between ends and means.

Gandhi to aid the pilgrimage to self-realization proposed 'ekadasha vrata' 11 vows: satya, meaning truth; ahimsa, meaning non-violence; brahmacharya, meaning celibacy or chastity; asteya, meaning non stealing; aparigraha, meaning non possession; sharirashtrama, meaning physical or bread labour; aswada, meaning control of palate; abhaya, meaning fearlessness; sarva-dharma- samanatwa- equal respects for all religious, swadeshi, and removal of untouchability. For him these are the nitya-karmas of the social within us.

Fasting or *Upawas* is 'remaining close to one's own self'. Relationships with external things create an attachment which unbalances a person and tends to take her away from her own self. Fasting helps a *satyagrahi* curb such longing. Thus we have physical fasting i.e. restraining food intake, fasting of the mind where you control the ingress of all kind of thoughts, and fasting for a social cause where you fast to restrain the significance of certain types of undesirable social dynamics. Thus, Gandhi writes, "There is nothing so powerful as fasting and prayer that would give us the requisite discipline, spirit of self-service, humility and resoluteness of will without which there can be no real progress".[144]

In a more contemporary sense the significance of satyagraha emerges in the notion of accountability i.e. liability and responsibility. When in 1936 Jawaharlal Nehru as congress president was complaining that he had to work with a committee constituted "against his better judgment", Gandhi reminded him, "If you are guilty of intolerance, you have more than your share of it. The country should not be made to suffer for your mutual intolerance".[145] In another occasion suggesting a rule of conduct Gandhi wrote, "We should cease to have any dealings with a person who breaks a promise". However, strictly speaking, accountability is not a term used by Gandhi. But his insistence on our being obligated for our thoughts and actions indicates the significance of accountability in his thinking. It can be argued that accountability is what makes him an 'evolutionary reformer' and not a 'revolutionary'. When Gandhi talks of sarvodaya, or swaraj, and satyagraha, he is engaged with being temporally accountable and responsible. We also find him stressing on the need to be involved in some form of manual labor even if it is part time, abhorring untruth, serving fellow human being, etc. Each of these is a concept pregnant with accountability on the part of the doer. Perhaps this is why he rarely speaks of development and modernization, inherent to which is co-lateral damage borne by the oppressed.

At the core of accountability lies our discretion and commitment in relation to our thoughts and actions. Gandhi suspended the 1921 noncooperation campaign when it turned violent, but did not bow to the brutality showered on the marchers during the salt satyagraha. Gandhi acknowledges the necessity of a continuous discourse regarding the why and how of a chosen 'action being subject to the obligation to report, explain and justify both to ourselves and to the community'. But he simultaneously stresses on the possibility of a cleavage between choice and results vis-à-vis thoughts and actions. Unlike choice, over which we have a measure of control, we have very little say over result because results depend upon a wider range of variables. Therefore choice becomes very important. But wise choice enjoins discretion i.e. keeping choice in harmony with norms and ethics. Since norms and ethics are related to situations, correct interpretation becomes crucial. Accountability enjoins a healthy understanding of norms and ethics combined with a commitment to make judicious choice in our social discourse. This underlines Gandhi's thinking about satyagraha.

Second, in accountability since the stress is on choice vis-à-vis results, it becomes a process of creative engagement and negotiation with the 'other' as the non-self who albeit excluded, nevertheless impinges upon decisions. In a slightly more complex way, while our capacity to act is an endowment, our capacity to choose is an entitlement. And these are always mediated by a threshold sense of inadequacy. When we accept this inadequacy and recognize that we cannot fulfill our baggage of expectation in totality, then we start becoming accountable to ourselves and others too. In Gandhian parlance the issue is sorted out by recognizing that your freedom is my limitation and my freedom is your limitation. We become accountable when to strive to take the antipathy out of this predicament. For a *satyagrahi* Gandhi described accountability as talisman: will the steps you contemplate restore to the poorest and the weakest man, control over his own life and destiny?[146]

Notes

1 *MPWMG*, Vol. II (1).
2 *CWMG*, Vol. 14 (176).
3 Gopal (1992, 138).
4 Ibid. (139).
5 *CWMG*, Vol. 10 (386).
6 Ibid., Vol. 32 (11).
7 See Parel (2007).
8 Vivekananda (1963, 1–2).
9 *Young India* (Oct. 31, 1921).
10 Ibid.
11 Nandy (2004, 19).
12 *Harijan* (Jul. 25, 1936).
13 Zaehner (1968, 65).
14 Ibid.
15 Ibid.
16 *Harijan* (Aug. 25, 1940, 260).
17 Ibid. (185–86).
18 *An Autobiography* (2004, 293). Sadagraha – insist with being as good; satyaagraha – obsession with truth as good, in the change from good to truth.
19 Parel (2007, 147). Also see, *An Autobiography* (2004, 189).
20 *An Autobiography* (2004, 188).
21 Parekh (1989, 177); *Young India* (Sep. 02, 1926).
22 *CWMG*, Vol. 62 (361).

23 Ibid., Vol. 37 (151–53).
24 Ibid., Vol. 14 (174).
25 *Young India* (Aug. 21, 1924).
26 *CWMG*, Vol. 54 (114).
27 *An Autobiography* (2004, 192).
28 *CWMG*, Vol. 44 (70).
29 Ibid., Vol. 87 (108).
30 *An Autobiography* (2004, 191).
31 Nayar (1948).
32 *MGTEW* (2008, 62).
33 *Harijan* (Nov. 21, 1936).
34 Bilgrami (2011, 106).
35 Kishwar (2006, 314).
36 *An Autobiography* (2004, 194).
37 Gandhi Rajmohan (2006, 229–34); Guha (2018, 105–10).
38 Parekh (1989, 179).
39 Gandhi (1928).
40 Ibid. (21).
41 Ibid.
42 Ibid.
43 *Young India* (Apr. 29, 1926).
44 Ibid.
45 Ibid.
46 Ibid.
47 Ibid.
48 Parel (2006, 151).
49 *CWMG*, Vol. 27 (151–53).
50 *MPWMG*, Vol. III (1987, 394).
51 *Young India* (Jul. 1921).
52 Parekh (2007, 93–101).
53 *MPWMG*, Vol. III (1978, 391).
54 *CWMG*, Vol. 14 (31).
55 Ibid., Vol. 40 (416–17).
56 Hingorani (1964, 61).
57 *CWMG*, Vol. 14 (207–8).
58 Ibid., Vol. 71 (207).
59 Hick and Lamont (1989, 231).
60 *CWMG*, Vol. 17 (31).
61 *Harijan* (May 5, 1946, 118).
62 *CWMG*, Vol. 27 (290–91).
63 Ibid. Vol. 21 (94).
64 Narayan, Vol. 4 (1968, 220).
65 *MPWMG*, Vol. II (1986, 183).
66 Gandhi (1959, 37).
67 Sorabji (2012); Veeravalli (2014).
68 Mahadevan (1990, 49).
69 *Young India* (Jun. 4, 1925, 191).
70 *MPWMG*, Vol. II (1986, 202).
71 Mahabharata, Shanti Parva, clxi. 8. 9, quoted in Mahadevan (1990, 52).
72 *MGTEW* (2008, 324).
73 Suhrud (2011).
74 *CWMG*, Vol. 54 (268).
75 *MPWMG*, Vol. II (1986, 180).
76 *Young India* (Nov. 13, 1924, 378).

77 *CWMG*, Vol. 30 (180).
78 *MPWMG*, Vol. II (1986, 70).
79 Ibid. (80).
80 Ibid. (176).
81 Ibid. (87).
82 Ibid. (160). Italics added.
83 Ibid. (163).
84 Ibid.
85 Ibid. (172).
86 *MGTEW* (2008, 54).
87 Ibid.
88 Ibid. (45).
89 *Katha Upanishad* (1987).
90 *CWMG*, Vol. 59 (401).
91 Iyer (1973, 215).
92 *MPWMG*, Vol. I (1986, 81).
93 *An Autobiography* (2004, 463).
94 *MPWMG*, Vol. II (1986, 212).
95 Sorabji (2012, 197–98).
96 Parekh (1989, 109).
97 *MPWMG*, Vol. II (1986, 237).
98 *Young India* (Sep. 9, 1925).
99 *Harijan* (Sep. 1, 1940).
100 Parekh (1989, 138).
101 Gandhi (1969, 202).
102 Ibid.
103 Veeravalli (2014, 3).
104 *MPWMG*, Vol. III (1987, 29).
105 *MGTEW* (2008, 311).
106 Ibid., Vol. III (1987, 4).
107 *Harijan* (Jan. 27, 1940).
108 *MPWMG*, Vol. III (1987, 8).
109 Ibid. (35–36).
110 Ibid. (36).
111 Ibid. (32).
112 Ibid. (58).
113 Ibid. (55).
114 Ibid. (80).
115 Ibid. (86–87).
116 Ibid. (96).
117 Gandhi (1928).
118 Ibid. (161).
119 Ibid. (162).
120 Guha (2013, 257).
121 Gandhi (1928, 165).
122 Ibid.
123 Ibid. (178).
124 Ibid. (315).
125 Ibid. (318).
126 Ibid. (319).
127 Ibid. (179).
128 Ibid.
129 Guha (2013, 275).
130 *CWMG*, Vol. 42 (380).

131 *Young India* (Nov. 5, 1931).
132 Parekh (1991, 149).
133 *Indian Opinion* (Dec. 1, 1914).
134 *MGTEW* (2008, 325).
135 Ibid. (327–30).
136 Puri (2015, 52–65).
137 *TEWMG* (1991, 192).
138 Ibid. (197).
139 Ibid.
140 Ibid. (196).
141 Ibid. (201).
142 Gandhi (1950, 172–73).
143 *TEWMG* (1991, 200).
144 *Young India* (Mar. 31, 1920).
145 Ibid.
146 *MPWMG*, Vol. III (1987, 609).

6
RELIGION
Case, brief, and argument

For Gandhi the issue of religion is not one of surrendering to awe of the transcendental but one of basking in this awe. It is in this revelling regarding creation, life, universe, humanity, and so on, that he sought insight, purpose of living, and ultimately *moksha*. Gandhi's essential spiritual quest was to be able to recognize the equilibrium between three seemingly distinct entities: the individual, the community, and the state or hegemonic political authority. Each of these is constituted by mutually volatile, unique and common features. The individual has to balance the personal and the social; the community has to balance a highly versatile unassimilated communitarian will, with the predilections of various individuals; the state has to resemble the hegemony and confirm to the ambitions of discrete leaders. Mediating all these are the notions of God, Truth, and Nature. The liberalism he perceived as a student in England, the racism of white Europeans in South Africa, the sufferings of the coolie Indian in South Africa, and the consequences of colonial rule in India, were all incorporated into an overarching quest for Truth, or and also of God. As a Hindu, in terms of spiritualism he had to specifically deal with the complex issues of power, renouncing and surrendering, and with its secular embodiment, authority, compromise, and abandoning. More specifically as far as religion was concerned he had to firmly take a position regarding the issue of superiority of one religion over others, which is, as a Hindu, the conundrum of caste. A moot question within this was the contentious issue of conversion because this not only had theoretical and practical connotations, it was also an issue he himself had to resolve at a personal level. In the early years, Gandhi was open to intense discourse, but he remained wary; in later years he was strictly against all conversion. For him, "The pity is we do not know religion, and if we know the principles, we have no grip over them".[1] Clarifying his position regarding the question of tolerance or equality of all religions he explains, "My position is that all great religions are fundamentally equal. We must have the innate respect for other religions as we have for our own. Mind you, not mutual tolerance, but equal respect".[2] As far as conversion was concerned, Gandhi wanted to stress an elemental point. "I want you to understand that you are labouring under a double fallacy: That what you think is best for you is really so; and that what you regard as the best for you is the best for the whole world. It is an assumption of omniscience and infallibility. I plead for a little humility".[3]

Gandhi in his progress from a *satyarthi* to a *satyagrahi* sought to recognize and articulate how religion is obtained and sanctioned in society, and how religion aids and abets capacities to read the innate and the inherent in society with or without coercing the reader to convert the contemporary into an instant agenda. In this he was convinced that the masses with their bias towards action are invariably well equipped to perceive the significance of existing and emerging trends in religions. But then the masses are also subject to enormous temporal coercion. Therein we find the contradictory problematic of religion: promise forfeit and the inevitable a veritable mosaic of morality, ethics, happiness, pity, mercy, and rituals. For Gandhi the resolution was, "there is only one God who is real. The real God is beyond conception. He neither serves nor receives service".[4] Effectively Gandhi considered religion as a give and a take, give as surrendering and take as renunciation.

The question thus becomes one of tension between ethics and religion or rather reducing religion to a problematic of theological ethics and perhaps in the process reducing religion to some exclusive system of ethics. Ethics is concerned with investigating the nature of right and wrong in human thought and action. The role of self-interest and religion in establishing ethical precepts by which issues of justice and freedom can be judged is the concern of moral philosophy. For Gandhi the query is: can and does religion help establish universal ethical principles? Perhaps the issue is one of moral conscience which can help distinguish 'good' from 'evil' and thus elucidate Truth, because Truth signifies the individual's in-self relationship of the personal with the social. Ethics, morality, and religion therefore have to be understood as conscious undertakings and a shaping influence mediating the individual's perpetually yoked personal and social beings. However, the most perplexing is the idea of God and its potential for ideological and theological determinism. The predicament here is in the influence this determinism can pose to human freedom. This is because we run into the dilemma of having to choose between God's ideas of human liberty and human being's idea of being liberty personified. More philosophically, does the idea and awe of God kerb or enhance our capacity to cognise ourselves? "God has indeed been used in the past to stunt creativity; if he is made a blanket answer to every possible problem and contingency, he can indeed stifle our sense of wonder or achievement. A passionate and committed atheism can be more religious than a weary or inadequate theism".[5] For Gandhi, the question of God was not a philosophical query; it was a day to day commonplace issue. "I often described my religion as religion of Truth. Of late, instead of saying God is Truth I have been saying Truth is God, in order more fully to determine my religion".[6] And "To be true to such religion one has to lose oneself in continuous and continuing service of all life".⁷ This inclusiveness of course must include one's own self and therein exists a difficulty.

Religion is a spiritual quest eternally unraveling, pointing to another milestone just a few steps beyond. While rituals claim to offer lasting solutions, religion itself is not an answer to anything, perhaps because it essentially aspires to set up the debate to find answers. And as an instrument to seek clarity it is mostly sheathed giving its possessor a feeling of security of having a weapon, never mind the ability to use it. Mystery, mystic, and metaphors often tend to obfuscate method, thereby making it even more difficult to be used as a conceptual tool by a curious and critical mind. In effect it ends up becoming an accoutrement and we remain contended that we possess it. But then as an accoutrement it is a pioneering mentifact always in the making: Hinduism hails Shaivism, Vaishnavism; Christianity has Catholics, Protestants, Lutherans; Islam offers Shia and Sunni; Buddhists wrap in Mahayana or Theravada. However, the accoutrement comes with dos and don'ts by means of Books such as Gita, Bible, and Koran, and so on. But then, we find that while they demarcate the necessary conditions, they are not as helpful regarding sufficient conditions in terms of equipping us with skills to negotiate our spiritual quest. Gandhi waded through a lot of 'ism' prone book-oriented discourse. Avoiding indoctrination, for him religion did not become an 'ism'. It became a part of his being as living itself. Having come to terms with the problematic of 'Truth is God' and 'God is Truth', the other quest that also needed understanding remained the issue of 'us also as Truth'. But this could not be easily accommodated under the idea of religion. Why? This is because it is an issue of the latent within us. Since in 'Truth' there can be no other, can there be an 'other' as 'God'? As such, the coalescing of 'I', 'other', 'God', and 'Truth' becomes the context of religion. For Gandhi, this contextualizing of religion became a narrative of involvement in service which would not discriminate and separate 'I' from the 'other', 'truth' from 'God', and 'quest' from 'being'. For him it is this quest as being which seeks to forge the personal and the social, thereby freeing each of us from the dilemma of living for oneself as distinct from living for society. Religion thus becomes a process model of 'conscious existence', the mindfulness which service makes us aware of and commends us to prospect as merit. Service by seeking to eliminate possession and possessiveness frees the personal in the individual from the constant harangue of the social. However, for Gandhi, while service recognizes the individual doer by converting the act into a *'nityakarma'* (rituals performed daily by Hindus), service itself becomes eligible for merit. Service thus insists on a negation of both, acquisitions that is possession and *daan* that is charity. Gandhi sought to free religion from the business of giving and taking by liberating it from the confusion of ethics and faith. By making morality a matrix of ethics and happiness, Gandhi made the person responsible regarding faith. This responsibility is a process of living in Truth, in God. But like relating to any process, religion too requires preparation, commitment, and total involvement. In many ways, it is a compliance of 'I' and 'me' to the vagaries of happenstance, as well as choice. The process mediating happenstance and choice is not easy. In a way religion can be described as demandingly inclusive and fragile but resilient. Intriguingly it is present at the moment before thought processes take over, mostly recognized in the passing by small nearly inconspicuous acts. For instance the hand moves to touch the forehead while passing in front of a temple. Society and individuals accept these seemingly unwitting acts as religious. Such witting and unwitting acts say a lot about an individual's faith and notion of ethics. Often the individual rather than using his thinking to comprehend truth uses it to consolidate faith.

Gandhi accepted all this and wanting to walk the talk, took the path realizing that it was like walking on a razors edge. However, he retained certain core aids: Vaishnava – Pranami faith of his mother and the Bhagavad Gita, which he acquired for himself; the sermon on the mount of the New Testament; selections from the Koran; Tolstoy's notion of labor and universalism along with humility to listen to the insight of all fellow travelers, as long as they did not hold him up or digress him from his quest. While searching for the sufficient conditions, Gandhi interacted with those who recognized the significant role of service beyond sectarianism; in this the Trappists were very encouraging. For him the quest was not to arrive but to recognize that you are always there. This conviction that I am there is not to be understood via acclaim, or holding forth. As Kabir puts it, "*Kabira khada bazaar, mange sabke khair; na kahu se dosti, na kahu se bair*": Kabir stands in the marketplace with good wishes for all, he has no friends and has strife with none. When the notion of the other withers away, 'I' 'me' 'we' 'thou' become empty jackets and you become like the Emperor, a person who needs a child to tell him he is naked. The guileless child was not making any judgement. She could not help being innocent. Gandhi sought this innocence through spiritualism.

Perhaps this is what he found from the BrihadAranyaka Upanishad: "*Asato ma sadgamaya; tamosomajyotirgamaya; mrityormaamritamgamaya*: from ignorance lead me to truth; from darkness lead me to light; from death lead me to immortality". Gandhi read it as truth is self-evident and self-sufficient; actually it is the path beyond the evident. The difficulty is with the distinctiveness of truth as evident and sufficient. Truth as evident is easily understandable. But that it is suffused with sufficiency has to be endorsed by the individual, invariably the personal within lags in accepting this. This in the Gita is the dialogic relationship between duty and expectation. Duty is evident; it is the notion of its being sufficient which remain perplexing because then it would overshadow expectations. This can be disconcerting, and the only way out it seems is faith, at least for Gandhi. "A *satyagrahi* will adhere to truth to the last. We may even lose the good opinion of others. We may let everything go. But we must not allow truth to forsake us". Perhaps this is why he feels that the search for satya can never be possible unless it is accompanied with ahimsa which fortifies us against anger and despondency, adjuncts of expectation.

Gandhi had very strong reservation regarding reification, alienation, and fetishism, particularly fetishism, which are all interestingly terms with a strong Marxist flavor. Beginning with Hind Swaraj and his take on professionals, doctors and lawyers in particular, transportation of goods and services by the railways and so on, we find him taking a strong position vis-à-vis what can be called human-generated dichotomies such as care and cure, aspirations and individualism, and so on. For him the underlying compulsion was of sustaining the *jiva* so as to recognize the atman. Fetishizing the processes of sustaining the *jiva* only comes in the way of the more fundamental issue of recognizing the atman, the true self. His stress on poverty and an uncompromising attitude towards possession and possessiveness was an essential element of this quest. Dharma a discursive practice defines the 'dynamic harmony' between *artha, kama, and moksha*. The *sthitapragna – jignasu – mumukshu* are qualifications of the *satyagrahi* who remains in peace with his own self and with the outside world. For him any process which fetishes individualism of the *jiva* is suspect. But to acquire such clarity takes time. In sarvodaya *sarva* the multitude, aspires for *udaya* that is rising or enlightenment. In other words starting from unawareness everyone rises to illumination rather enlightenment. Gandhi translates Ruskin's 'Unto This Last' not as 'antodaya', the welfare of the last person but as sarvodaya, 'welfare of all'. Perhaps Gandhi was seeking to stress that there is no first and no last? If he did, he would have to consider the social system to be value neutral and thereby undermine his need to interrogate it.

A crucial question regarding religion centers on the nature and quality of connect between personal faith and the prevailing social world, particularly whether these are in conflict or in concord? Gandhi felt that reconciliation is not only possible but necessary. A major constraint is the tension between faith, the anxiety of day to day living, and mankind's penchant for certainties. Truth he suggests mediates between these variables. For him since truth cannot be appropriated, provided truth obtains, there is no issue of either insider or outsider manipulating the discourse of religion. When truth prevails it is never a question of either/or, but one of moreover/and, where the moreover retains an influence with its considerable regard for afterthought. Therefore Gandhi remained partial to ethical reasoning. Consequently, he never accepted any religion as superior to another, nor would he accept conversion to another religion. The conscience of the individual is an ever evolving narrative between the tolerant and the intolerant, faith and reason, assurance and anxiety and obligations and protests. Gandhi sought meaning in tradition, but never ignored the 'small, still voice' or the 'inner voice' within.[8] He wrote in *An Autobiography*, "What I want to achieve – what I have been striving and pining to achieve these 30 years – is self-realization, to see God face to face, to attain *Moksha*. I live and move and have my being in pursuit of this goal".[9]

Gandhi's essential thrust pertaining to his understanding of religion and the creed thereof *comes* out clearly in his refusing to accept that any particular religion is superior to others, and its corollary, that unless you subscribe to it you can never really understand or gain from it, more so because religion moves from the mind to the heart. Gandhi explains, "Religion is a matter of feeling or the heart and, therefore, not a matter of argument".[10] Then again, religion "is a matter of reasoning, the mind, the intellect. It may shift from time to time without reaching the heart".[11] Therefore Gandhi reasoned, "All religions are divinely inspired, but they are imperfect because they are products of the human mind and taught by human beings. The one Religion is beyond all speech. Imperfect men put it into such language as they can command and their words are interpreted by other men equally imperfect".[12] Hence, "we have not realized religion in its perfection, even as we have not realized God. Religion of our conception, being thus imperfect, is always subject to a process of evolution and reinterpretation. Progress towards Truth, towards God, is possible only because of such evolution".[13] Obviously this necessity of respecting and being sensitive to processes foregrounds tolerance. However, while discussing the issue of 'Equality of Religions' Gandhi prefers to remain cautious. "Tolerance may imply a gratuitous assumption of the inferiority of the other faiths to one's own and respect suggests a sense of patronizing whereas *ahimsa* teaches us to entertain the same respect for the religious faiths of others as we accord to our own, thus admitting the imperfection of the latter". And he concludes, "But being only seekers, we prosecute our quest, and are conscious of our imperfections".[14] For him the idea is of equimindedness; caution necessitates care while being judgmental and arriving at hasty conclusions. He argues, "That anything that we cannot understand is necessarily wrong" is the root of the problem.[15] God for him neither serves nor needs service; as such there should be less of theology and more of Truth. With an abiding faith he maintains, "Man has within his breast an impulse for good and a compassion that is the spark of divinity".[16] And he concludes, "Personally, I do not regard any of the great religions of the world as false. All have served in embellishing mankind and are even now serving their purpose".[17] The question therefore is: 'why this enormous dependency and longing for religion and some transcendental godhead?' Perhaps this is an elemental requisite to discover the meaning of living. Gandhi was even more candid: "The central experience of life will forever remain the relationship which man has to God and it will never be superseded or replaced by anything else, just as human bodies will never free themselves from the law of gravitation".[18]

In all this for a Hindu, and Gandhi remained one, an elemental issue is that of *samskara* or disposition. A most common affliction of humanity is of having a propensity to desires, even at the cost of discretion. Fulfilling desires becomes a necessity, an addiction, and a compulsion, with not being able to do so leading to frustration. Gandhi sought clarity regarding every social-personal act so as to clearly elaborate the relationship of the act with actual individual satiation which instigated the act. This clarity he reasoned would elaborate the relationship of the act with actual human satiation the raison d'être of the act. But such clarity is difficult because human acts are instigated by assorted nebulous desires. Further we tend to relate them to even more tenuous memories and histories. The problem is with the fact that we are constantly creating a 'desire – act – experience – event – memory – history' continuum. To cope with such creativity we prefer to bunch details of acts into chronicles, which then tend to take a life of their own, and then to justify and sustain, generate their own set of desires. Not surprisingly individuals end up becoming very 'desire driven' persons. But they now also have a predicament; they now have to deal with a cluster of desires only some of which might be their own. We of course try to restrict ourselves to what we know or assume we know, a knowing which is relentlessly persuaded by the above-mentioned continuum.

Gandhi hopes to avoid this two-fold problematic: a disposition towards desires and an over dependence just on what we know or assume we know. Since life is transient his focus is on the present. "What may be permissible at one time, or in one place, may not be so at another time, and in another place. Desire for fruit is the only universal prohibition. Desirelessness is obligatory".[19] Gandhi would prefer to put a moratorium on desiring; but that is not possible. Our access to the present has to first overcome our transitory own habits which then can help us negotiate our life from moment to moment. However, these habits are resilient and tend to oppose when confronted. Moreover habits do give us a crutch however specious and transitory to face the unknown.

Tryst with faith

Gandhi's tryst with religion was a lifelong involvement. It started with his Vaishnava mother Putli bai, who besides Vaishnavism was also influenced by the Pranami faith and nurse Rambha dai who convinced him of the efficacy of Ramanama. While the significance of Ramanama evolved ever since Rambha *dai* gave it to him to ward off fear of the dark and the unknown, the dormant Pranami influence was to emerge conspicuously in village Paniala near Noakhali where Manu Gandhi, remembering the song as it was sung in the Sudama temple, inserted the term Allah into *Ishwar allah tero naam*.[20] This early exposure to distinct theologies left a strong impression in that Gandhi found it easier to respond openly to his subsequent spiritual yearning. However, when he left for England, he was a Hindu with only a modicum of knowledge about his religion. In his words, "I knew of Hinduism what my parents taught me, not directly but indirectly, that is, by their practice, and I knew a little more of it from a *Brahmin* to whom they sent me in order to learn *Rama Raksha*".[21] It was in England that he conspicuously encountered the idea of religion, theology, spiritualism, and so on. Here, while still a student he started becoming aware of what all these complex cognitive issues meant to people and above all what it could mean to him. It began with Sir Edwin Arnold's *The Song Celestial*, a translation of the *Bhagavad Gita*, meeting H. P. Blavatsky and Annie Besant of the Theosophical society and becoming a member of the London Theosophical Society, becoming aware of and member of the London Vegetarian Society, and so on. In this eclectic mix Gandhi managed to keep a clear head regarding religion, philosophy, and its practice. Later in South Africa as a *satyarthi*, he became critically aware of the distinct constituents of religion, philosophy, and practice.

Gandhi approached the diversity of religion from a historical perspective. For him religion is more than just a cognitive act of the mind; it is a dialogue of the immanent and the transcendent. Historically religion is an evolving expression of mankind's quest for a better life. In this complex medley, to locate his own self, Gandhi began with his existential location as an Indian Hindu. This comes out clearly when early 1905 he as an aspiring *satyagrahi* gave a series of lectures on Religion to the members of the Johannesburg Lodge of the local Theosophical Society. He began with an exposition of Hinduism, went on to Buddhism and to the role of Kabir and Nanak, describing them as necessary course correctives of Hinduism. He conceptualized his talks around the theme, 'three assaults on Hinduism, and coming from Buddhism, Islam, and Christianity'. In these lectures his ideas particularly about God was relatively cautious. Much later in 1940 while talking with a missionary who wanted to know about 'things one should avoid in order to present the gospel of Christ' that is push the transition towards spirituality, he was much clearer. "I do not regard God as a person. Truth for me is God, and God's Law and God are not different things or facts, in the sense that an earthly king and his law are different, because God is an idea, Law Himself. Therefore it is impossible to conceive God as breaking the Law. He therefore does not rule our actions and withdraw Himself. When we say he rules our actions, we are simply using human language and we try to limit Him".[22] Continuing he further elaborated that while, "I literally believe that not a blade of grass grows or moves without his will", he also believed that man as the Gita teaches us "is the maker of his own destiny".[23] And as such while man has freedom of choice as to the manner in which he uses that freedom, he is no controller of results. This apparent freedom and its inbuilt restrictions were the core guiding principles for Gandhi. As for the messengers of God, "What did Buddha do, and Christ do, and also Mahomed? Theirs were lives of self-sacrifice and renunciation".[24] Perhaps Gandhi preferred to distinguish the messenger from the message, choosing not to either abnegate or appropriate spirituality and authority.

Such clarity of course came after decades of systematic efforts. Over the years he studied the important works of all the major religions. He became so intimate with the essential ethos of Jainism, Buddhism, Christianity, and Islam that by the time he was in his mid-fifties he found that, "It is a very strange thing that almost all the professors of great religions of the world claim me as their own".[25] But he was to explain that while "All this is extremely flattering to me.... For me, however, I regard myself as one of the humblest of Hindus".[26] In effect, while Hinduism helped him enunciate his religious and spiritual aspirations, Gandhi genuinely sought to learn from the insights of all religions. The first of course was the receptivity to Islam which he picked up from his mother's *Pranami* sect association. It was in South Africa that this openness helped him associate easily with his Mohammedan peer. It must be remembered that over the twenty years that he stayed in South Africa, almost all his mass meetings were organized in the premises of Mosques. In terms of ideas he cognized the Prophet as a seeker of Truth, a fakir who had renounced everything, one who along with his family and companions suffered privations voluntarily and "whoever walked in God's fear and who had boundless compassion for mankind", all qualities Gandhi respected highly.[27] Beyond these qualities of the prophet, in terms of actual practice he was very appreciative of three specifics of Islam: practice of egalitarianism, stress on daily prayers and pilgrimage, and saving a part of one's earnings to be offered to the needy. "The key-note of Islam was, however, its leveling spirit. It offered equality to all that came within its pale, in the manner that no other religion in the world did. When, therefore about 900 years after Christ, his followers descended upon India, Hinduism stood dazed.

It seemed to carry everything before it. The doctrine of equality could not but appeal to the masses, which were caste-ridden. To this inherent strength was also added the power of the sword".[28] While he was appreciative of the internal qualities of Islam he was equally critical of its usage of the sword and practice of conversion. He was particularly critical of some of the practices such as the penalty of stoning to death which he felt went against reason and universal sense of justice. But these he reasoned were interpolations because of interpreters, and a reluctance of these interpreters to be open to criticism.[29] Besides, within Islam he could not discern clarity regarding the distinct roles of the state and religion. This is important for a diverse multi-religious country like India. This was particularly significant in South Africa where the state and church albeit intimate, remained distinct. Gandhi had experienced the importance of this separation while in England.

Gandhi's response to Buddhism was equally straight forward and matter-of-fact. Two concerns dominated his inquiry. Why Buddhism was necessary since Hinduism was already available? The second pertained to what precisely did the Buddha do to so actively impact the social milieu? Besides, Gandhi was captivated by the beatific composure of the exalted one; he was undoubtedly influenced by the serenity of Buddha. However, he explains, "In my opinion Buddha lived Hinduism in his own life".[30] "Gautama was himself a Hindu of Hindus. He was saturated with the best that was in Hinduism, and he gave life to some of the teachings that were buried in the Vedas and which were overgrown with weeds".[31] But he was also very alive to the fact that his knowledge about Buddhism was meager. He also accepted Prof. Kosambi's criticism of Edwin Arnold's *The light of Asia*, the book from which he had abridged his information about the Buddha. However he remained convinced that Buddhism "is a part of Hinduism. Buddha did not give the world a new religion; he gave it a new interpretation. He taught Hinduism not to take but give life".[32] His reasoning was as follows. Much like a Banyan tree drops roots from branches to convert them into new trunks while retaining its original trunk, Hinduism too has over the course of history dropped many such trunks in the form of Buddhism, Jainism, Sikhism, the renderings of Kabir, the Brahmo Samaj, and so on. Each trunk while being part of a network with the mother trunk is also capable of independent existence. Perhaps it is in this sense that Gandhi could claim that, "It is my deliberate opinion that the essential part of the teachings of the Buddha now forms an integral part of Hinduism".[33]

The problem as he saw in all these is what he explains as, "The priest has ever sacrificed the prophet".[34] 'The priest clung to the letter and missed the spirit'. But is this the core problem? Is it just a question of letter and spirit? When Gandhi insists that the masses with their feet in reality and not philosophy were able to distinguish between the selfish Brahmins and the Buddha, is he calculatingly blending rhetoric to simplify a complex phenomenon? The issue becomes more easily said than done when Gandhi insists that he is able to make such claims because of "being myself also one of the masses living in their midst";[35] it sounds very much like a prophet appropriating the right to sermonize. But then Gandhi always remained alive to the problematic of the contingent relationship of spiritualism and ritualism within religion. Above all, he never doubted that people were philosophy literate in that they did not have to struggle to coax and cajole meanings out of religion. Besides, for the masses it is relevance to *'action'* that is day to day living, which informs meaning to religious discourse, not epistemology. Gandhi remained convinced about the efficacy of the gospel of work in preference to that of contemplation.[36]

However regarding Buddhism Gandhi was more specific. The Buddha while not teaching of any one God was not an atheist. The Buddha was against empty rituals, and his message of mercy and pity has to be translated into modes of living. He rejected the idea that Buddha did not believe in God. "In my humble opinion such a belief contradicts the very central fact of Buddha's teaching. In my humble opinion the confusion has arisen over his rejection, *and just rejection*, of all the base things that passed in his generation under the name of God".[37] He felt it was a question of interpretation and one of cleansing and rejecting of practices such as animal sacrifice, which had become part of Hindu religion. Gandhi sought to draw attention to Buddha's rejection of the prevailing attitude of appeasing God through 'temptation and bribes'. For him Buddha, "emphasized and redeclared the eternal and unalterable existence of the moral government of this universe. He unhesitatingly said that the law was God Himself".[38] In short, Buddhism was an effort at re-energizing within Hinduism the eternal principle of God which insidious practices had reduced to some kind of a superior being similar to that of 'Kings of earth'. The Buddha essentially was reconverting the contemporary which had corrupted age old wisdom. To explain he refers to the 'great word *Nirvana*'. "*Nirvana* is undoubtedly not utter extinction. So far as I have been able to understand the central fact of Buddha's life, *Nirvana* is utter extinction of all that is base in us, all that is vicious in us, all that is corrupt and corruptible in us. *Nirvana* is not like the black, dead peace of grave, but the living peace, the living happiness of a soul which is conscious of itself, and conscious of having found its own abode in the heart of the Eternal".[39] The moot question then is the harmony between living and thinking and further, why and how should this be mediated. The Buddha wanted to make humanity recognize its responsibilities and jurisdiction towards itself, the community and nature. Gautama wanted to make the threshold a thoroughfare, thereby making the assimilation of owing and owning of the processes and structures of living into a harmonious, contemporary agenda, integral to the comprehension of suffering. This necessitates mindfulness and self-control because suffering mediates the very purpose of life; its flipside is simple ephemeral happiness. But then happiness implies altruism, love, and compassion: wisdom. Perhaps this is what Gandhi means by 'simple living and high thinking': wisdom as the foregrounding of the contemporary, eventually to become the message of *khadi*. Perhaps Gandhi felt that being at peace with suffering is the beatitude of the Buddha. Sadly Gandhi's philosophical perception of suffering has been erroneously converted into an overt indulgence in povertism.

The other insight Gandhi obtained from Gautama was about ahimsa. Buddha was particularly critical about animal sacrifice. Gandhi appreciated this and wanted to make this an all pervading social ethos preferably evolving into vegetarianism. As such he was not happy that while Buddhists will not kill a single animal, they "do not mind others killing the animals for them and dishing the carcasses for them for their food".[40] But was Gandhi becoming judgmental? Perhaps in his efforts at seeking to recognize, as he put it, the significance of 'the inexorable law of cause and effect', he was imposing himself upon nature with a presumption about suffering and himsa! Gandhi spoke about the inevitability of the law of gravitation; perhaps one needs to recognize many other such laws of nature which impact life and living.

Gandhi's debate with Christianity was more dialogical in nature. It was deeply influenced by people's capacity for the social, historical, and contemplative, while accepting the constraints of social and personal conditions. Perhaps this was because he had to rediscover his own roots, and for him this process was mediated by Christianity. It started when he went to England as a student and continued throughout his life encompassing the whole range from philosophy to the problematic of conversion. Overall it remained highly nuanced covering specific dialogues with post-industrial revolution liberals in London; Christian philosophers, priests, and social workers such as the Trappists in South Africa; Bible quoting racists in South Africa; the Church in India and abroad; Indian Christian converts; and many individual Christian priests and colonial rulers in India. Some became very good friends, and his first biography was written by a Christian priest, Rev. Joseph Doke. There was a time when he was drawn close enough to Christianity for some to even think that he was contemplating conversion. In many ways his progress from a *satyarthi* to a *satyagrahi* in South Africa benefitted from his understanding of Christianity and Christians as individuals; Christianity incidentally was an integral part of the South African hegemony.

His engagement with Christianity was dynamic and vibrant. For twenty years, in the absence of Hindu philosophers with whom he could have interacted on a day to day basis, it was Christianity, Christian writers, and lay Christian thinkers which served as the mediating platform for many of his spiritual reflections. Coming from a background where philosophical divergences of religious beliefs and practices coexisted with equally profound similarities in belief, it was in Christian Britain that Gandhi slowly but surely found his calling. It was in his dialogues with Christianity that he was able to create the intellectual space to not only come to terms with his own self, but also to recognize the moral ambiguity of modernism. In many ways it not only made him aware of what he did not want as a conscious social being, but also made him aware of what he wanted. Instead of becoming a theologian he was able to separate God from rite and sacrament where clarity is often usurped by rituals. Being an objective sympathetic outside observer, Christianity in many ways made him a true Hindu who could go beyond the awe and anxiety of ritual religion and also acquire a hermeneutic. The Sermon on the Mount, serving humanity without ostentation, suffering without bitterness, formal surrenderance, and the celibacy of priests, and so on, in many ways led him to enhanced clarity regarding complex concepts such as satya, ahimsa, tyaag, brahmacharya, and *tapasya*. In the process, Truth in his hermeneutics gained a transpersonal cognition and he was to ascertain, 'Truth is God'. However, for an individual the issue is not truth, but its verification. This was the problematic Gandhi sought to unravel; and in this the contribution of Jesus, Christianity, and its philosophy and practices is evident. In all this the role of the Trappist remains significant. After a visit to the Trappist monastery he wrote, "The principle of liberty, equality and fraternity is carried out in its entirety. Every man is a brother, every woman a sister".[41] "While everyone worked side by side, ate the same food and dressed in similar fashion: The most prominent feature of the settlement is that you see religion everywhere".[42] "The Trappist pattern represented for Gandhi a dynamic and creative fusion of ascetic ideals with the practical concerns of service to and management of the community".[43] Perhaps this is where in Gandhi's thinking the association or link between God, religion, priest and people as service, was introduced. Much later he was to write, "Man's ultimate aim is the realization of God and all his activities, social, political, religious, have to be guided by the ultimate aim of the visit of God. The immediate service of all human beings becomes a necessary part of the endeavour, simply because the only way to find God is to see Him in His creation and be one with it. This can only be done by the service of all".[44]

Besides recognizing the significance of service as an essential element of religious practice, from the practitioners' of Christianity, Gandhi also gained knowledge of the meaning and purpose of conversion, fidelity to a particular religion, and the meaning of contemplation and silence. All of these he was to realize later were sentiments, as much political as religious. Conversion that is rerouting to the right spiritual path is a power equation of the conversant enlightening the ignorant. It is a narrative seeking to reorder inter and intra personal relationships so as to confirm to emerging patterns of societal narration, hegemony, and authority. Service and the politics of service are more complex. It is like holding a mirror to a viewer with the service provider both outside and within the frame. In the process, albeit framed, the viewer, the regulator, and the medium each remain independent of the other. The process is not necessarily transparent and equanimous; necessity is dictated by premeditated conjunction of local and non-local interests. Fidelity of commitment is post-factum serendipity. To illustrate, in South Africa, Christianity was propagated via various denominations. The role of the priest extended from being representative of Christ on earth to being representative of people who appealed and prayed to God on behalf of people. While the priest represented himself, what is the real role of the people in such placations? Silence is even more complex, and the first time Gandhi recognized it being practiced systematically by religious groups was when he met the Trappist monks. Silence in many ways is an adjunct of speech or talking and must not be confused with pause or non-talking. Silence gives individuals and institutions, space to communicate. Essentially, while talking is listening by the social of the self, silence is listening by the personal of the self. Later in life Gandhi employed silence as a systematic practice. Besides these there was the question of religious theology and ethics, that is, whether involvement in religion meant separating theology from ethics. From the very life of Christ, Gandhi recognized the distinction between moral life and actions and abstract religious concepts.

"Where there is faith there can be no self-sufficiency".[45] And over the years, "not only did Gandhi not confuse abstract ethical principles with faith, but he did not even confuse the actions of a person with the person itself".[46] Christianity not only helped Gandhi recognize the significance of religion and spiritualism towards self-realization, but the praxis of Christianity also helped him recognize the need to unshackle theology itself. The book, the praxis and the priest were all temporal. Perhaps the thrust has to be on recognizing that in temporal terms one has to be accountable to somebody or something other than God. Possibly this was the call to listen to 'the inner voice', a presence which nevertheless was an absence which he could not explain and which remained beyond reason and comprehension.

The liberal intellectual milieu of England encouraged the faculty of choice. The diversity of intellectual discourse in South Africa, a potpourri of various intellectual strands from Europe, was very conducive to enquiry particularly of the spiritual-religious variety. The Christian Missionaries zeal to convert and liberate souls added to the potency of the mélange. Gandhi found this energizing and challenging and used it judiciously and maturely as he progressed from a *satyarthi* to a *satyagrahi* particularly in the way he re-appropriated Hinduism. For him in this effort the seminal text was the Bhagavad Gita. The process however was rather eclectic because he worked simultaneously with an assortment of notions, concepts, philosophies, and ideas. Ultimately however the issue would devolve into self-knowledge and self-realization. Towards this over time he "created two distinct realms of spiritual knowledge; one though spiritual, religious, and moral was not only communicable, it was capable of emulation and replication. This was the scientific realm of experiment. There was yet another realm of his striving, which was known only to himself and his Maker. This was the realm of *Sadhana*".[47]

Gandhi's transition from a *satyarthi* to a *satyagrahi* evolved around three core spiritually charged concepts: satya, brahmacharya, and ahimsa. Along with these were the more secular concepts such as swaraj, sarvodaya, swadeshi, and so on. Mediating all these was his unique notion of satyagraha where *agraha* encompasses both the other as insistence and one's own self as obsession. In this conceptual progress, it was the Gita which became his foremost inspiration; it's a book which he always carried, and of which in spite of his busy schedule he managed to memorize the first 13 chapters. Perhaps this was one religion related icon which Gandhi explicitly venerated. However, for all his sincerity and faith, he still maintained: "I exercise my judgment about every scripture, including the Gita. I cannot let scriptural text supersede my reason. Whilst I believe that the principal books are inspired ... nothing in them comes from God directly.... I cannot surrender my reason whilst I subscribe to Devine revelation".[48] The shastras he reasoned are not mere intellectual products to be explained by learned men; "For understanding the meaning of the shastras, one must have a well-cultivated moral sensitivity and experience in the practice of their truths".[49] Thus, while the Gita certainly meant coming to terms with the fundamental query of *purushartha* consisting of artha that is economic emotional social security, kama that is pleasures which satisfy the senses and the mind, dharma which is a feeling of being in harmony with all that one comes in contact with, and moksha that is freedom from all possible fetters particularly of likes and dislikes, for Gandhi the quest stretched from simple issues of day to day living to profound issues of renouncement and surrenderance, more in the sense of aura rather than that of achievement.

In South Africa as an emerging leader he had to anticipate various and at times opposing interests which necessitated engaging with motives. While the 'what' and 'how' were not very difficult, the 'why' was not so. This is where the notion of choice, which liberal England had offered, became significant. To liberate himself he chose to drop the shackles of his profession. By the end of the 19th century Gandhi was well into his *satyarthi* phase and reasonably conversant with the Gita which he had started memorizing. He identified two core concepts from the Gita: equability and aparigraha or non-possession which helped him conceptualize and explain his social involvement both to himself and also to others. In the process he also became aware about the problematic of affection and attachment along with the more demanding desire to possess, own and experience relationships accordingly. He recognized these as part and parcel of acquiring an 'attitude': a curious and very individual mix of desires and its consequence. The Boer war, the brutality of the Zulu rebellion, his incapacity to understand his wife's outlook towards caste and notions of purity, and so on, put a big question mark on his discernment of the personal and the social within. He had to choose between the humdrum of a lawyer's life and the haunting call of the *mumukshu*. Thus, began a lifelong process, where, with the help of 'The Song Celestial', Gandhi found his calling: that of an intrepid itinerant mystic social worker or in his terms a *satyagrahi*. The holism is reflected in his clarity regarding his religiosity; "most religious men I have met are politicians in disguise; I however who wear the guise of a politician am at heart a religious man".[50] But this religious man cultivated a rare quality; while he remained a skeptic about religious rituals, he was a genius in terms of detecting and revealing the quintessential spiritual. It is in terms of this quality that we find Gandhi recognizing that, while violence always reaches a level of incompetence, ahimsa doesn't. As he was to declare, "There is an indefinable, mysterious power that pervades everything. I feel it though I do not see it. It is this unseen power which makes itself felt and yet defies all proof because it is so unlike all that I perceive through my senses. It is proved not by extraneous evidence but in the transformed conduct and character of those who have felt the real presence of God within. Such testimony is to be found in the experiences of an unbroken line of prophets and sages in all countries and climes. To reject this evidence is to deny oneself".[51]

Gandhi unlike most religious leaders or a mystic was neither looking for liberation for himself from birth or rebirth, nor was he looking for unity with God as the primary raison d'être of his quest. While moksha remained an aspiration, it was satya and ahimsa its means, which remained his explicit mission. His was and he repeated this often, a quest of love, not as an acquisition but as an abiding obligation. Accordingly, while reading texts like the Gita, he was not bothered so much about what has been said or unsaid, but of merging like salt in water; while the letter was important it was the spirit which for him was of prime concern. Experiencing this as ontics was perhaps his motivation. Further he sought this experience as a complex relationship of individuals, family, neighbourhood, and community. While accepting that the experience could be individual, he rejected the utility of experiences which depended on isolation. For him experience had to have the organic flavor of the contentious and contiguous traits of intentions, integrity, self-interest, mutual trust, transparency, tranquility, and so on. This assortment which he negotiated without becoming a part of is what made him a mystic.

Religion is a tense configuration of an ethereal core and a temporal manifestation expressing as an institution. As an institution, it is both an organization and a structured pattern of accepted behaviour or relationships. Sustaining it are practices, rather rituals, which can range from the laudable to the deplorable, depending on how one views the otherworldly core. Role, authority, position, and specifics articulate a complex discourse projecting what the religion stands for. But then what is the site of this discourse? For the *satyarthi* Gandhi it was society of which he was an element; for the *satyagrahi* Gandhi the site was himself, of which society was an extension. This fundamental shift in the connection to religion from the social to the personal, although his apparent involvement in society became more pronounced as a *satyagrahi*, is a paradigm shift in Gandhi which was as we will see the impact of the Bhagavad Gita: "The human body is the battleground where the eternal duel between Right and Wrong goes on. Therefore it is capable of being turned into the gateway to freedom".[52] Religion begins as implicit at a propositional level that is stated for the purpose of discussion and then as it develops into a discourse it evolves into requiring it to be explicated that is analyzed and explained into a proposition, a rounding back into itself. Explaining the role of a wise man, the Bhagwat Gita says, "The man who sees worklessness in work [itself], and work in worklessness, is wise among his fellows, integrated, performing every work".[53]

In his social transformation involvements in South African, Gandhi soon realized that human relationships are governed by norms of permanence and contingency and that these are constantly mediated by the disruptive and prescriptive in which religion plays a significant role by stressing principles which are non-negotiable. Complicating this of course is the problematic of prevailing privileges of sections and individuals seeking to appropriate a spirit of legitimacy, for instance deciding on what comes first, personal gratification or social contentment. For Gandhi it seems the way out of such dichotomies is in surrenderance, which is accepting a benign sense of being and conceding consciously the art of becoming. In existential terms religion for him is not only to mitigate the coercion of talent and its twin vanity. Perhaps the Gita offers a meditative way when it proclaims, "Serenity, benignity, silence, self-restrain, and purity of the spirit – these constitute austerity of the mind".[54] However, in the cacophony of religious ardor it is important to emphasis the resilience silence provides. As Gandhi explains, "Silence is essential for one whose life is an incessant search for truth. Silence also helps one to suppress one's anger as perhaps nothing else does. . . . True self-restraint is the fruit of silence consciously pursued".[55] Truly silence is hearing the self.

God and the wise person

By the time Gandhi actually wrote the *Anasaktiyoga or The Gospel of Selfless Action*, his interpretation of the Bhagavad Gita, he was already using insights from the Gita to design and articulate many of his ideas such as satya, ahimsa, satyagraha, swaraj and so on. A question therefore does emerge: was his interpretation a further elaboration or was it a summation of his essential understanding and as such should form the basis of evaluating his usage of the text. Gandhi himself considered all his latest interpretations as the more authentic. In his words, "this rendering is designed for women, the commercial class, the so-called Shudras and the like, who have little or no literary equipment, who have neither the time nor the desire to read the *Gita* in the original, and yet who stand in need if its support".[56] "At the back of my reading there is the claim of an endeavour to enforce the meaning in my own conduct for an unbroken period of 40 Years".[57] It appears as if he was speaking to both the *satyarthi* and the *satyagrahi*. And this time unlike when he was reading Ruskin or Tolstoy, he was re-narrating and interpreting the *message* of the Gita which while impacting him in many very complex ways, was for Hindus that is a majority of Indians, a powerful prevailing moral philosophy. Gandhi's reading of the Gita was that of a devotee. His was a devotion of love not supplication; a devotion to both formal ideas and to common sense which the Gita expostulates. He recognized that the earnest reasoning of Krishna is way beyond remonstration. His devotion was a solemn effort to re-qualify real life-processes not just as an exercise, but as a shaping influence upon his own being. In his reading he was not concerned with the historicity of the Mahabharata as a war, or of Krishna and Arjuna as concrete entities. Recognizing the distortions in our material world, his essential approach to religion and the reading of the Gita was to come to terms with the apparent incompatibility between religion as a set of transcendental otherworldly ideas and the transactional real world. For him the Gita is as material as the real world. Therefore he reasons, "I venture to submit that the *Bhagavad Gita* is a gospel of non-cooperation between forces of darkness and those of light".[58] Clarifying on the notion of non-cooperation "he argued that Duryodhana had good people on his side, as evil by itself cannot flourish in the world. It can do so only if allied with some good".[59] Expounding, Gandhi said, "This was the principal underlying non-co-operation that, the evil system which the Government represents, and which has endured only because of the support it receives from good people, cannot survive if the support is withdrawn".[60] This inclusivity for Gandhi was the core norm of social creativity. Good and evil are not exclusive, and this holds as much for institutions as for individual human beings. Therefore for Gandhi, "My religion is a matter solely between my Maker and myself. If I am a Hindu, I cannot cease to be one even though I may be disowned by the whole of Hindu population. I do, however suggest that non-violence is the end of all religions".[61] Gandhi thus shifts the focus of religion from ends to means by stressing on the elemental role of ahimsa. Further, this highlighting of means makes religion/philosophy inseparable from the practitioner, and the end is self-realization. He succinctly argues, "Boycott of beef-eaters may have been proper in the past. It is improper and impossible today. . . . Many a man eating meat, but observing the cardinal virtues of compassion and truth, and living in the fear of God, is a better Hindu than a hypocrite who abstains from meat".[62]

To learn from the Gita and contextualise it for the present, Gandhi sets aside the historical connotations of the text. "Krishna of the *Gita* is perfection and right knowledge personified; but the picture is imaginary. That does not mean that Krishna, the adored of his people, never lived. But perfection is imagined. The idea of a perfect incarnation is an after growth".[63] For himself the need and the privilege to translate the Gita was also clear. "At the back of my reading, there is the claim of an endeavour to enforce the meaning in my own conduct for an unbroken period of forty years".[64] Moreover since religion has a considerable influence on society, the issue of *adhikaritva* authority or qualification becomes an important component of Gandhi's approach to religion. Besides this was his thinking that this uniquely Indian text while having a universal appeal, has a lot particularly for the Indian masses, provided of course one is clear about one's spiritual motives. Therefore he argued that, "Only he can interpret the *Gita* who tries to follow its teaching in practice and the correctness of his interpretation will be in proportion to his success in living according to its teaching".[65] His commitment to the Gita remained transparent. "The *Gita* for me is a perennial guide to conduct. From it I seek support for all my actions and, if, in a particular case, I do not find the needed support, I would refrain from the proposed action or at any rate feel uncertain about it".[66] Consequently Gandhi attributed his clarity regarding concepts such as ahimsa, satya, non-possession, brahmacharya, and so on to his reading of the Gita. In a way while the Gita grew on him he too immersed into it. He claimed that, "As far back as 1889, when I had my first contact with the *Gita*, it gave me a hint of satyagraha, and as I read more, the hint developed into a full revelation of satyagraha".[67] Perhaps he was prone to post factum serendipity; or is it a case of Gandhi mixing up the intuitive and the reasoned?

Gandhi's interpretation had some fundamental strands: the text essentially espouses ahimsa non-violence rather than himsa and war; the Pandavas and the Kauravas are in many ways similar to the differing personal and the social with their mutually contradictory desires, attitudes, and notions of change and continuity within us; and above all, the skirmish between the social and the personal is not one of evil opposed to good for no evil is possible without the aid of the good and as such is a question of harmony of the individual as a living being. Ultimately, "Man is not at peace with himself till he has become like unto God. The endeavour to reach this state is the supreme, the only ambition worth having. And this is self-realization. This self-realization is the subject of the *Gita*, as it is of all scriptures".[68] Nevertheless, while Gandhi was clear about not mixing up the allegorical and the historical, he did try to glean some historical clarity from the allegory of war. As he put it, "When the *Gita* was written, although people believed in ahimsa, wars were not only not taboo, but nobody observed the contradiction between them and *ahimsa*".[69] Times have changed; it is time to change! And this can also leave Gandhi, his thoughts, and actions in a limbo?

From the Shastra: Bhagavad Gita

For Gandhi the Gita was an abiding day to day conscientious commitment. It was not just a question of studying the nature of existence, but also of understanding the nature of transition towards self-realization. In this he preferred to unload the baggage of whether the text was a *shruti* or *smriti*. Consequently it might be worthwhile for us to understand the import of some of the verses which inspired him in his conceptual quest.

The Bhagavad Gita is a narrative of an episode from the Mahabharata. And in this tale it transpired thus: Arjuna Pandu's son, desiring to be placed between the two armies, addressed Krishna his conscience, "halt the chariot, unfallen, that I may scan these men drawn up, spoiling for the fight, that I may see with whom I must do battle in this enterprise of war" (1:22).[70] On the field of justice, what did they do? (1:1). "I see them here assembled, ready to fight, seeking to please Dhritarastra's baleful son, by waging war" (1:23).

Thus, addressed by Arjuna the contemplative within him transported him to halt between the two armies (1:24, 25). This symbolic location between two armies is the site from where Gandhi proceeds; but first he has to make a choice, that of avoiding prevarication. This compulsion is the necessity on which Gandhi compiles his world view and social praxis.

Many priests and experts of theology considered Gandhi to be an upstart out to malign Hindu religion. Some others such as Ambedkar felt Gandhi avoided the fundamental problems of Hinduism such as caste. While both have a point, for Gandhi, the issue was one of relating to religion in terms of inclusivity and personal integrity; moreover, there remained the issue of bias and reflexivity, rather avoiding the circularity of cause and effect. A core text of Hinduism thus begins with confronting the self to begin a process of reflection and awareness. Like Arjuna he wants to see as to who are those 'others' with whom he has to struggle. For him the effort is not to just garner some odd evidence. It became an issue of self-realization. As such, he sees Arjuna's self-confrontation as a fundamental problematic. He recognizes the hazards faith in a text can endanger. He was ready to put together his own miscellany and blend of hagiography and philosophy which would follow the principle of 'taste of the *khichdi* is in the eating'; but then eating is a narrative of its own because some might want to snatch away even your *khichdi*. The Bhagavad Gita helps him understand this snatching away of legitimate needs. After all, 'legitimate needs' expound a tale of their own; a distinct narrative of exclusivity and inclusivity which pervades wants and needs, ends and means, rights and duties, and give and take to conclusively re-apportion the personal and the social.

For Gandhi, Arjuna along with Krishna the contemplative within him wades into the threshold separating the two armies where the insiders and the outsiders encounter. And he wants to know the nature of the skirmish at this threshold. Was it the eternal problematic of a moment needing or having to be replaced by another? Or was it more prosaic in that it was to please somebody, something or some notion? For Gandhi the location between the armies is the eternal predicament of the human being and he hopes the Gita can aid in prospecting a resolution. "I regard Duryodhana and his party as the baser impulses in man, and Arjuna and his party as the higher impulses. The field of battle is our own body. An eternal battle is going on between the two camps, and the poet-seer vividly describes it. Krishna is the dweller within. Ever whispering to a pure heart".[71] The Gita thus is a treatise aiding enlightenment. Our predicaments are solvable, but require constant personal effort and contemplation.

"There as they stood, the son of Pritha saw fathers, grand sires, teachers, uncles, brothers, sons, grandsons and comrades" (1:26).

Fathers-in-law and friends in both armies; and seeing them, all his kinsmen, thus arrayed, the son of Kunti was filled with compassion (1:27, 28).

And he said to his conscience, "when I see this mine own folk standing before me, spoiling for the fight; my limbs give way, my mouth dries up, trembling seizes upon my body, and my hairs stand up in dread" (1:29, 30).

"I cannot stand and my mind seems to wander" (1:30).

And then addresses himself, "were we to lay low our own folk, how can we be happy" (1:37).

Totally distraught he decides to lay down his arms (1:47). "Krishna, how can I fight Bhisma and Drona in battle, [how assail them] with [my] arrows? for they are worthy of respect" (2:4).

But the armies are drawn. Can he lay down his arms? Will the war stop? There seems to be an element of inexorability. This element of inevitability which goes beyond the individual is a fundamental concern and burden of every individual; as is its corollary, 'can this inevitability be influenced, controlled and modified'? Above all can an individual opt out? This is the core problematic of choice. Every individual is beset with the personal and social vying with each other. Choice seeks to make them concur and the hope is to make them agree more often than not. But in real life these remain a dilemma because the inspiration behind them is different.[72]

Approaching serendipity he beseeches Krishna the contemplative within him to realign him; he preferred and chose not to make desirable discoveries by accident.

"My very being is oppressed with compassion's harmful taint. With mind perplexed concerning right [and wrong] I ask you which is the better course? Tell me [and let your words be] definite [and clear]. I am your pupil and put all my trust in you. So teach me" (2:7).

And Krishna the contemplative possess the parable: your words seem to be wise but you don't talk like a wise man, for wise men remain the same in pleasure as in pain (2:11,15). Arjuna is reminded of sameness in pleasure and pain. How is he different from those on the other side of the threshold? "Of what is not there is no becoming; of what is there is no ceasing to be: for the boundary-line between these two is seen by men who see things as they really are" (2:16).

He continues, "Vanquished by dejection and delusion, devoid of wit, your innermost self has been upset by what is all too human; pity has seized you because you see your kinsmen enter into the jaws of death".

The contemplative further counsels, "of what is not there is no becoming; of what is there is no ceasing to be; for the boundary-line between these two is seen by men who see things as they really are" (2:16). But Arjuna is beset with a numbing torpor of compassion. Why does compassion, an otherwise venerated quality, become a 'harmful taint'? This is because compassion authorizes a qualification which necessitates purity; it is a purity which can only be attained by a sacrifice of the waywardness of the self which is normally dominated by expectations, a restless mind, and confused personal obligations. Arjuna gives in, sacrifices his ego which he had achieved, and sustained no doubt by acclaimed competences. He requests Krishna the contemplative to impart and enlighten. The contemplative in turn asks him to first learn how to distinguish between wisdom and a wise man. Wisdom is acquired; it is a matter of interpretation for it is touched by the temporal. It is transactional. The wise man knows the limitation of this acquisition. The contemplative reminds Arjuna about the sameness of all binaries: self and the other, ends and means, and so on. Above all he brings to mind the exaggerated credence of the binary give and take, wherein the driver's seat is allocated to give. Sameness informs that you cannot give more than you can take. The issue is of recognizing the characteristics of the contingent 'being'. However, this appreciation cannot be reduced to a discourse of *sad and asat*, Being and Not-Being; the wise see 'things as they really are'. As such the past cannot be re-created with some correctives and adjustments. Parameters of the past were aligned to serve a purpose; these are not for one to tinker and appropriate. Seize the moment with integrity, for that is all that is wise; above all, neither the act or the mind is wise.

Arjuna has reached the ledge. Under this the threshold beckons. But now he has to distinguish between recognition and realization, same and similarity. "As a man casts off his worn-out clothes and takes on other new ones, so does the embodied (self) cast off its worn out bodies and enters other new ones" (2:22).

To recognize is an act of understanding of what, how, and where, while to realize is to comprehend the why of an event. Recognition is a cognitive act of perception and acknowledgement of something as true or valid and recognizance is an obligation which is binding. To realize is to be able to link these two into a commitment by giving a reality to the binding obligation; in the social context it is the binding relationship of the individual to the processes of change and continuity. Simultaneously for the individual it also means that during the processes of social transition, acts of transgression have to be recognized, and not compounded by post-factum justifications. Realization strikes when the individual is able to comprehend that to be an agent of a process and to intercede are distinct. Oneself, involvement, site of involvement, understanding of this site and authority to know the site, all become issues. Garbs and wraps are caste off and the *satyarthi* becomes a *satyagrahi*; the *satyarthi* now is able to pause and propose alternatives. This pause is the gaining of an attitude which comes with its own recognizance or binding obligation: "Herein no effort goes to seed nor is there any slipping back" (2:40).

Here then is the issue of will. "The essence of the soul is will, and it is really single, but many-branched and infinite are the souls of men devoid of will". (2:41) Gandhi explains, "When the attitude ceases to be one and undivided and becomes many and divided, it ceases to be one settled will, and is broken up into various wills of desires between which man is tossed about".[73]

"The essence of the soul is will, – [but the souls] of men who cling to pleasure and to power, their minds seduced by flowery words, are not attuned to enstasy. Such men give vent to flowery words, lacking discernment, delighting in the Veda's lore, saying there is naught else. Desire is their essence, paradise their goal, – their words preach [re-]birth as the fruit of works and expatiate about the niceties of ritual by which pleasure and power can be achieved" (2:42–4). The necessity to escape from the clutches of rituals and the illusion these engender by covering up the core motivation of desires needs to be comprehended. The contemplative suggests enstasy "that type of 'inverted' mystical experience in which there is experience of nothing except an unchanging, purely static oneness. It is the exact reverse of ecstasy which means to get outside oneself and which is often characterized by a breaking down of the barriers between the individual subject and the universe around him".[74] This is the pause of silence which Gandhi aspired.

All nature is made up of the three 'constituents': satva, rajas, tamas. The contemplative suggests, "Have done with them, Arjuna: have done with [all] dualities, stand ever firm on Goodness. Think not of gain or keeping the thing gained, but be yourself" (2:45). Here is 'service' as distinct obligation to the personal and the social of one's own self. In the process, a necessity is not fetishized nor an involvement reified. "As much use as there is in a water-tank flooded with water on every side, so much is there in all the Vedas for the Brahman who discerns" (2:46). Amidst plenty one tends to overlook or fail to properly appreciate the essential or rather what the source of the necessity offers. The seekers discernment is sorely tested. Will the water tank be ignored?

"[But] work alone is your proper business, never the fruits, [it may produce]: let not your motive be the fruits of works nor your attachment to [mere] worklessness" (2:47). The quest is for yoga or evenness that is sameness-and-indifference beyond just controlled involvement; more in the sense of detachment.

The query still remains, "What is the mark of the man of steady wisdom immersed in enstasy? How does he speak, this man of steadied thought? How sit? How walk? (2:54). The contemplative suggests, "When a man puts from him all desires that prey upon the mind, himself contended in the self alone, then is he called a man of steady wisdom" (2:55). The problem is the inseparability of the human and his desires. The wise man is above and aside, but very much there; he recognizes desires for what they are. And in true humility accepts the limitation of 'what I can do'; he is humble about our vaunted competence to 'choose and change', strictly abnegating the urge to exult in any such ability. The wise man is able to discern the intrinsic from the incidental; what belongs by its very nature is not confused with what is likely which could happen because of the fortuitous conditions created by one's actions.

"Whose mind is undismayed [though beset] by many a sorrow, who for pleasures has no further longing, from whom all passions, fear, and wrath have fled, such a man is called a man of steadied thought, a silent sage" (2:56). "Who has no love for any thing, who rejoices not at whatever good befalls him nor hates the bad that comes his way – firm-stablished is the wisdom of such a man" (2:57). "And when he draws in on every side his senses from their proper objects as a tortoise [might draw in] its limbs – firm-stablished is the wisdom of such a man" (2:58).

"Let a man [but] think of the objects of sense – attachment to them is born: from attachment springs desire, from desire is anger born" (2:62). "From anger comes bewilderment, from bewilderment wandering of the mind, from wandering of the mind destruction of the soul: once the soul is destroyed the man is lost" (2:63). "But the disciplined soul, moving among sense – objects with the senses weaned from likes and dislikes and brought under the control of *Atman*, attains peace of mind" (2:64).[75] Verily *krodhatyaag* leads to ahimsa and *trishna tyaag* to brahmacharya; together these lead an individual to satya.

"As the water flows into the sea, full filled, whose ground remains unmoved, so too do all desires flow into [the heart of] man: and such a man wins peace – not the desirer of desires" (2:70). "The man who puts away all desires and roams around from longing freed, who does not think, 'This I am', or 'This is mine', draws near to peace" (2:71).

"Therefore detached, perform unceasingly the works that must be done, for the man detached who labours on the highest must win through" (3:19). "For only by working on did Janaka and his like attain perfection's prize. Or if again you consider the welfare [and coherence] of the world, then you should work [and act]." (3:20).

"Whatever the noblest does, that to will others do: the standard that he sets all the world will follow" (3:21). "In the three worlds there is nothing I need do, nor anything unattained that I need to gain, yet work [is the element] in which I move" (3:22). *Loka-samagraha* or the maintenance of the world is the domain of the *satyagrahi*, the exemplar.

"The order of the four *varnas* was created by Me according to the different *gunas* and *karma* of each; yet know that though, therefore, author thereof, being changeless I am not the author" (4:13).[76]

"Krishna, fain would I know the truth concerning renunciation and apart from this [the truth] of self-surrender" (18:1).

"To give up works dictated by desire, wise men allow [this] to be renunciation; surrender of all fruits that [accrue] to works discerning men call self-surrender" (18:2).

All attachments to what you do and all the fruits of what you do must be surrendered. This is my last decisive word. (18:4).

In effect if such is a wise person, then, can such a wise person say 'I will not'?

For Gandhi the very first verse of the Gita is very indicative for the seeker, and he regarded himself to be a seeker of knowledge, the field of the wise person. For him, "The human body is the battlefield where the eternal duel between Right and Wrong goes on. Therefore it is capable of being turned into the gateway of freedom.... The Kauravas represent the forces of Evil, the Pandavas the forces of Good. Who is there who has not experienced the daily conflict within himself between the forces of Evil and the forces of Good?"[77]

Arjuna very specifically asks: "[What is] nature? [What the] person? [What] the 'field' and [what] the 'knower of the field'? This, Krishna, would I know. [What too is] knowledge? [What] that which should be known?" (13:0)[78] To this Krishna replies; "The body is called the 'field' and he who knows it is the 'knower of the field', or so it has been said by those who know it" (13:1). And Krishna the contemplative adds: 'I am the knower of the field in every field'. This is an explicit question and its context is vast. It indicates the essential theme Gandhi has in mind. However Gandhi does not refer to this verse in his Anasaktiyoga. Why he did not will remain an abiding albeit significant querry.

The narrative of the Gita is a complex text pertaining to both transactional and transcendental concerns. For Gandhi, "I venture to submit that the Bhagavad Gita is a gospel of noncooperation between forces of darkness and those of light".[79] In effect it is a narrative of a struggle which is "raging all the time, even today".[80] It is in a way an effort to bridge the gap between the perplexed and the contemplative. It is not attrition but rejuvenation. The Gita permits, "freedom even in the phenomenal realm with a choice to resist impulses, check passions and lead a life regulated by reason".[81] Gandhi the seeker sought to paraphrase it as a cluster of insightful conceptuals, each helping both the person and the social. These are ahimsa, equanimity and non-possession, sthitpragnya, action or service, svadharma, lokasamgraha, tyaag, surrenderance; as derivatives, these are prayer, fasts, caste and gunas, and sarva dharma samanvaya. For the personal and the social, a dichotomy between the desire to help oneself and helping others persists. Should the desire to help oneself be less than the desire to help others? This is a fundamental which remains for the individual to adopt where even the contemplative as Krishna is helpless.

Aparigraha or non-possessiveness: as Gandhi saw it

Aparigraha means non-accumulation. Gandhi's basic thrust in this is to show how possessiveness not only restricts our attaining our potentials but also makes us immune to others sensitivities. While the tendency to acquire is a basic instinct, in our quest for social security we tend to convert this into hallowed processes of possessiveness and accumulation. Possessiveness is the twin process of acquiring and retaining, while simultaneously disregarding 'social owing' without which no individual in society can aspire to start the processes of acquiring and retaining.

For Gandhi, "non-possession is allied to non-stealing". He argues, "a thing not originally stolen must nevertheless be classified as stolen property if we possess it without needing it".[82] The problem according to him is, "the rich have a superfluous store of things which they do not need, and which are therefore neglected and wasted; while millions starve to death for want of sustenance. If each retained possession only of what he needed, no one would be in want and all would live in contentment. As it is, the rich are discontented no less than the poor. The poor man would fain become a millionaire and the millionaire a multi-millionaire".[83]

He therefore suggests a radical reorientation. "Possession implies provision for the future. A seeker after truth, a follower of the law of love, cannot hold anything against tomorrow". And, "The rich should take the initiative in dispossession with a view to universal diffusion of the spirit of contentment. If only they keep their own property within moderate limits, the starving will be easily fed and will learn the lesson of contentment along with the rich".[84] There is also a spiritual dimension to his thinking. "From the standpoint of pure truth, the body, too, is a possession. It has been truly said that desire for enjoyment creates bodies for the soul and sustains them. When this desire vanishes, there remains no further need for the body and man is free from the vicious cycle of births and deaths".[85]

A corollary to this is his understanding of 'voluntary poverty'. "Civilization, in the real sense of the term, consists not in the multiplication, but in the deliberate and voluntary reduction of wants. This alone promotes real happiness and contentment".[86] This in real terms means that if you must possess things, "you must hold them at the disposal of those who want them". Moreover, "you have also got to be content with what the world will give you". In this way, "the richest man is really one who, possessing nothing, has everything at his disposal". Ultimately for Gandhi a want is a progeny of '*mama*' the acquiring personal which is the obverse of '*swa*' the social within us. The want separates the '*mama*' from the '*swa*', the '*I*' from the '*me*'. The moot question therefore is the role of civilization in breeding the '*mama*'.

Practices: prayer, worship, meditation

Gandhi a seeker and a man of faith had a genuine and abiding confidence in the efficacy of prayers. For him it sustained humility, helped recognize the source of compassion, and while confronting one's ego, reaffirmed one's seeker hood. As a practice, prayer "brings a peace, a strength and a consolation that nothing else can give. But it must be offered from the heart".[87] As such a prayer orients our own selves to sustain our fundamental quest as human beings. Consequently, Gandhi prayed to his "Higher self, the Real self, with which I have not yet achieved, complete identification". Prayer is not an end. It is "the very soul and essence of religion", and therefore, "the very core of man's life".[88] It is an act and remains so, for it is by nature a thanksgiving. For Gandhi, "Heartfelt prayer steadies one's nerves, humbles one and clearly shows the next step".[89] "Prayer is the only means of bringing about orderliness and peace and repose in our daily acts". He writes, "As the body needs food and feels hungry, so the soul needs and feels hungry for prayer".[90] In the temporal progress of the deha-atman combine, while the deha is sustained by material consumables, the atma depends on prayers: both are sustained by oblations. For Gandhi prayers, worship and meditation amount to inner purification and thanksgiving.

Humanity has an abiding spiritual aspiration. And worship is a method of giving recognition and form to these aspirations. Imagination is what makes form and spirit the two fundamental aspects of worship graspable. Worship thus is a mutual process of imagination and spiritual aspiration. But a moot question remains. Given that the intelligence we depict as God, to be God has to be formless and without attributes, why then do we take recourse to such attribute-prone imaginations? Gandhi clarifies this as follows. "I am intellectually conscious of this" that God is nirguna, but still, "I cannot help dwelling upon the attributes of God. My intellect can exercise no influence over my heart".[91] Accepting the dichotomy between the personal and the social, Gandhi elaborates, "Krishna of the Gita is perfection and right knowledge personified, but the picture is imaginary. That does not mean that Krishna, the adored of the people, never lived. But perfection is imagined. The idea of a perfect incarnation is an aftergrowth".[92] In effect, worship helps people grasp the dichotomies between the temporal (temporal) and the eternal (social) within themselves. Therefore Gandhi writes, "Fundamentally God is indescribable in words. Man's conception of God is naturally limited. Each one has, therefore, to think of Him as best appeals to him, provided that the conception is pure and uplifting". To worship is a benign engagement with the 'perfect'. But like all such benign engagements, this too has the potential of becoming a paradoxical mix of the real and the virtual.

Preoccupied with our existential demands we tend to ignore a lot of that which we are. Meditation is an effort to re-appropriate these and try and delve in the inner self. Gandhi writes, "God is not some person outside ourselves or away from the universe. . . . He abides in our hearts and is nearer to us than the nails are to the fingers".[93] For Gandhi meditation has a three-fold significance: it helps us recognize the time, space and form aspects of existence; it helps us relate to the Absolute; and it indicates the eternal, which we are.

In his conception of God and/or Truth, Gandhi felt that the universe was pervaded by intelligence higher than human reason. Prayers recognize this immanence. Therefore prayers help us contain our ego and enhance our spiritual awareness. Thus it also becomes an expression of gratitude. There is another deeper meaning to thanks giving and this becomes evident when prayer is "offered from the heart". Most pray when the will is not able to handle our existential confusions, contradictions and so on. Thanks giving become prayers "offered from the heart" even when we are able to handle our existential confusions and contradictions; this is positive not cringing gratitude.

"Prayer is an impossibility without a living faith in the presence of God within".[94] In this sense it is an act of inner or self-purification. "The object of prayer is not to please God, who does not want our prayers or praise, but to purify ourselves",[95] writes Gandhi. And this purity means, "the triple purity" – purity of thoughts, words, and deeds. The hope in turn is to control what Gandhi called "subtle passions" and "dormant passions" such as longing, greed, anger, and so on. In his own life he says, "By a long course of prayerful discipline, I have ceased for over forty years to hate anybody".[96]

Lastly, Gandhi felt that prayer as a discipline was a must for a *satyagrahi*. "The person whose life is dedicated to service and who has burnt his or her egoism lives in the spirit of prayer. Devotion to duty is itself prayer". Therefore while religion is not a duty, it is the duty enshrined within religion which prayer addresses as *nityakarma*.

Sarva Dharma Samanatwa

Gandhi believed in god. He was spiritual and non- sectarian. For him 'god is truth'. It is not qualification or normative, it is axiomatic. And while truth is the end, ahimsa is the mean to this end. As he put it "I believed in the essential unity of man and for that matter all that lives". And, "religions are different roads converging to the same point. What does it matter that we take different roads, so long as we reach the same goal? Wherein is the cause for quarrelling?"

But while "ahimsa as a means is our supreme duty", the realization of the Truth is a process of discovery. For him, "As long as I have not realized this Absolute Truth, so long must I hold to the relative truth as I have conceived it. That relative truth must meanwhile be my beacon, my shield, my buckler".[97] He reasoned, "Man's conception of God is naturally limited. Each one has, therefore, to think of Him as best appeals to him, provided that the conception is pure and uplifting".[98] This relative truth manifests as religion. And as such is just the harbinger and passage.

Gandhi recognizes the two conjoined but distinct aspects of religiosity: *Sanatana* and Parampara. Sanatana as the Sanskrit term indicates refers to eternal, the same, always valid and contemporary. Since truth and ahimsa are at the core of all religiosity and spiritualism, there is sameness, integral and contemporary to all spiritual, religions quests. For him the spiritual infusing all religions is fundamentally the same. Parampara on the other hand refers to the contextual. It reflects the constraints of conviction, time, and place; Parampara in Sanskrit refers to nitatwapravaha i.e. eternity in flow. Thus for Gandhi, "instead of boasting of the glorious past, we express the ancient moral glory in our own lives and let our lives bear witness to our past".[99] The core of religiosity is fundamental while the various traditions as manifest in various religions and sects are temporal and transitory. The Parampara is to help us engage with and recognize the eternal; in Gandhi's terms the relative truth aids to recognize the absolute Truth. As he put it, "we therefore have a duty to live up to truth as we see it at this time". His Sarva Dharma Samanatwa and Sarva Dharma Prayers recognized these sensitivities of people engaged in various practices of relative truth. So while he remained true to the fundamentals of his religion, he encouraged congregational prayers which included texts from various religions. In the ashrams, prayers were held every day; mornings between 4:15 and 4:45 and evenings between 7:00 and 7:30. And in these prayer meetings which he scrupulously attended, he prayed with whoever chose to attend. In many ways this was his recognition of the 'conjoining' of the personal and the social. It also made the renunciant aware of what renunciation meant. He wrote, "For a congregational life a congregational prayer is a necessity and, therefore, form also is necessary". "Congregational prayer is not intended to supplant individual prayer.... Congregational prayer is an aid to being in tune with the infinite. For man who is a social being cannot find God unless he discharges social obligations and the obligation of coming to a common prayer meeting is perhaps the supremest".[100] For Gandhi ultimately it is the recognition of the commonality of the core sympathies of both the transactional and the transcendental which should inform our engagement with God as god.

Caste system or *varna-ashrama vyavastha*

For Gandhi the concept of *varnashrama vyavastha* is different from the present practice of caste as a system of societal hierarchy. The first is he writes, 'a rational scientific fact' while the latter is 'an excrescence, an unmitigated evil'. Caste is the most complex and confounding social ethos impacting the India socio-economic milieu. It is all pervading, substantial and critical to every process of social interaction, transition and transformation. Gandhi recognized this and responded at various levels: concept, belief, customs, and practices. Initially tentative, involvement became clearer as to what he should do and more importantly how much he could do. While he never compromised in his attitude towards untouchability, he did not assume a position of absolute confrontation. Recognizing that he could not throw the baby (religion) with the caste sullied bath water, he opted for a process of gradual de-legitimization, persuasion, and reflexivity. One of his major handicaps was that caste is a social phenomenon in which the protagonists of every jati, which also refers to caste, stubbornly maintain exclusivity, and claim spiritual tradition and origin lore to legitimize their temporal, personal privileges, and social agenda. Complicating any radical stance is the problem that Gandhi remained sensitive to every individual, preferring to convince rather than force an alternative. However, for him, while the caste system had evolved into a pernicious parody poisoning religion, the spiritual aspiration of the people remains inviolate beyond all contradictions.

Gandhi wrote, "The *rishis* after incessant experiment and research arrived at this fourfold division – the four ways of earning one's livelihood. The different professions can easily be brought under the four main divisions – that of teaching, of defending, of wealth producing, and of manual service".[101] The 'modal view' of the varna-*ashrama vyavastha* is derived largely from sacerdotal Hindu texts. In this system, varna caste stands for the four castes: Brahmin, kshatriya, vaishya, and Sudra while ashrama stands for stages in life beginning with brahmacharya (student), *grishasta* (householder), *vanaprastha* (retiree), and *sanyasa* (renouncer); the caste system is hierarchic in the order – Brahmin, kshatriya, vaishya, and lastly sudra.

While the ashram or stages aspect is left to the individual, the occupation-pollution-purity-birth mandated caste has evolved into a self-serving heuristic matrix. Complicating the issue is the fact that there is no universally acknowledged single caste hierarchy pattern. Very complex systems of jatis which runs into thousands have emerged wherein each jati internally characterized by equality has different hierarchical elaborations vis-à-vis other jatis and does not accept any caste ordering. In practice the prevailing hegemony dictates the norms. But the sudras always remained at the bottom. Over the centuries, in practice the ideal-model got diluted. People found different meaning for their duties. The Brahmin ignored the significance of rituals and performed his duties to earn a living; the Kshatriya used his skill to acquire temporal power; the vaishya's focus became piling of wealth as a means of security and so on. These divisions instead of being on a horizontal plane on which all were standing on a footing of equality, as the ideal might have expected, became vertical relatively independent sections of relative mutual inequality. The sudra however had to serve all the three; as society evolved, the terms of service was determined and enforced by the top three. A major problem emerged, when in an ethos which believed in rebirth and Karma, duty instead of being based on worth and disposition, became birth-centric. As society and occupations became more complex, birth and purity-pollution became the core values which mediated inter social 'we-they' discourse. Obviously the most powerful prevailed in which the Brahmin led. While jati, profession, job descriptions evolved, birth-centric restrictions became stringent and some of the sudras became *avarna*.

However, the process was not that ingenuous. Large sections of people don't easily accept being dominated. The four-fold system blossomed into thousands of jatis, with each of these historical ensembles relating broadly to at least one particular caste. While they drew ideological rationale of purity-pollution, endogamy, commensality, and so on from the original model and its elaboration in various texts, injunctions on marriage, rituals, occupation, and intra and internal social relationship norms were dictated by the group's self-interest and the capacity to sustain it. By the 19th century it had become a perversion eating into the very vitals of the larger society. The village became segregated with various castes living in exclusive zones. Access to these areas was restricted and to the lower castes was either denied or strictly regulated. The stratification and differentiations became further complicated with the emergence of a plethora of exclusive profession related hierarchy conscious jatis. These jati hierarchies might share many things in common but leave scope for disagreement in terms of primacy. It is difficult to place them in a continuum. While the avarna would certainly refuse to accept that his condition is a direct result of his past life/lives, others would insist it did. Involvement in professions such as scavenging and cremation was used to sustain notions of impurity and thereby not only sustain segregation but also ensure sustainability of an essential service. Historically necessary but menial jobs were foisted on the dasa or slave, and then these were scripturally approved to sustain a religious veneer.

Ideally the Varna system is based on Guna i.e. qualities and karma i.e. duty. Prakriti i.e. the cosmic substance consists of three constituent qualities called Gunas. These are sattva, rajas, and tamas, and in human beings manifest as the composition and the disposition of the mind. They are at the core of all change. Sattva stands for the goodness and refers to contemplativeness. Rajas denote passion and stands for ambitions, energy, enthusiasms, overcoming resistance, and accomplishment. Tamas stands for restraints and is the restraining and binding i.e. holding back potency of nature. These Gunas co-exist and don't happen separately. While their functions intermingle, at any given instance one or the other may predominate. And this dominance leads to individuals differing in their aptitudes and attitudes. Valorisation of aptitudes and attitudes leads to hierarchies which then gets scriptural sanctity. Thus considering the three together when we have a situation where in order of dominance first is Sattva, then rajas and then tamas, we have a contemplative, thinking person: a Brahmana. If the order is rajas followed by sattva and tamas we have an active, ambitious, goal-oriented person. This person will be enthusiastic, desirous of success, but considerate about others: a Kshatriya. If the order is rajas, tamas, and sattva, we will have an ambitious person whose primary goal is to acquire and retain. Such a person will not be given to deep thinking, but such a person might not be very considerate about the well-being of others: a Vaishya. Lastly when the order is tamas, rajas and sattva we will have a simple person not given to any initiative of any sort: a Sudra. Problems begin when we project these speculative stereotypes as hereditary natural qualities of human beings. In Hindu society, the above-mentioned combinations of gunas are justified by a karma based hierarchy. The Brahmana teaches and officiates at rituals. He is the priest and is supposed to dedicate his life to acquiring tranquillity of thought through meditation and self-restraint over personal conduct. The Kshatriyas' role is that of an administrator. He ensures society's security thereby protecting dharma. The Vaishya who deals in commerce, wealth, agriculture provides the material needs of society. The Sudra servers and provides the labour to accomplice various societal activities. These are very complex propositions with too many imponderables and history tell us that such thinking has resulted in horrendous and abominable exploitative social practices. There is another simpler myth-based origin theory. As per the purusasukta legend, the metaphor refers to the Brahman and Kshatriya emerging from the head and arms respectively of purusa, the primeval being, while the vaishya emerged from the thigh and Sudra from his feet.

Gandhi recognized all this. He agreed that the system for all its unity and concord regarding the diversity of functions had evolved into a "hideous travesty". For him it is a "dead letter today" and has to go. But herein was the dilemma. How was one to prune the excesses of the moral-code of the varna- jati system while retaining the purity of Hindu dharma? Obviously those who benefited from the system were reluctant to forgo the benefits. Gandhi tried to respond at various levels, and mostly did not succeed. While his intentions were not suspect, their applicability remained suspect. For Gandhi social norms and individual norms were analogues. A firm believer in rebirth, perhaps he was not ready to accept that while society came with steeped in history, an individual essentially made history.

However, Gandhi sought to redraw the balance between community and individual privileges. Accordingly he felt restrictions were to be placed on sections of the community becoming perennial interest groups. He wanted the untouchable communities to seek a new identity and towards this accepted the name Harijan. He was wary of legislative measures to resolve the problem because such measures other than being essentially political tend to perpetuate interest groups. Moreover it gave an exalted position to the state as an arbitrator. He preferred a gradual, inclusive cleansing process. Ethics for him evolve over time and cannot be replaced in days. He therefore started by questioning the locus standee of the religious leadership. "I am not required to accept the ipse dixit or the interpretation of pundits".[102] Thereby throwing open the discourse about dharma he argued, "In dealing with the problems of untouchability during the Madras tour, I have asserted my claim to being a sanatanist Hindu with greater emphasis than before".[103] For Gandhi, "caste has nothing to do with religion. It is a custom whose origin I do not know and do not need to know for the satisfaction of my spiritual hunger. But I do know that it is harmful both to spiritual and national growth".[104] According to his "interpretation of Advaita", it "excludes totally any idea of superiority at any stage whatsoever. I believe implicitly that all men are equal born". The dilemma however was regarding replacing the caste system with another system to help an individual acquire a non-humiliating identity and also relate to a profession. If it were not the caste system it would be the responsibility of the family, community, or the state or some free market system? Gandhi could not visualize the contours of such an alternative system. Perhaps he was apprehensive about an alienated motile individual even more than a caste subjugated one? Above all, his preoccupation with the political due to his involvement in the colonial struggles left him with little time to work out a systemic solution to remove this anomaly.

Isa vasyam

Gandhi accepted that most religious texts while aiding insight remain difficult and demanding for most folk. He himself took time to internalize such texts. On the other hand we also have a typical human problem: a very resilient compulsion to possess which creates a feeling of security. While his reading of the Gita and his elaboration of the concept of *Aparigraha* or non-possession does question the illusionary nature of security through possession, Gandhi still needed to debunk and expose the very 'act of acquiring' as a restraining if not debilitating predicament of humanity. For this he needed to question the very notion of freedom to acquire itself, because acquiring assumes that things are freely available, extras just waiting to be appropriated. For clarity regarding this fundamental query Gandhi turned to the first shloka of the *Isa vasyam Upanisad*. Since this was during the Vaikom satyagraha period he put it forth as, "I should like to apply this mantra to our own condition in virtue of the proclamation".[105]

After the proclamation regarding the demands of the avarnas by the Maharaja of Travancore as a response to the Vaikom satyagraha, Gandhi addressed a number of meetings in the region. Besides encouraging the political subtexts of the changing relationship between savarnas and avarnas, he was keen to help initiate a more meaningful dialogue about religion and spiritualism which inspires both. Towards this he posed a simple albeit percipient question: "have we or have we not something that will answer the demands of the most philosophic among the Hindus or the most matter-of-fact among them?"[106] And he suggested, "I have now come to the final conclusion that if all the Upanishads and all the other scriptures happened all of a sudden to be reduced to ashes and if only the first verse in the *Ishopanishad* were left intact in the memory of the Hindus, Hinduism would live for ever".[107] Although he had learnt by heart the verse when incarcerated in the Yerwada Jail, its significance captivated him during the vaikom satyagraha. Seeking to help people understand the fragile relationship between spiritualism and ritualism he declared, "It is not enough that the savarnas and the avarnas continue to go to the temples just as they are doing now. Hitherto people have gone to the temples more by way of formality than from conviction. They have not reasoned out for themselves why they needed to go to the temples".[108]

The first verse of the *Ishopanishad,* while exploring the larger notion of *purushartha,* specifically clarifies regarding the unabridged freedom to own to ensure security. The verse reads: "*Isa vasyam idam sarvam yat kinca jagatyam jagat; tena tyaktena bhunjitha, ma grdhah kasya svid dhanam*". All this that moves on earth is to be covered with the lord; with that given up, protect yourself, covet not, for whose is the wealth?

The shloka has four quartets. The first points to 'all this that moves on earth': the temporal world and all that emanates from it and its implication for human beings. Contextually 'this that moves' points to change and continuity, while remaining open to choice as a factor to tinker this matrix of change and continuity, and 'that moves' is symptomatic of the temporal. The second quartet discusses 'to be covered with the lord'. The intent is to underline that it is not necessarily covered, but has to be covered. Latent in this is the fact that mankind is not necessarily the only purpose of creation. The issue here is the role and nature of transition and transformation enjoined on the human being. Therefore the moot question is 'does man have a choice'? It can be argued that the world is already covered and as such this urge to cover, that is to consciously be involved in the processes of change and continuity, is futile. The choice on the other hand can extend from a temporal intervention to an idealist involvement. Gandhi reads this together to mean, "All this that we see in this great Universe is pervaded by God".[109]

The third quartet translates as, 'with that given up, protect yourself'. This refers to transition which is temporal, but seeking a representation of the mortal's path to the immortal. This involves choice and choice necessitates renouncing something in favour of something else. As against control of transition by possession, renunciation encourages thinking about the implication of such a desire. "Man is not asked to abandon the temporal world and see the eternal beyond it. He is asked to see this very world as the self of all in each. To realize the world as the self, the self has to be realized as the lord".[110] Gandhi divides this section into two and translates it to read thus: "Renounce it and enjoy it. There is another rendering which means the same thing, though: Enjoy what he gives you".[111]

The last section translates as: 'Covet not, for whose is the wealth?' For Gandhi this was Gita all over again. "As I read the *mantra* in the light of the *Gita* or the *Gita* in the light of the *mantra* I find that the *Gita* is a commentary on this *mantra*".[112] Admiring this, in his speech at Quilon he gushed, "It seems to me to satisfy the cravings of the socialist and the communists, of the philosopher and the economist.

I venture to suggest to all who do not belong to the Hindu faith that it satisfies their cravings also".[113] Perhaps in this not coveting there is something also to be said about inequalities and equalities. Earlier in 1931, Gandhi had written, "Inequalities in intelligence and even opportunities will last till the end of time. . . . But if inequalities stare us in the face the essential equality is not to be missed. Every man has an equal right to the necessaries of life even as birds and beasts have. And since every right carries with it a corresponding duty and the corresponding remedy for resisting any attack upon it, it is merely a matter of finding out the corresponding duties and remedies to vindicate the elementary fundamental equality. The corresponding duty is to labour with my limbs and the corresponding remedy is to non-cooperate with him who deprives me of the fruits of my labour. And if I would recognize the fundamental equality, as I must, of the capitalist and the labourer, I must not aim at his destruction".[114]

For Gandhi private property as possession and thus power is a suspect equation. *Aparigraha* refers to private possession and competence which is generally acquired through access to possession. But labour on which everything depends is an elemental competence which is independent of private possessions. This is the dynamic actuality of the separation of the personal and the social. Therefore "*kasya svid dhanam*": whose is the wealth? Does it belong to the personal or the social? Does this mean disavowing private property? Not exactly. For Gandhi, "I can only possess certain things when I know that others, who also want to possess similar things, are able to do so. But we know – every one of us can speak from experience – that such a thing is impossibility. Therefore, the only thing that can be possessed by all is non-possession, not to have anything whatsoever. In other words, a willing surrender".[115] As for resolving the squabbling personal and the social, he deduced, "If we can erase the 'I's' and the 'Mine's' from religion, politics, economics, etc., we shall soon be free and bring heaven upon earth".[116] This is the only possible protection possible because it brings harmony between the personal and the social by restricting the 'mine'.

The question is can wealth be vested on some, and as such remain vested, but held as that belonging to the people and as such *Isa*? History tells us that this is difficult. What then is the way out? For Gandhi, obviously, it is not revolution but Trusteeship, inclusive rather than exclusive re-ordering. Gandhi preferred to believe in the human being rather than concepts and manmade systems which respond to none and become self-serving when they are not already serving some well-meaning altruistic logic. This premise of Gandhi can certainly be questioned. But then Gandhi was not laboring under any need to elaborate any theory. "I understand the *Gita* teaching of non-possession (Aparigraha) to mean that those who desired salvation should act like a trustee who, though having control over great possession, regards not an iota of these as his own".[117] For Gandhi while the world is an imperfect place, how to handle perfection remained a problematic. And he was not ready to outsource this, preferring idealism if necessary. This way only the human being and not some malaise or a system can claim advantage. The paradox is that the wise and the not-wise might act similarly: one consciously, the other unconsciously.

A contemplative dialogue

Religion obligates conviction. It is this conviction, rather 'being steeped in conviction' which Gandhi sought. But convictions come with paradoxes and uncertainties; seemingly contradictory statements may bear out to be well founded. Perhaps this is because religion is the vernacular of the human narrative, which when local predicates an elemental vibrancy. But it also encourages the upstart and the avaricious in man and therein rests its appeal and flaw, a characteristic example of which is the caste system.

The articulation of the caste system essentially revolves around the purpose of agency and action. While the purpose of agency in the case of caste is to provide mechanisms and a clear code of inner coherence and cohesiveness to the numerous discrete castes as independent social entities, the purpose of action whether inter or intra caste is to ensure the sustenance of their traditions and objectives. In reality the purposes of agency and action differ from the ideals of Gandhi. The actual it seems reflects the ideal as a cruel parody. Gandhi seems to bypass this when he claims, "The callings of a Brahmin – spiritual teacher – and a scavenger are equal, and their due performance carries equal merit before God and at one time seems to have carried identical reward before man. Both are entitled to their livelihood and no more".[118] Even more specifically he insists, "I believe in *varnadharma* which is the law of life. I believe that some people are born to teach and some to defend and some to engage in trade and agriculture and some to do manual labour, so much so that these occupations become hereditary. The law of varna is nothing but the law of conservation of energy. Why should my son not be a scavenger if I am one?"[119] For him, "The essence of Hinduism is contained in its enunciation of one and only God as Truth and its bold acceptance of ahimsa as the law of the human family".[120]

The difficulty for Gandhi was with his brief for Hinduism. "*Varnadharma* acts even as the law of gravitation";[121] at various times he felt the caste system has saved 'Hinduism from disintegration'.[122] It was problematic for him to reconcile aspirations vis-à-vis Hinduism and the purposes of agency and action of discrete castes as found prevailing in reality. In a way the core problem lay somewhere else. "The law of varna is the antithesis of competition which kills".[123] Religion for Gandhi at any given time is an imperfect intercession to establish contact with God. This becomes clear from what he had to say about *suddhi*. "I believe in the equality of all the great religions of the earth. I regard no man as polluted because he has forsaken the branch on which he was sitting and gone over to another of the same tree. If he comes back to the original branch, he deserves to be welcomed and not told that he had committed a sin by reason of his having forsaken the family to which he belonged".[124]

However Gandhi did recognize that these justifications were palliatives. In practice therefore, "I have gone no-where to defend *varnadharma*, though for the removal of untouchability I went to Vaikom".[125] Conversely in terms of world view his justification was weaker. "A religion has to be judged not by it's worst specimens but by the best it might have produced. For that and that alone can be used as the standard to aspire to, if not to improve upon".[126] He sought to go by the best that Hinduism stood for while exposing and discarding the worst. This however becomes a specious argument as was argued by Ambedkar. Ambedkar chose to focus on the purposes of agency and action of the discrete castes and ask as to why within Hinduism, 'the worst number so many and the best so few'; perhaps the ideal of religion itself is flawed?[127] Gandhi's rhetorical position that, "if the *Shastras* support caste as we know it today in all its hideousness, I may not call myself or remain a Hindu since I have no scruples about interdining or intermarriage",[128] begs the problem. He seems to suggest that within Hinduism there are auto-correct mechanisms. But then Gandhi fails to mention as to what these might be. Further will individual tinkering and intervention rectify the nature of the caste system itself? It is like trying to shave with the aid of a cracked mirror.[129] While Gandhi personally liberated himself, his 'evolutionary revolution' seems to have left caste to sort out its mess.

India has been more of a civilization than a nation. Over centuries as a society it has been fecund and prolific sustaining a wide diversity of people, regions, and cultures. As people settled and the civilization consolidated, a complex pan Indian ethos of diversity and unity emerged wherein people while retaining their basic distinctiveness learned to cooperate and coordinate around similarities. Every region while developing and retaining local cultures, language, heritage, and religions, accepted certain pan Indian practices albeit with a local flavour. While Hinduism emerged as the broad pan Indian religion, it precincts covered a wide spectrum allowing individuals and communities to follow diverse philosophies and traditions. This diversity is indicative of its capacity to be assimilative, reflective, and accommodative. However it came with a price; in its essential structuring, among commonalities spread over regions is the ubiquitous caste system. By accommodating different food habits, cultural practices, and regional susceptibilities, Hinduism incorporated diversity; by enjoining the caste system it ensured a pan Indian similarity. All this was further assimilated via a broad range of texts and rituals espoused in the *shruti, smriti,* and puranas. As a matter of fact, it is the particularized similarities of the caste system, as practiced, which significantly helped sustain the Indian civilisation, its transition and its claims of being a nation. While retaining its inherent logic of guna, varna, and jati, caste provided the pillars, columns, and beams to structure the Indian social formation. In the process every region while sustaining its regional particularities was able to sustain a pan Indian sensibility. However, it must be recognized that not every localite could communicate at a pan Indian level. Religious practices while similar were not the same; food habits for instance reflected local resource profiles. Caste in short provided consensus, cohesion and identity to the idea of India. And it came with its own ethos of inclusion and exclusion. For the twice-born it was a pact of give and take while simultaneously keeping the aspirations of polity under scrutiny, a pact from which the sudras and avarnas were assiduously keep out.

Over centuries in India, two parallel civilizational discourses, one local-regional and another pan Indian emerged, competing and complimenting each other. The caste system substantially facilitated this. While people did travel, most lived their lives within small geographic regions with their own language, rituals, culture, and exclusive do's and don'ts. An essential parameter of commonality was provided by the caste system which incidentally was adaptive permitting the emergence of new jatis. But it was the sanctity of exclusiveness of caste divisions and its binding links with Hindu religion which ensured the pan Indian linkages. Caste offered sanctity to inter regional hierarchies and a platform for intra-regional discourse. Shankaracharya could pick Brahmins from Kerala to man temples in the Himalaya; but even after a millennium, albeit without malaise, they are still identified as coming from the south. Religion and ritual similarities offered equality of status to various corresponding castes thereby ensuring debate and discourse. Caste thus played and plays a strategic role in our much-acclaimed unity in diversity.

However the processes were not all that simple. First, there were local efforts (bhakti movements) to rework the immensely exploitative caste hegemony. With the arrival of powerful monotheistic ideologies backed by force, Hinduism and the caste system came under severe stress. But it survived because the opposing ideologies preferred to compromise and use the mute efficacy of the all-pervading caste system which offered access to local hierarchies along with enabling a pan India reach and mobilization potential. All the new religions while rejecting the philosophy, implicitly accepted caste as a practice. Today this is under stress because the polity centric notion of nation is seeking to replace the hegemony of caste and a nation is not as adaptive as civilization. Since independence we are still sorting out as to who is an Indian. We have constitutionally banned caste while retaining its ethos as casteism. Gandhi had a dilemma: Mahomedans, Sikhs, Europeans may remain as such in perpetuity, but will untouchables remain untouchables in perpetuity?[130] We are still trying to answer this.

Notes

1 *Harijan* (Nov. 28, 1936).
2 Ibid.
3 Ibid. (Jul. 18, 1936).
4 *TEWMG* (2009, 157).
5 Armstrong (1993, 378).
6 *TEWMG* (2009, 461).
7 Ibid. (159).
8 *CWMG*, Vol. 55 (255).
9 *An Autobiography* (2004, xii).
10 Ibid. (541).
11 Ibid.
12 *MPWMG*, Vol. 1 (1986, 543).
13 Ibid. (542).
14 Ibid.
15 Ibid. (545).
16 Ibid. (519).
17 Ibid. (497).
18 Ibid. (459).
19 *The Gospel of Selfless Action* (1970, 134).
20 Bose (1972).
21 Ibid.
22 *Harijan* (Mar. 23, 1940).
23 Ibid.
24 *TEWMG* (2009, 148).

25 *MPWMG*, Vol. I (1986, 480).
26 Ibid.
27 Ibid. (512–13).
28 Ibid. (469).
29 Ibid. (477–79).
30 Ibid.
31 Ibid. (493).
32 Ibid. (476).
33 Ibid. (492).
34 Ibid. (477).
35 Ibid. (481).
36 *CWMG*, Vol. 62 (85).
37 *MPWMG*, Vol. I (1986, 494). Italics added.
38 Ibid.
39 Ibid.
40 Ibid. (495).
41 *CWMG*, Vol. 1 (180–86).
42 Ibid.
43 Thomson (1993, 40).
44 *Harijan* (Aug. 29, 1936).
45 Ignatius (1987, 276).
46 Ibid. (275).
47 Suhurud (2012, 48).
48 *CWMG*, Vol. 70 (116).
49 Ibid., Vol. 33 (85).
50 Prabhu and Rao (1945).
51 *Young India* (Oct. 11, 1928).
52 *The Gospel of Selfless Action* (1970, 135).
53 Zaehner (1968, 188).
54 *The Gospel of Selfless Action* (1970, 359).
55 Ibid.
56 Ibid. (126).
57 Ibid. (127).
58 *CWMG*, Vol. 21 (116).
59 Suhrud (2012, 91).
60 Ibid.
61 *CWMG*, Vol. 28 (47).
62 *Young India* (Apr. 8, 1926).
63 *The Gospel of Selfless Action* (1970, 128).
64 Ibid. (127).
65 *CWMG*, Vol. 39 (142).
66 Ibid., Vol. 32 (71).
67 Ibid., Vol. 18 (50–51).
68 *The Gospel of Selfless Action* (1970, 129).
69 Ibid. (133).
70 All quotations from the Gita (Ch.:Verse) are from Zaehner (1968).
71 *The Gospel of Selfless Action* (1970, 136).
72 See Gandhi's views on history in Chatterjee (1983, 6–7).
73 *The Gospel of Selfless Action* (1970, 159).
74 Zaehner (1968, 143).
75 *The Gospel of Selfless Action* (1970, 168).
76 Ibid. (199). Also see *Young India* (Nov. 24, 1927).
77 *The Gospel of Selfless Action* (1970, 135).
78 Ibid.
79 *MPWMG*, Vol. III (1987, 129).
80 *CWMG*, Vol. 37 (76).

81 Gopal (1992, 25).
82 *MPWMG*, Vol. III (1987, 473).
83 Ibid. (473–74).
84 Ibid. (474).
85 *MGTEW* (2008, 92).
86 Ibid.
87 *CWMG*, Vol. 41 (46).
88 Hay (2000, 147).
89 *CWMG*, Vol. 25 (361) and Vol. 42 (412).
90 Ibid., Vol. 43 (363).
91 Ibid., Vol. 50 (201).
92 Ibid., Vol. 41 (94).
93 Ibid., Vol. 50 (203).
94 *Young India* (Dec. 20, 1928, 420).
95 *Harijan* (May 26, 1946, 156).
96 *Young India* (Aug. 6, 1925, 272).
97 *An Autobiography* (2004, xiii).
98 *CWMG*, Vol. 50 (200) and Vol. 88 (145).
99 Parel (2009, 159).
100 *CWMG*, Vol. 42 (13).
101 Gandhi (1950, 366).
102 Parekh (1989, 224–25).
103 Ibid. (224).
104 *Harijan* (Jul. 18, 1936).
105 *CWMG*, Vol. 70 (304).
106 Ibid. (298).
107 Ibid.
108 Ibid. (314).
109 Ibid.
110 Gupta (1991, 16).
111 *CWMG*, Vol. 70 (298).
112 Ibid. (298–99).
113 Ibid. (298).
114 *Young India* (Mar. 26, 1931).
115 *CWMG*, Vol. 53 (398).
116 *Young India* (Sep. 23, 1926).
117 *An Autobiography* (1927, 394).
118 *Harijan* (Jul. 18, 1936).
119 Ibid. (Mar. 6, 1937, 27).
120 Ibid. (Jul. 18, 1936).
121 Ibid. (Mar. 6, 1937).
122 See Kolge (2017).
123 *Harijan* (Mar. 6, 1937).
124 Ibid. (Sep. 25, 1937, 273).
125 *CWMG*, Vol. 35 (523).
126 *Harijan* (Jul. 18, 1936).
127 Ambedkar (1937, 57).
128 *Harijan* (Aug. 15, 1936).
129 Guru and Sarukkai (2012).
130 Gandhi (2006, 361).

7

TOWARDS A WORLD VIEW

Sarvodaya, *Hind Swaraj*, swadeshi, social service

By the time Gandhi acquired the credentials of a *satyagrahi*, he had a broad understanding of what was wrong with the social milieu. Interrogating a series of awareness events, he was now becoming firmly committed to self-realization and expressing his social involvement as a conscious desire to serve. He was becoming an interlocutor. An interlocutor is a person in a vision-mode. The mode indicates the mission i.e. aspirations impregnated with purpose. He seeks a path, and Gandhi's *Hind Swaraj* is an instance of conspicuously articulating a path i.e. vision and mission. The interlocutor while being distinct is not necessarily an exemplar. His is an evolving paradigm. He has a path of his own which he shares. He writes only a chapter reflecting his world view. But this is a distinct chapter, and then he edits the chapters contributed by others critically sympathetic with his world view. However, his editorial indicates an analysis which is not a replication of his own chapter. The other contributors retain their identity, aspirations, and visions while being critically sensitive to the sentiments and sanctity of the editor's path. In their own ways they help propagate and maintain a common path. The contribution of each being distinct and symbiotic, the process creates a distinct synergy which adds that little bit more to the sum total. The distinctness of the various contributors lends an aura of plurality and diversity to the common analysis making it that much more resilient, symbiotic, and full of promise.

But the interlocutor needs to prepare for the journey. Brahmacharya was Gandhi's preparation of himself as an interlocutor. While he remained transparent about it, he was also clear that not all can follow him. An added complication in Gandhi's case is with his insistence on experiments and their validity for himself and others. As a member of civil society and at times as its representative, the interlocutor mediates between the people and the state; this is an onerous task which nevertheless is essential. At times the distinction blurs and the interlocutor walks the thin and sharp edge. People while following him find it difficult to distinguish between his personal chapter and the editorial. But Gandhi had one great asset; while he was open to ideas, he could not be hustled. He would retain the right to choose to be a leader or interlocutor. For Gandhi, his quest of self-realization would have to be the conclusive consideration. Paradoxically, for the people it could mean that he had to be the ultimate leader. He tended to sustain the paradox by seeking to comprehend the personal within him only through the social prism.

The *Indian Opinion* offered a perfect platform for Gandhi to initiate a debate and dialogue, and also to offer access to ideas and experiences. And he used it to the hilt. While at a personal level Gandhi preferred to express around satya, ahimsa, brahmacharya, *vrata,* and so on, his social half soon started to formulate sarvodaya, swadeshi, swaraj, and the larger notion of social work. Gandhi was becoming clear that struggles and satyagraha, while being rejuvenating and transformative, could not be restricted to infrequent skirmishes with the state, occasioned by some travesty of justice on the part of the authorities. The state should not appropriate the monopoly to choose the time and place for the skirmishes. The struggles had to have a larger and more substantial cause and vision. For this he needed to elaborate a world view. This is where the cluster of sarvodaya, swadeshi, swaraj, and much later, the constructive programme played a seminal role in his personal evolution as a *satyagrahi*, and perhaps one can say, 'of a rare vintage!' Through each of these concepts, Gandhi sought to underscore the immense significance of personal and social freedom for self-realization. The 'pilgrim after truth' needed both a mission and a vision. Gandhi had to formulate as to how social interaction between individuals and groups could become an effective social force as a social criterion wherein it can aid the individual or group to overcome fear, hypocrisy, and hatred. How, for instance, could swaraj become a state of being of individuals and nations? All this meant a critical and creative look at individual entitlements and endowments vis-à-vis that of the community.

Sarvodaya

Gandhi's conceptualization of sarvodaya began as a part of his ongoing praxis of self-realization. Inspired by John Ruskin's 'Unto This Last', he bought a farm, named it Phoenix and got down to practicing the principles laid out therein. These principles were that the good of the individual is contained in the good of all; that a lawyer's work has the same value as the barber's inasmuch as all have the same right of earning their livelihood from their work; that a life of labour, i.e. the life of the tiller of the soil and the handicraftsman is a life worth living. He recognized that "the first of these I knew. The second I had dimly realized. The third had never occurred to me. *Unto This Last* made it as clear as daylight for me that the second and the third were contained in the first".[1] To this unambiguousness much later while discussing Ruskin on education he mentions six requisites: pure air, clean water, and clean earth as essential things, and gratitude, hope, and charity as virtues.[2] Such were the convictions which lead to the conceptualization of sarvodaya, a concept which he hoped would truly liberate social discourse.

What is crucial is his recognition of the fundamental nature and inclusive role of 'labour' as physical and 'affections' as the emotional in our lives. For Gandhi it also became clear that labour is not just an input into a profession; it cannot be hierarchized and ranked as inferior or superior, and labour remains an inalienable element of our liveability, livelihood, and being. While Ruskin did help crystallize his views, this clarity was also influenced by the independent thinking, profound morality and the truthfulness of Leo Tolstoy's *The Kingdom of God is Within You*.[3] Perhaps by the time he read Ruskin, Gandhi was already thinking not only about the ends and means binary, but also of the needs and wants binary. This can be assumed because in his argument it is the import of the role of labour-labourer context which becomes undeniably significant. "The phrase Unto This Last would have been translated in Gujarati as *Antyodaya* or the welfare of the last person. Gandhi does not translate it as *Antyodaya*, but as *sarvodaya*".[4] The *satyagrahi* Gandhi was rapidly recognizing the philosophical, moral, and pedagogical implications of his involvements and writings; perhaps he was also coming around to accept that taking a position enjoins taking a side, and thereby facing an 'other'.

It was Tolstoy who put him firmly on the path of prospecting the praxis of simplicity and simple living. While this simplicity and simple living is not innocence, it should also not be confused as minimalism or denial. It is a complex nuanced ethos leading to personal and social reorientation, leading to self-realization. A year after he bought the Phoenix farm and much before he published the summary of *Unto This Last*, writing in the *Indian Opinion, 2 Sept. 1905*, he had summed up Tolstoy on simplicity as follows:

1 In this world men should not accumulate wealth;
2 No matter how much evil a person does to us, we should always do good to him. Such is the Commandment of God, and also His Law;
3 No one should take part in fighting;
4 It is sinful to wield political power, as it leads to many of the evils in the world;
5 Man is born to do his duty to his Creator; he should therefore pay more attention to his duties than to his rights;
6 Agriculture is the true occupation of man. It is therefore contrary to divine law to establish large cities, to employ hundreds of thousands for minding machines in factories so that a few can wallow in riches by exploiting the helplessness and poverty of the many.

Each of these Gandhi internalized, and as was his wont, he reinterpreted it to blend into and serve his overarching notions of satya, ahimsa, and God. Thus, when writing the *Hind Swaraj* perhaps recollecting Plato's Apology and the Socratic principle "that it is better to suffer harm than to inflict it on others",[5] he wrote that the core of Tolstoy's teaching was "real courage and humanity consists in not returning a kick for a kick" and "to return injury for injury does harm both to ourselves and to our enemy".[6] Latter he was to explain, "We are our own slaves, not of the

British. This should be engraved in our minds. The whites cannot remain if we do not want them".[7]

From Tolstoy, Gandhi picked up a couple of significant values. Tolstoy "did what he preached'; and secondly, "He strove uncompromisingly to follow truth as he saw it, making no attempts to conceal or dilute what he believed to be the truth".[8] While delivering a speech on Tolstoy's Birth Centenary, reiterating the need to harmonize words and deeds, Gandhi cautions, "Our non-violence is an unworthy thing. We see its utmost limit in refraining somehow from destroying bugs, mosquitoes and fleas, or from killing birds and animals. We do not care if these creatures suffer, nor even if we partly contribute to their suffering".[9] For this one needs to cultivate a firm mind, courage, and resolute spirit: all precepts which Tolstoy imparted. Moreover, such a resolve can only be cultivated if one practices self-restrain, non-violence, and bread-labour or 'manual labour' i.e. the labour essential for meeting the basic needs of human life.[10] The simple meaning of bread labour for Gandhi is that the right to eat is directly related to bending one's back and working. "The doctrine of bread-labour asserts the moral imperative that one must earn one's bread by the sweat of one's brow: he has no right to eat who does not bend his body and work. Bodily labour is a duty imposed by nature on mankind. And one who eats but does not do any manual work in effect steals food";[11] "Perhaps the most important use that Gandhi made of his doctrine of bread-labour was to decry what he called the glorification of leisure".[12] For him the issue was not one of necessary leisure, but the tendency to measure one's involvement in labour vis-à-vis the leisure it gave in return.

Labour, affection, and the craftsperson

All his life if time permitted Gandhi remained a voracious reader. He had developed a capacity to get at the heart of a text, systematically gleaning precise and succinct insights from it. Assimilated and rendered as discernments he used these insights to design and also suggest to others a meaningful life. Gandhi paraphrased *Unto This Last* as sarvodaya and summarizing the text published it as a series of nine articles in the *Indian Opinion* between 16 May and 18 July 1908;[13] sarvodaya stands for 'the well-being of all' or 'welfare of all' or 'the advancement of all'. Ruskin had borrowed the title from the parable of the workers in the vineyard in St. Mathew 20:1–16.[14] Introspective, philosophical, and moral in tone and essence, the exposition looks into the "nature of economic motivation, the meaning of wealth, and the place of honesty, truth and natural justice in its acquisition, distribution and enjoyment. *Unto This Last* was a critique of, not an alternative to, capitalism".[15] This book along with Ruskin's 'A Joy Forever: And Its Price in the Market', had a considerable influence on Gandhi's conceptualization of the *Hind Swaraj*.[16]

The preface opens with an outright refutation of the West's exclusive promotion of physical and material happiness. Ruskin rejects the unjustified acceptance of the quest for prosperity of the greatest number even if it be at the cost of a minority because it has no sanction in moral law. This untenable acceptance and justification of the greatest number thesis is because "people in the west do not believe it to be wrong if it (i.e. prosperity) is secured at the cost of the minority".[17] Gandhi finds Ruskin effectively countering such arguments. Besides, in the book he also recognizes some hard lessons for Indians who have taken to imitating the west. "We do grant that it is necessary to imitate the west in certain respects. At the same time there is no doubt that many western ideas are wrong".[18] Even the great urge to go 'out to distant lands to make money' ends up with Indians becoming engrossed in the pursuit of self-interest and actually does 'more harm than good'.[19] Gandhi's reading of Ruskin convinces him that the flaw is due to the ignoring of moral laws and common sense.

At the heart of the problem is the fact that "Man suffers from many delusions; but none so great as his attempt to formulate laws for the conduct of other men disregarding the effects of social affection, as if they were only machines at work".[20] Sustaining this kind of thinking are political economists who "assert that social affections are to be looked upon as accidental and disturbing elements in human nature; but avarice and the desire for progress are constant elements".[21] This distortion and misrepresentation stems from an iniquitous if not motivated mixture of essentially caring human nature with the conception of man as a money-making machine. "Man's affections constitute an inner force. The laws of demand and supply are formulations concerning the external world. The two, therefore are not of the same nature".[22] It has to be understood that, "Affection has a different kind of effect on man and acts in a different manner".[23] Simply put, "knowledge of the laws of exchange is of no help in determining the effects of man's social affections".[24] Taking strong objection to considering man as a mere body, a machine, the treatise declines to exclude human affections from economics which is undoubtedly a crucial human social practice. In essence man is not a machine. He has a soul, and this is 'the predominant element' within him. And as such it has to be given due prominence while analyzing humanity.

A moot issue in all this is the complex economic relationship between the employer and the employee and how this universally accepted, fraught with tension relationship, affects or impinges on their independent and mutual interests. The nature of this relationship can either be symbiotic, synergetic, or antagonistic. The economic affairs of men however cannot be determined only by the principle of profit and loss. The more encompassing notion of justice must provide the foregrounding. But human justice always includes affection as an inalienable constituent. "The relation between master and operative depends upon this element of affection",[25] an actuality ignored by economists. Strictly speaking supply and demand along with profit and loss can never make a man work at optimum. "The master-servant nexus must not be a pecuniary one, but one of love".[26] "Kindness should be exercised for the sake of kindness; the reward will then come unsought".[27] In short, to optimize the benefits of economics we need to explicitly recognize the function of 'affection' between employer and employee.

The problem of economics as the economists see it is that economics has to be posited on a disjunction between the employee and employer so as to comprehend and sustain their economic relationship and assert its relevance as a mode of discourse. The ambiguity is with one fundamental premise: the claim that profits are the basis of all incentives for the entrepreneur-employer. Consequently fluctuations, manipulations, returns, and security of employment all impact wages, and the only issue at stake is the surplus the whole production process generates. All compulsions and consequences are measured against the quantum and subsequent control of the surplus economics generates. Economics thus ends up eulogizing the self-aggrandizement of the employer, a very one-sided affectionless unethical enterprise. Affection has to be an important integral criterion to help economics remain true to ethics without which it becomes an act of exploitation. Shifting from the general master-servant nexus to specifics, Gandhi looks into the role of professionals such as doctors, soldiers, clergymen, and the trader. Among the professionals he invariably finds a higher level of morality compared to that amongst the traders. It seems as if, "Trade is always associated with unscrupulousness".[28] Perhaps trade is mendacious by definition?

Even though the trader has a socially useful function, "we take it for granted that his object is to fill his coffers". "It is also accepted as a principle that the buyer must offer the lowest possible price and the seller must demand and accept the highest".[29] The only way out of this trust deficit is possible when the trader like the professional accepts that, "Both have work to do- each a duty to perform – irrespective of whether or not they get the stipend or the profit".[30] Duty and work cannot and should not be separated. But then "this requires a great deal of patience, kindness and intelligence",[31] particularly because every trader knows that it is never clear as to what people want and can afford. While these nitty-gritties have more complex tenets, at the core always is the urge to create individual wealth. The economist might keep extolling this as a virtue, but Gandhi feels most businessmen don't even "know the meaning of the word 'rich'. They do not realize that, if there are rich men, there must also be poor men. People sometimes believe, mistakenly, that by following certain precepts *it is possible for everybody to become rich*".[32] The simple fact is that "the power of the rupee you own depends on another going without it. If no one wants it, it will be useless to you. The power it possesses depends upon your neighbour's lack of it. There can be wealth only where there is scarcity. This means that, in order to be rich, one must keep another poor".[33] At the root of all this is the generally evaded core riddle of power and possession. "Careful reflection will show that what we really desire through acquisition of wealth is power over other men – [power] to acquire for our advantage the labour of a servant, a tradesman or an artisan. And the power we can thus acquire will be in direct proportion to the poverty of others".[34] Therefore, we need to take a harder look at the problematic of surplus through profit maximization, the fickle nature of circumstances which can render anyone a pauper or debtor and the unscrupulousness latent in the manipulability of supply and demand. Above all, we need to recognize and understand that "Cash in the hands of an individual may be a token of perseverance, skill and prosperity or of harmful luxuries, merciless tyranny and chicanery".[35] Consequently economics without ethics is only a façade and half-measure at best.

Gandhi's reading is a stinging critique of the entrepreneur-consumer-market-based notion of development.

Gandhi's analysis is straight forward. "Wealth is like a river".[36] How you use it depends upon the nature of intervention, discretion, and a commitment to non-appropriation of resource and returns for selfish ends. "The principle of regulating the circulation of wealth is ignored altogether by economists".[37] It is not enough to live by the laws of demand and supply. "God has endowed man with understanding, with a sense of justice".[38] Therefore, economics should have a human first approach. He reasoned that we can for instance pay interest for labour to a labourer just like we are ready to pay interest for a loan. After all, for every economic activity the entrepreneur has to acquire capital and labour. For capital he pays interest to those who hold capital such as banks, etc. Whenever he pays interest, this interest he pays is above the capital taken as loan. Similarly a labourer holds labour in stock. Just like the capital is returned at the end of the job the labour of the labourer too becomes free at the end of the specific job. As such, why shouldn't the entrepreneur pay an interest beyond the cost of labour he uses as he does to capital? After all even for dead labour as machinery he pays rent. This interest as an extra can render justice to the labourer for whom his capital is his labour.

In the concluding part Gandhi critically puts in perspective society's one point agenda of indiscriminate creation of wealth and its associated focus on industrialization and who should be held responsible for the consequences, most of which incidentally are unpleasant. For him, "it is the rich who are responsible for the immorality of the poor".[39] This happens because it is not possible for everyone to become rich even by honest means. Not surprisingly, most 'turn in desperation to fraud'. The only way out of this knot is to accept that "there is no wealth besides life. That nation is wealthy which is moral".[40] While summing up the insights from Ruskin, Gandhi takes a critical but creative look at India, Indians, and the new spirit amongst the western educated Indian youth. He ponders about the dichotomy amongst the Indian elite regarding the lofty aims of swarajya on the one hand and the desire to accumulate wealth by emulating the industrialization processes of the west on the other. Questioning the half-baked notion of swarajya prevalent amongst Indians he cautions: real swarajya consists in restraint. This means being moral, truthful, and responsible towards duties. We are ruled by the British because of our disunity, immorality, and ignorance. Swarajya is a harmonious blend of economics, politics, and culture which to be sustained requires appropriate disposition and capacity. After all, "true economics is the economics of justice. That people alone will be happy which learns how to do justice and be righteous under all conditions of life";[41] and "there is no wealth besides life".[42]

Accepting that real swarajya is a valid and just demand, his only reservation concerns the means of achieving it. For him real swarajya can be attained only by righteous means. For Gandhi the issue pertained to the ambiguity of aggrandisement vis-à-vis the good of all. While every person should have the possibility of being able to give vent to their innate abilities, these have to accept the hegemony of the 'good of all'. For Gandhi there cannot be any one aspect, certainly not the creation of wealth which should dominate the calling we term 'human'. Sarvodaya for Gandhi presupposes a moral code: a purity of means for the achievement of ends, particularly economic well-being. Moreover this code enjoins an obligation towards the recognition and practice of bread-labour which means labouring with one's own hands. Above all, an arbitrary separation as intellectual or labourer 'has no sanction in divine law' which remains the final arbitrator. In effect any system which downgrades labour is ungodly.

Alienated from the systems which use labour as an input, alienated from the products or commodities his labour produces, and antagonistic towards the employer who brings them into the production process, the labourer soon loses his respect for his own labour, shuns it, debunks it, and along with hatred for the employer, the employee-labourer loses all his respect for labour itself. The labourer, labour, and the product of labour become distinct and separate. Recognizing this, Gandhi sought to harmonize the relationship with an attitude of genuine receptiveness towards labour. The labourer accordingly is encouraged to respect his contribution and also relate positively to the products of labour. This of course means questioning the market-oriented industrialization processes which lead to alienation of the labourer and reification of commodities. Gandhi's attitude towards machinery stemmed from this problematic of the labourer becoming redundant due to his systemic alienation from the product and losing his respect for both his labour and product of his labour. At a more emotional level, by stressing on the need to do physical labour or bread labour as he called it, Gandhi sought to question the contempt for labour particularly amongst the intellectuals. Perhaps this was Gandhi's effort to understand the fast-emerging money-capital-oriented class system.

In sarvodaya as a concept, perhaps Gandhi was envisioning a craftsperson: an identity which can suit every person by encouraging individual creativity and criticality. A craftsperson never demurs from labour, is constantly creative, produces for her own self as also for the community, but not for some amorphous market. She does not focus on profits, lives tradition with a keen eye for innovation, and will not commandeer the environment. Such a person is an educing self constantly learning and teaching while being at peace with the community. For her, 'give and take' is spontaneous and sustainable because it is a tripartite deal between the craftsperson, the community, and the environment. Sarvodaya means unabridged access to bring forth the craftsperson quiescent within each and every one of us. It is also a practice which through self-help liberates us to nurture the potential latent within us.

Swadeshi

Following Ruskin, in sarvodaya Gandhi's focus was on the processes of the political economy and the nature of economic practices such as profit and loss, supply and demand, employer-employee relationship, quantum of returns, and so on. In swadeshi on the other hand the focus shifts to the organization of the political economy, and as such, the discourse is about politics. In swadeshi well-being as 'benign power' is the core issue because such power can become coercive depending on the nature of the local social configurations. Thus, while swadeshi is not an overbearing and dogmatic concept, it is also not necessarily benign. Swadeshi essentially tries to project the significance of the local as a graspable historio-geographic entity, and Gandhi using swadeshi tries to revitalize the local as a site of benign power. This narrative exemplifies a man's innate responsibility towards his neighbour. This not only necessitates a refocusing as far as the personal is concerned, it also reconfigures the social within each individual necessitating the abjuring of selfishness and self-interest. Gandhi reasoned that the issue has to be one of access and not control, encourage potential and not exclusivity. To rephrase, swadeshi encourages a dynamic debate within a community regarding what the community considers as 'wants and needs'. Of course this comes along with contradictions and histories reflecting the distinctive local reality of the community. Gandhi "refused to believe that there could be an objective social knowledge independent of the knowers or an objective history impervious to the moral choice of individuals. Institutions could never be designed so perfectly or scientifically, he once pointed out, that they would obviate the need for individuals to be good".[43] Swadeshi therefore is no static reasoning.

In Gandhi's conceptual repertoire, swadeshi is an important component. Distinct from the European doctrine of nationalism and its focus on the state, its import lies in that it elaborates the socialilty[44] of natural necessity and of the socialness of choice by an individual. For Gandhi, the ever present palpable community and therefore the social within all of us is a non-alienable given. Our social and individual practices along with our memories and aspirations emerge and relate us to our community in very comprehensive ways. "For Gandhi every man was born and grew up in a specific community with its own distinct ways of life and thought evolved over a long period of time. The community was not a mere collection of institutions and practices but an ordered and well-knit whole informed by a specific spirit and ethos".[45]

Swadesh refers to the unity of two terms, *swa* meaning one's own and *desh* meaning the local society of which we are a part. *Desh* in many ways refers to a territorial-cum-civilizational unit with its own memories, histories, aspirations, and uniqueness. Swadeshi thus symbolizes "the way an individual related and responded to his *desh*".[46] Besides the territorial identity, swadeshi invokes sharing and sustaining a way of life and articulates a conspicuous moral, economic, and political narrative. The moral corresponds to a neighbourhood ethos; economics corresponds to encouraging self-subsistence; and the political refers to local leadership. In effect "swadeshi means reliance on our own strength.... 'Our strength' means the strength of our body, our mind and our soul".[47] Further it necessitates an active abjuring of indifference and insensitivity to the limitation of fellow locals while encouraging an abiding clarity which distinguishes self-interest from selfishness. "The swadeshi spirit sanctioned legitimate self-interest but not selfishness".[48] The spirit of swadeshi flows in harmony with swaraj and swadharma. The subtle nuance of swadeshi can be found located in the way people are able to relate their traditions with emerging aspirations and design alternatives exclusively intended for themselves. The nub of this is the instinctive understanding between members of a community who not only enjoy familiar daily contacts but share sincere expectations. Perhaps it is this appreciation about the potential of swadeshi which encouraged Gandhi to devote his attention exclusively to India although his message had an international import. After all, "Our capacity for service is limited by our knowledge of the world in which we live".[49] For Gandhi all social relationships emanate from the local and are foregrounded on service.

What swadeshi stands for is clearly spelt out in the 'New Constitution of the satyagraha Ashram' written in 1928 although Gandhi had been using the concept previously. "Man is not omnipotent. He therefore serves the world best by first serving his neighbour. This is *swadeshi*, a principle which is broken when one professes to serve those who are more remote in preference to those who are near. Observance of *swadeshi* makes for order in the world; the breach of it leads to chaos. Following this principle, one must as far as possible purchase one's requirements locally and not buy things imported from foreign lands, which can easily be manufactured in the country. There is no place for self-interest in swadeshi, which enjoins the sacrifice of oneself for the family, of the family for the village, of the village for the country, and of the country for humanity".[50] In effect, swadeshi is a social norm beneficial to all because it abjures the rapacity of profit motivated unbridled competition. It also helps us take a hard look at our needs and wants. While the local and the universal need not sustain antagonism, they certainly can encourage harmony. Thus it is both a responsibility and a necessity. "I refuse to buy from anybody anything, however nice or beautiful, if it interferes with my growth or injures those whom nature has made my first care".[51]

For Gandhi swadeshi is not just a political movement. It is essentially an ethos which includes swaraj, swa-dharma, and swa-deha. The relationship linking deha the body with desh is swadeshi dharma, a pact between the individual and society. Swadeshi recognizes the spirit of nationality but not as an ideology of nation-state nationalism. To serve elite hegemony, nationalism as an ideology with a geographic entity at its core, needs clarity and justification regarding its identity and role because in this brief, nationalism as an article of faith gets transformed into the driving ideological justification to acquire hegemonic power with the state as its vehicle. In this process, an elemental issue such as neighbourhood rather neighbourliness is deliberately ignored. Neighbour is the spatial extension of the social within us. The personal ranges over this creating communal equations and relationships. This linkage gives a constituency and a consistency to the social being that we are. But how far is the boundary of this constituency? Can it easily stretch on and on into the blurred horizon of a nation? Perhaps this is why Gandhi preferred the primacy of a cohesive neighbourhood community to that of a political nation. The cohesiveness of a community can be expressed through various core sentiments which remain unique to it because they are the products of diversity, priority, access, commonality, history, and ecology. Simply put, while a neighbourhood-community exudes organic social processes, a nation nurtures political structures.

All this however, does not mean that the political is irrelevant or inconsequential. For Gandhi the significance of swadeshi is in the way it relates to self-rule, independence, and satyagraha, all concepts alive with political overtones. For satyagraha, "swadeshi in every sense is necessary".[52] Given this it is necessary to be clear about the distinctions Gandhi sought between political nationalism and the swadeshi-swaraj connotation. Gandhi seeks a marked distinction in the usage of swaraj and swarajya[53] in which swarajya stands for home-rule and swaraj is self-rule; *Rajya* is country or realm while *Raj* suggests 'to reign', 'to rule over'. "The idea of reigning in the sense to 'rule ourselves' is basic to Gandhi's idea of swaraj".[54] For Gandhi, "it is swaraj when we learn to rule ourselves". Moreover the aspiration of home-rule is very definitely political in its connotation. But, self-rule foregrounds the larger range or spectrum of individual human practices. If swaraj as Gandhi visualized has to be 'experienced by each one for himself', then obviously it has to be rooted in the entirety of the milieu so that it is recognized by people of all sections. Moreover, it is in this need for credibility that we find Gandhi insisting that to be viable, all interventions towards social transformation must have a local flavour with clearly discernible economic parameter. Khadi and the Charkha were his preferences.

Basically self-rule and home-rule draw attention to the need for harmony between the personal and the social. Swadeshi, by encouraging and nurturing the symbiosis between the individual and the local, furthers self-rule while being agreeable to home-rule. This harmony of the individual and the local, which swadeshi helps nurture, can in turn spread into neighbouring communities via what Gandhi called 'oceanic circles'. For Gandhi, "it is through swadeshi that we shall get swaraj".[55] It can be argued that in swadeshi Gandhi was seeking some sort of dynamic conservatism, which while not rejecting change and the new, remains wary of the consequences of individual- and economic-centric initiatives on the less endowed in society. Access and appropriation of resources in a community needs transparency and should be receptive to local opinion. For Gandhi, swadeshi helps in such local community-level interrogation. To illustrate he takes the case of Hinduism as a local religion: "Hinduism has become a conservative religion and therefore a mighty force because of the *swadeshi* spirit underlying it. . . . By reason of *swadeshi* spirit, a Hindu refuses to change his religion not necessarily because he considers it to be the best, but because he knows that he can complement it by introducing reforms".[56] One can argue that Gandhi while stressing about the resilience of Hinduism chooses to be generous. In a way it is the same with swadeshi too. Swadeshi also needs its practitioners to be accommodative. The homogeneity of the spirit of a community remains a disputatious issue! It is this disputatiousness which could both restrict the import of swadeshi while contradictorily encouraging internal adjustments and reorganization.

Swadeshi suggests non-possessive appropriation, a seemingly contradiction in terms. The alert individual pursues work. But although the individual is sustained by the work, it is not for him to crave for the fruits. Critical recognition of the distinctness of sustenance and craving, needs and wants, are what non-possession enjoins. The appropriation is to assert a right and duty to work; non-possession stops at the steps of exclusivity. Such being the nature of the local it can complement demands for change by introducing non-appropriating alternatives. And since "swadeshi means reliance on our strength",[57] it encourages sustainable choices. Therefore at the core of swadeshi is the benign potential of the local. It is the capacity to be at peace. It debunks the flattery of development as also the need to have to live up with the political expectations of a nation or a world or global-village. Above all, as a consequence of swadeshi orientation, pride in the local acts against self-pity and the exhausting arguments of universal standardization used by development discourse. Swadeshi seeks to highlight all aspects of the local reality while avoiding any prejudice. This recognition of reality or satya is a way to encourage people's involvement. It is a call to seek your own path. This does not mean shunning the beaten path or prospecting a new path. It is only a call to remember the significance of the unique you and therefore the import of self-realization. Swadeshi does not permit the personal within us to avoid the social, nor does it encourage the social to intimidate the personal. This logic holds for the community in its eternal search of freedom to be able to express; the community has to be sensitive to every individual's legitimate claims to belong and perform to the best of their abilities. Although social change and continuity is a given for any community, it is not a matrix of the inevitable. Swadeshi is a notion which is wary of falling into the trap of feeling undeveloped and therefore having to accept new societal goals. It is wary because these goals are set by the pervasive conception of modern nation and by those who claim to be developed. In change centric debates of growth, evolution, and maturity, while we are allowed our discourse of 'what we don't want', the discourse of 'what we want' draws its meaning, contribution, and sustenance from somewhere else. Swadeshi cautions us about ubiquitous systems such as the market and is equally illuminating about the role of experts who sell experiences and dreams ostensibly to structure for us 'what we need'.

Swadeshi essentially is the flourishing and enduring of diversity of natural and social life. Gandhi while stressing the notion of ethics over economics was perhaps warning about the tendency of economics to subsume every other form of human practice, be it political, cultural, or environmental. Swadeshi would not permit the individual to be reduced to a hapless parody, groaning under the weight of tradition, bereft of wisdom and requiring mediation to lighten the burden. As we have seen, Gandhi perhaps was warry of the manipulability of notions such as scarcity, inefficiency, the lure of free markets and non-transparent intervention by powerful forces of hegemony. Swadeshi suggests a focus on care and of traditional wisdom against that of cure by opaque mechanistic systems. Swadeshi seeks to make clusters of 'commons' it's abiding threshold. These commons are neighbourhoods which allow inhabitants to live on their own terms, where the social context is not hijacked under the notion of nation or universalism. Perhaps swadeshi re-establishes the need to be careful and avoid dis-embedding concepts from their contexts of order and meaning.

For Gandhi the import of swadeshi is not so much about the form and certainly not about chauvinism. It is the spirit of nurture which is his concern and Gandhi sees this in the community's economic life, its religious predispositions, and the vibrancy of its neighbourhood connectivity. For him, swadeshi is that spirit in us which restricts us to the use and service of our immediate surroundings. Gandhi explains, "Thus, as for religion, in order to satisfy the requirements of the definition, I must restrict myself to my ancestral religion. That is, the use of my immediate religious surrounding. If I find it defective, I should serve it by purging it of its defects. In the domain of politics, I should make use of the indigenous institutions and serve them by curing them of their proved defects. In that of economics I should use only things that are produced by my immediate neighbours and serve those industries by making them efficient and complete where they might be found wanting. It is suggested that such swadeshi, if reduced to practice, will lead to the millennium".[58] Gandhi as we have seen preferred the individual to systems.

For the individual, swadeshi is a yajna, a service, and also an eternal abiding duty. It is resilient and its spirit evolves to meet the demands of the age and the place. Although aware of the drawbacks of religion where a Hindu would 'rather die of thirst than drink water from a Mohammedan household', for Gandhi, swadeshi is a "religious discipline to be undergone in utter disregard of the physical discomfort it may cause to individuals".[59] This is because for Gandhi, "swadeshi is the only doctrine consistent with the law of humility and love". Perhaps, sometimes Gandhi forgets the *satyarthi* and talks exclusively to the *satyagrahi*. However, overall he insists that while swadeshi builds on proximity, it demands discretion, because only then can it become both inclusive and exclusive. However, he does warn, "even swadeshi, like any other good thing, can be ridden to death if it is made a fetish".[60] Therein lays the lure of swadeshi: discretion and non-fetishism. After all, "swadeshi is the law of laws enjoined by the present age".[61]

Swaraj

The '*swa*' in swaraj includes both the personal and the social of the individual. However, in swaraj while the social is the guest turned host, the personal is the one who came home, rather the ostensible prodigal who never left. *Hind Swaraj* is a dialogue between the guest turned host and the prodigal who stayed back. It is not just a critique which as an agenda is also a document; it has an intention backed by a civilization. But then can intentions dictate instruments of agreement? While they might rely on empathy to be recognized for what they are, intentions can never be the last word. Intentions are like arrows which can only indicate direction. It is for the seeker to follow through, walk the path, and act. In the *Hind Swaraj* the traveler, intentions, and the path form a tripartite seeking an alliance. *Hind Swaraj* itself is the pointer to the ontology of a possible civilizational destiny with a rather difficult prognosis. But then an ideal principle and its manifest reality can render consequences sterile. In *Hind Swaraj* Gandhi was trying to invoke his own civilizational self, beginning with the claim that consequences cannot be sterile.

July 1909 to lobby for the rights of Indians in Transvaal, Gandhi travelled to England from South Africa. When he landed on 10 July he found the expat Indian community in a high state of excitement. On 1 July, Madanlal Dhingra, an engineering student, had assassinated Sir Curzon Willie a senior army officer and civil servant in imperial service. Dhingra as a patriot had sought vengeance for his countrymen. As a part of his programme Gandhi met highly placed Indians, British liberals, and many others along with ideologically influential Indians such as Shyamaji Krishnavarma and Vinayak Damodar Savarkar. It was during this period that he got further acquainted with the writings of Count Leo Tolstoy with whom he was profoundly impressed and soon got into a serious mutually rewarding exchange of ideas which Gandhi cherished throughout his life.

This was also a period when his popularity in South Africa, England, and India was growing. While his biography by Rev. Joseph Doke was published, Henry Polak, his *satyagrahi* collaborator, was campaigning in India about his satyagraha struggles in South Africa stressing on the extraordinary personality of Gandhi as a leader. However, as far as his main purpose of being in England was concerned he made no headway. While the imperial bureaucracy stone walled him, General Smuts just refused to accept that Asiatics should be placed in position of equality with Europeans. Such were the types of issues engaging Gandhi when he wrote the *Hind Swaraj*.

However, the most significant event during his visit was his interaction with the expat Indian community and his discussions regarding violence as a means of struggle for overthrowing colonial rule. Gandhi the *satyagrahi* was recognizing that to be fundamentally contributive and meaningful he had to return to India. Not only did he draw his essential inspiration from India, his discourse had to reach out to Indians in India to acquire appropriate significance and impact. His discussions with the extremists brought out in stark reality the twin issues of impatient and violence. He ran into what these days might be called a reality check. He was particularly taken aback at the hostility between the moderates and the extremists within the Indian community regarding the strategies and tactics the Indian national regeneration and the independence narrative should adopt. While he was for consciously designing and articulating a narrative of Indian independence aspiration, he was totally against violence as an integral element of this storyline. For him no violent event should be allowed to mar and mark the regeneration and independence initiatives. While he accepted the reality of the subjugation of large sections of the Indian masses as a consequence of colonial hegemony, he untiringly refused to accept that physical elimination of the colonizers and re-appropriation of the nation-state space would solve the problem of exploitation. The brown sahib he reasoned could and would be as bad as the white original. For him it was a question of philosophy, policy, and practice where the term *native* would neither be an asset or a pejorative.

Gandhi wrote *Hind Swaraj* while returning from England to South Africa on board SS *Kildonan Castle*, between 13 and 22 November, 1909. The book is a product of intense cognitive and passionate churning and perhaps tapascharya, a term Gandhi would have preferred. Working continuously he wrote the book over ten days at a stretch. His involvement was so intense that when his right hand tired, he continued writing with his left hand. The text spread over 20 chapters, was scripted in Gujarati, and was formatted as a conversation between an editor and a reader. The context is Hind while the content explicates swaraj. The narrative is in many ways Gandhi's vocalization of a call to which he responded. In later years he would talk of the 'small voice' which not only clarifies but proposes a response. This call essentially is a moment of submission and surrender to the inner self and he responded because, as he claimed, he could not help himself.

Hind Swaraj was for Gandhi a release from 'restraint'. Perhaps Gandhi was seeking to harmonize experience and expectations wherein aspiration as hope is a step beyond the scope of being vented through measly learned skills. In the foreword he writes, "I have written because I could not restrain myself. I have read much, I have pondered much, during the stay, for four months in London of the Indian Transvaal deputation. I discussed things with as many of my countrymen as I could. I met, too, as many Englishmen as it was possible for me to meet. I consider it my duty now to place before the readers of *Indian Opinion* the conclusions, which appear to me to be final".[62] Through *Hind Swaraj* Gandhi was asserting the primacy of duty over rights. Therefore he is able to assert, "These views are mine, and yet not mine. They are mine because I hope to act according to them. They are almost a part of my being. But, yet, they are not mine, because I lay no claim to originality".[63] Besides he concludes with a three-fold assertion, "The only motive is to serve my country, to find out the truth, and to follow it".[64] He was thus ushering in the rights of the social within himself, a social which was always chasing an ideal. However, the onus and nuances of intensity and restraint are not exactly the same for the personal and the social. This is exemplified in the shift in distinctions between the Gujarati version and the English translation and comes out clearly for instance in his preference for the term civilization as translation of *sudharo* or for choosing passive resistance instead of satyagraha. Gandhi's thrust however is to neither nurse grievances or to ignore the source of such grievances. In the end we find him concluding, "What we want to do should be done, not because we object to the English or that we want to retaliate, but because it is our duty to do so".[65] Truth is in the action as duty. Interestingly he also translates *daya-bal* as love-force while *daya* literally refers to compassion. Perhaps love is a certitude that resides somewhere between compassion and humility, each unencumbered by certitudes? But then there are other not so subtle issues regarding texts and translations. These pertain to some fundamental questions. Why did Gandhi write the *Hind Swaraj*? For whom was it intended? Why in Gujarati? Why unlike the Gujarati version was he circumspect about publishing the English version in the *Indian Opinion*? Was it just pandering to pragmatism? Is *Hind Swaraj* some kind of political theology?

As an interlocutor each of these queries finds resonance in his sense of purpose and perhaps also in his tentativeness. In electing to write in Gujarati, Gandhi sought expediency in the most intimate, familiar and was least resistive to chart the most unfamiliar and foreign. In a way this is indicative of his conviction of the need to balance the known and the unknown of the personal and the social. Perhaps initially the choice of language was as unpremeditated as the reason to write the *Hind Swaraj*; "I have written because I could not restrain myself". But by the time he had to decide about publishing the English version, the social asserted its opinion. While he wanted to be true to his convictions, as an individual interlocutor he could not take others for granted. The reasoning was clear, albeit a bit polemical. "*Indian Opinion* represents the Transvaal Passive Resistance struggle and generally ventilates the grievances of British Indians in South Africa. It was, therefore, thought desirable not to publish through a representative organ, views which are held by me personally and which may even be considered dangerous or disloyal".[66] Gandhi did not allow himself the liberty to confuse his vision and mission, stressing that these need not be or even appear to be the same for all. Although he was relatively clear as to why he wrote, "The only motive is to serve my country, to find out the truth, and to follow it",[67] it took some time for him to assert this.

The title of the book consequently had an eventful journey reflecting and unfolding Gandhi's expectations. In 1909 it was titled *Hind Swarajya* which by 1914 became *Hind Swaraj*; in 1919 it appeared under the title 'Indian Home Rule'. By 1921 Gandhi's journal *Young India* confirmed the title as '*Hind Swaraj* or *Indian Home Rule*'. The shift from swarajya to swaraj and Home Rule brought the individual's personal on par with the social political; the term swarajya had tilted the focus to favour the collective. Moreover the term swaraj had already become a part of the Indian political narrative. Bal Gangadhar Tilak had invoked it and in 1906 Dadabhai Naoroji declared swaraj as the objective of the Indian National Movement. Interestingly while the authorities given their proclivities proscribed the book, stalwarts such as Gokhale and later even Nehru were not particularly impressed by the book. This absence of enthusiasm is noteworthy. Gandhi in *Hind Swaraj* was seeking to separate the significance of intervention and involvement from the narrow dictates of political success. As a *satyagrahi* he recognized the inevitability of the perpetual sequence of change and continuity of the social milieu. Within the larger discernment of civilization *Hind Swaraj* does a critical appraisal of the sequence as envisaged by the notions of tradition, modernization, and development. Gandhi preferred '*sudharo*' to denote civilization. But, "Unlike the word 'civilization' the word '*sudharo*' in Gandhi's usage is not directly anchored in the idea of a 'civitas' as the center of order and upholder of virtue".[68] Gandhi was appropriating a potential role for choice. For him, social transition is not just a pre-determined concatenation of chance and necessity. In *Hind Swaraj* this element of choice is facilitated by the notions of eternal, contemplation, and innocence: the eternal provides, contemplation sustains, while innocence puts forth the original. Choice escorts chance and necessity to mediate change and continuity in social transformation.

Disturbed by the conspicuous acceptance of violence by the extremists and the obdurate polemics between them and the moderates, in the *Hind Swaraj* Gandhi sought to put forth his opinions about the larger universe of social concerns of which gaining independence is just a chapter. This was his contemplative dialogue where philosophy, policy, and practice of social structuring, transition, and transformation were distinguished and analyzed as expressions of civilization as reform. Within the parameters of change, continuity, chance, and necessity, Gandhi's concern was with choice as catalyst. While for the individual this choice aids in a maturing of personality, for society it means expounding and refinement of civilization.

Gandhi wrote from the heart, but the heart has no time to pause. For a writer it is a non-stop continuum from memory to moment and back again. Gandhi remained non-partial to both; continuity as memory and change as moment had to be in concord. This harmony accompanied by conscious choice comes with corresponding responsibilities because conscious choice is a deliberate act of intervention. Perhaps Gandhi was being a trifle diffident when he says, "I don't know why '*Hind Swaraj* has been seized in India".[69] It was seized because it connected a world view to economic and political policy and the nature of social practices which connected the rulers and the ruled. It also helped people make sense of hitherto disjointed information floating in the milieu to try and put together a mission. Nothing could be more scurrilous to an imperialist. A text which 'reads', 'ponders', and 'dialogues' can be the seed bearing a far reaching narrative. Further when he says, "These views are mine, and yet not mine. They are mine because I hope to act according to them. They are almost a part of my being. But, yet, they are not mine, because I lay no claim to originality",[70] his intentions are clear, never mind the clarification.

The chapters of the *Hind Swaraj* can be bunched into three clusters:

Cluster I includes Ch. 1: The Congress and its Officials; Ch. 16: Brute Force; Ch. 18: Education; Ch. 19: Machinery and refers to practice i.e. what or ground norms of on-going political, economic, social, and cultural processes.

Cluster II includes Ch. 2: The Partition of Bengal; Ch. 9: The Condition of India (cont.): Railways; Ch 10: The Condition of India (cont.): The Hindus and the Mahomedans; Ch. 11: The Condition of India (cont.): Lawyers; Ch 12: The Condition of India (cont.): Doctors and refers to intentions i.e. the how of the colonial mission.

Cluster III includes Ch.3: Discontent and Unrest; Ch.4: What is Swaraj?; Ch.5: The Condition of England; Ch.6: Civilization; Ch.7: Why was India Lost?; Ch.8: The Condition of India; Ch.13: What is True Civilization?; Ch.14: How can India become Free?; Ch.15: Italy and India; Ch.17: Passive Resistance and refers to philosophy and the larger vision incorporating the why of the imperial project and design.

The three cluster each focus on information, knowledge, and wisdom respectively. The information in Cluster I is comprehended as knowledge in Cluster II, and the wisdom in Cluster III brings in the self and helps it to relate to the knowledge availed in Cluster II. In the conclusion Gandhi suggests how a *satyagrahi* should relate with intervention urges, both as a generic issue and as per the Indian specificity. The term '*chutkaro*' or release, deliverance, and escape is very illustrative of this.[71] When Gandhi insists that "I do not think of a third party" he is emphatically stressing on how to negotiate from knowledge to wisdom. *Hind Swaraj* is an epistemic offering of a *satyagrahi* which while interrogating the benefits of the colonial system, seeks to offer a more meaningful sustainable civilizational system in oneness with the local. Above all, the *Hind Swaraj* is a dialogue between a *satyagrahi* and a *satyarthi*.

Hind Swaraj: a reading

A *satyagrahi* considers work i.e. involvement, participation, occupation, or profession as service, both to self and to society. Gandhi conflates the self and society and thereby dissociates work from the obligations of personal returns. But this process remains problematical because the distinctness of the individual and what it signifies in terms of self-interest includes benevolence. Gandhi tries to circumvent this potential contradiction at least conceptually through a conscious acceptance of the non-possessiveness of ahimsa which for him is an integral qualification of service. He further suggests that since in satyagraha there can be no 'other', doing good to another is doing good to oneself. Thus the apparent one-way compassion while serving an 'other' becomes a two-way bond of love. In service Gandhi anticipates mutuality, an empathy which encompasses the personal and the social coexistence of the individual. As such for Gandhi the individual, *Hind Swaraj* had to be written irrespective of what the British government did to it. "To do otherwise would be for me to be a traitor to truth, to India, and to the Empire to which I own allegiance. My notion of loyalty does not involve acceptance of current rule or government irrespective of its righteousness or otherwise".[72] As far as he is concerned his loyalty is for the "ancient civilization of India".[73]

Implicit within the narrative of the *Hind Swaraj* is an overarching sense of simplicity and innocence where innocence is the actual take off point; metaphorically the darkness underneath the lamp is the springboard of illumination all around. Gandhi begins from this spot to either perish in the flame or walk forth assured of the lamp's illumination. "The seed is not always seen. It works underneath the ground, is itself destroyed, and the tree which rises above the ground is alone seen".[74] The seed falls, stays under the soil, under the snow, drought, or rain, only to sprout with all the inner consistency and promise of the mother plant; yet not a single leaf of the thousands that the daughter brings forth would be the same as each other or with those of the mother. While retaining the spirit and the form of the old, the daughter although distinct, hails the old as the new. This is the awesomeness of innocence which Gandhi seeks to summon.

In the foreword Gandhi acknowledges, "I have written because I could not restrain myself. I have read much, I have pondered much, during the stay, for four months in London of the Transvaal Indian deputation. I discussed things with as many of my countrymen as I could. I met, too, as many Englishmen as it was possible for me to meet. I consider it my duty now to place before the readers of *Indian Opinion* the conclusions, which appear to me to be final".[75] This indicates three distinct issues: a compulsion, an insistence or obsession, and a transition. For him, "The only motive is to serve my country (*inalienability of compulsion*), to find out the truth (*an obsession and a pledge*), and to follow it *(the transition)*".[76] The *satyagrahi* had truly arrived. He further clarifies these in Chapter I. Accepting that there indeed is an urge for National Independence or Home Rule which refers to both individual and collective self-rule and self-governance, Gandhi elaborates on how to acquire these rights, a process which cannot be impatiently rushed. The stress is on 'impatience'; the seed represents the tree but this tree needs to sprout and grow! As such, "the people's will has to be expressed; certain sentiments will need to be fostered, and defects will have to be brought to light".[77] But, for these the involved participants will have to understand the popular feelings, give expression to it, arouse desirable sentiments amongst people, be fearless in the endeavour and expose popular defects. Above all, the process has to be grounded in our own pasts. Stressing the enabling nature of history in our transition, Gandhi cautions, "It is a mark of wisdom not to kick against the very step from which we have risen higher. The removal of a step from a staircase brings down the whole of it".[78] Further he argues that in social transition there can be no shortcuts spurred on by impatience. This is a possibility with which perhaps an individual could indulge and get away, but society as a whole cannot. In a more practical way Gandhi elaborates three very pertinent cautionary issues. The first is that, "I can never subscribe to the statement that all Englishmen are bad".[79] For a *satyagrahi* committed to satya and ahimsa, blanket hatred is a sinkhole. This hatred of a particular 'other' has the potential of transforming into a hatred of all 'others', a perfect prescription for self-centeredness. Secondly, Gandhi concedes that trust has to be created and acquired. For him the fact that the Reader in his text is "suspicious is not a matter of anxiety".[80] However, getting rid of this anxiety has to be a social praxis. Thirdly he accepts that while the congress has the political potential, it is for the people to seize the opportunity. And this is possible only through ensuring community level ethical and moral values along with a commitment to stick to such values.

Instead of getting stuck with what comes first, fear or violence, Gandhi probes the more generic notion of fear, its origin, usage, and prevalence as agency. Essentially fear aids and abets our wants and end and thereby fashions a 'desired end' to justify itself. Therefore the moot question is the generic 'what do we want?' This actually refers to the fundamental problematic of intention and motives. To paraphrase these in the context of colonialism the question is, 'do we want the same things which the British wanted while colonializing India?'[81] Obviously we do not. From this follows the question: can we follow the means adopted by the British to obtain a desired end? Once again obviously we cannot. This contrast therefore necessitates a paradigm shift in our understanding of means and ends and wants and needs. *Hind Swaraj* seeks to clarify this paradigm shift by bringing a third binary rights and duties to make acquisition and processes of acquiring a sustainable non-antagonistic process. Obviously we will have to address the fundamental problematic of intentions and motives; the exploited too harbor motives. Therefore, it is necessary to understand the threshold pertaining to the relationship between the oppressor and the oppressed in the unfolding of motives. For Gandhi, the way forward lies in questioning the intentions behind social responses during events. He is particularly concerned about the oppressed becoming co-partners in the motive which sustains oppressive systems. No oppressor can sustain oppression if the oppressed refuse to play the game. The question therefore is to understand what blurs the threshold between the oppressed and the oppressor.

This is a complex phenomenon and requires a proper appreciation of the mutuality of the oppressed and the oppressor. To seek clarity Gandhi analyzes the case of education and machinery. In 1905 the Maharaja of Baroda initiated bold and imaginative measures for the spread of modern education and literacy. Gandhi writes, "Maharaja Saheb and the other greats who lead us, are striving towards education for all, their motive is pure".[82] After all the "ordinary meaning of education is knowledge of letters".[83] But the question is 'what will a peasant do with knowledge of letters'? Further such education gives him access to information which the education he acquires might not make him competent to analyze. While this logic does appear to be instrumentalist and a dismissal of the potential of people, Gandhi nevertheless did have a very valid dilemma for which he needed an answer.

The problem as the *Hind Swaraj* sees it is in the controlling of the senses and the nurturing and maturing of the human mind. Concern of education should be about what it does to a learner at a given moment of time and how transparent this process is to the learner. He feels skills by themselves can be self-defeating for an individual although they could have some relevance to society. This dichotomy has to be recognized and the linkage between knowing, known, and the knower has to be explicit. Modern education splits them into separate entities and handles them separately. While knowledge of letters is useful, it should not become a fetish.[84] This is where motives or intentions come in. Gandhi elaborates, "Reforms, retrogression, progress would happen in the natural course; but one effort is required, and that is to drive out Western civilization. All else will follow".[85] Thus for him education has to articulate the making of Indian civilization the import of which is the Indian. It has to stop becoming an instrument of so-called modernization and development, a parody of the west.

In Chapter 19, Gandhi makes a similar argument regarding machinery. Like education machinery too separates man from his occupation as also from the products of his occupation. The intention of technology-machinery and industrialization is the creation of wealth and leisure. It is this preoccupation which not only destroys nature the source of all resources and life itself, but also progressively improvises large sections of society by utterly warping notions of needs and wants. Rather candidly he observes, "We will have to admit that moneyed men support British rule; their interest is bound up with its stability. Money renders a man helpless".[86] The problem is not in the creation of wealth for society. The evil lies in the urgency to accumulate and appropriate it as fast as possible.

Cluster II probes and evaluates the deceptive nature of the modernization paradigm and its surrogate, the market system. Social practices to bear fruit have to articulate through self-serving policies. In these five chapters, Gandhi elaborates on how colonial policies serve only the masters, but given their inherent contradictions, they also aid in awareness rising thus encouraging people to become critical about such policies. One such policy, the partition of Bengal shook the British Empire. The swadeshi movement and the ensuing events led to conspicuous and critical political awareness. Not only the British but even the Indian National Congress was forced to respond to the peoples demands which went way beyond their hitherto polite and hopeful petitioning. "After the Partition, people saw that petitions must be backed up by force, and that they must be capable of suffering. This new spirit must be considered to be the chief result of Partition".[87]

But resolving emerging conflicts can result in other contradictions. Gandhi describes this possible upshot; "The Partition has not only made a rift in the English ship, but has made in ours also. . . . Our leaders are divided into two parties: the moderates and the extremists".[88] These factions distrusted each other and mocked each other. Whether it is the colonial masters or the home grown elite, both sought to convert the people into images of their making. And while the elite are not a single or even a relatively composite group like the colonial powers, they are equally a product of self-interest and contradictory aspirations. As for the people, Gandhi humbly salutes them for their growing self-confidence vis-à-vis both the British masters and the local elite. However, it was this call to evaluate and re-dedicate along with a sweeping civilizational analysis which led to the proscription of the book and Gandhi's initial reluctance to publish the English version in the Indian Opinion. Apparently resolving of conflicts and contradictions are not necessarily of the same order.

While partition was a state policy initiative and the people responded against this through the call for swadeshi, the Indian elite were nurturing a split personality. The all-out ingress and consolidation of the market system and its hegemonic structures, the creeping authority of market-oriented professionalism, and the dogmatic influence of cognitive religious practices were systematically marginalizing large sections of the people while providing the elite with enormous opportunities of self-aggrandisement. In Chapters 9, 10, 11, and 12, Gandhi elaborates how and why this was happening. He specifically analyzes the role of railways, lawyers, and doctors and the schism between the Hindus and Mohammedans. Gandhi marshals his critique around three coordinates: self-sufficiency, self-help, and self- realization. He finds all of them warped, flawed and leading to the mercies of non-accountable progressively alienating systems such as markets, consumerism, and modernization, and so on. He therefore concludes, "Railways, lawyers and doctors have impoverished the country, so much so that, if we do not wake up in time we shall be besieged from all sides".[89] His concern was about how 'civilisation de-civilises' via creeping consumerism and how it creates an ethos which fudges the distinction between wants and needs. The individual is not left with any discretion and choice regarding necessity and inclination, both are usurped by norms set by the system. He explains, "The holy places of India have become unholy. Formerly, people went to these places with very great difficulty. Generally, therefore, only the real devotees visited such places";[90] even religion it seems serves consumerism. Arguing that the railways did not unite us, he writes, "We were one nation before they came to India.

One thought inspired us. Our mode of life was the same".[91] The railways and the markets changed our mode of life and by making our wants and needs dependent on them; 'they divided us'. It is the lure of mobility which is behind all this. Gandhi's reasons are inclusive. Firstly, "I should, however, like to add that man is so made by nature as to require him to restrict his movements as far as his hands and feet will take him". Secondly, "God gifted man with intellect that he might know his Maker. Man used it to forget his maker. According to the limits set by nature I can only serve my immediate neighbours, but, in my conceit, I pretend to have discovered that I must with my body serve every individual in the universe."[92] And he concludes, "In making this attempt, man comes in contact with different natures, different religions, and is unable to bear that burden".[93] In other words, man is responsible for creating his difficulties. However, Gandhi is rather laboured regarding how to handle this legacy of History and burgeoning desires. While the need to make intentions explicit is understandable, the competence to do so is another matter. To use his analogy, when for instance will the clay pot be baked enough to make it unbreakable? It is the nature of the social milieu to change and thereby ensure entropy to sustain itself and avoid stagnation. The issue is about creating trust and confidence so that intentions aren't malignant. This is what Gandhi hopes when as cited above he says, "God gifted man with intellect that he might know his maker." The essential problem behind Hindu Mohammedan strife is because the social ego dwarfs the personal and the transactional is obliged to play second fiddle to the ostensibly transcendental. People forget that restrain and discretion are essential to freedom and self-realization. Above all, the problem is the notion of history or rather what the emerging hegemony insists is history. Moreover history cannot be reproduced because society is never the same; we can only learn from history and ensure that it is not fabricated. This is only possible through assimilation. There is nothing like inborn enmity. It is a post-factum mischief. While one must accept that there can be no tabula rasa in terms of social memory, the point is to accept this with equanimity and grace. And if one is honest one finds that all religions can offer meaningful solutions. When we don't know what we genuinely want and when we are not confident of our own selves, we end up allowing others to make decisions for us. And of course, we suffer the consequences. Ahimsa, himsa, and protection are essentially secular manifests of the art of living. This works as much for the human beings as for the cow. Obviously this means being clear as to who will decide about what is 'living' and its privileges. Will it be the personal or the social? The dilemma is that both can be self-serving and narcissistic.

Gandhi is even more scathing about lawyers and doctors. "My firm opinion is that the lawyers have enslaved India, and they have accentuated the Hindu-Mahomedan dissensions, and have confirmed English authority".[94] While he agrees that many lawyers are good human beings, the problem is with the profession itself and the nature of its engagement. A lawyer has a trade only when there is animosity, quarrel, and enmity. Removing these would mean eliminating the lawyers' profession. Gandhi states the paradox clearly, "The parties alone know who is right. We, in our simplicity and ignorance, imagine that a stranger, by taking our money, gives us justice".[95] Actuating this is our refusal to become self-reliant as individuals and as social beings. The same situation avails in our dependence on doctors. We fall sick because we indulge. The Doctor solves the problem, and we go home and indulge all over again. Over time, we become dependent on medicines and such other doctor-initiated cures. We destroy our capacity to take care of ourselves and thereby we emasculate ourselves. Like an addict we become slaves of the doctor-ordained medical system.

Lastly, the *Hind Swaraj* through ten chapters (3, 4, 5, 6, 7, 8, 13, 14, 15, and 17) seeks to draw attention to a larger vision, that of the why of the prevailing imperial hegemonic system. Through a dialogue with this system Gandhi narrates a vision of his own. With Hind as the context and swaraj as the content, Gandhi sketches a world view wherein swaraj is projected as a civilizational ethos. Swaraj in many ways is an ideological dialogue within the self, wherein the personal distinguishes and separates habit, habitat, and habitation while the social remains concerned with their linkage, which is with the lifestyle. In *Hind Swaraj*, Gandhi seeks to stand aside, disagree, and also resist the hegemon. It kind of becomes a dialogical narrative because it not only opens the narrative to the subordinated, but also unsettles authority. By distinguishing the obvious from the truth Gandhi tries to distinguish a manoeuvre from a position. For instance, while analyzing education or the construction of railway systems, Gandhi draws attention to both the reasons behind the original event and its later interpretive construction. Further, he is able to indicate the significance of evolving memory of these events, particularly in the way we relate to such memories. Gandhi is particularly concerned about re-dressing old social structures and processes in a new garb with unknown intentionalities. For him the crucial narrative is that of how the shared practices of the colonizer and the colonized are structuring our 'being'. In the process the *Hind Swaraj* helps us ask fundamental questions. What is the impact of imperialism on our historical memories? How does this past constitute and impact our present identities? By resorting to some essentialist national identity will we be going back to some imagined past? Will such selective and imagined reconstruction further confuse our reading of the present, particularly that of power and subjection?

The narrative of *Hind Swaraj* begins with recognition of emerging unrest and the inevitable demise of the prevailing social order. However Gandhi clarifies, "Unrest is in reality discontent. . . . This discontent is a very useful thing".[96] Unrest aids reform, but it comes with a human cost; it can lead to death, imprisonment, banishment, and so on. In discontent and the unrest, Gandhi finds that the promise of social potentialities is unlocked because society at such occasions is at a crossroad and has to choose its direction and path. He implicitly accepts that we cannot procrastinate. If we do so the discontent will consume us. The unrest is the pause; it is for us to choose the next note. The choice of creating a genuine Hindustan or a caricature '*English-sthan*' will depend on how we understand swaraj and the difficulties that practicing it entails. Severely criticizing the parliamentary system of England, Gandhi urges a critical and creative understanding of civilizational systems, particularly those of so-called modern civilization and its claim of meaningful change and limitless progress.

This is where Gandhi's dialogue format stands out and gives better insight to the problematic of applying the notion of civilization to periods of transition. Thus for him the issue is, 'are we at a cross-road leading to a frontier through uncharted paths, or do we have the choice of walking a well paved road which has already been traversed by others'? The issue is not just an either/or choice and it cannot be bunched into one overarching concept such as modernization. Gandhi puts it succinctly, "It is not due to any peculiar fault of the English, but the condition is due to their – rather Europe's – modern civilisation. This civilisation de-civilises".[97] In *Hind Swaraj,* Gandhi is wary of the promise of modern civilization. For him, unravelling human potential is not in the giving of any one idea or individual. *Hind Swaraj* is not seeking to be a pioneer or follow some exclusive proven path. Gandhi prefers a healthy blend of continuity and change based on local histories and genius. "Unlike the word 'civilisation', the word '*sudharo*', in Gandhi's usage is not directly anchored to the idea of a 'civitas' as the centre of order and upholder of virtue".[98] Clarifying he urges, "Let us first consider what state of things is described by the word 'civilisation'. Its true identity lies in the fact that people seek to find in engagement with the material world and bodily comfort true meaning and human worth".[99] Perhaps this is where the claim and paucity of civilization lies?

Over all, Gandhi rejects modern civilization, damning it as being consumerist, irresponsible, irreligious, and above all immoral. For him, it is unsustainable and beset with internal contradictions. For him given time it will self-destruct. Therefore, the issue is one of course correction. Civilization is not an incurable disease, although it can be an undesirable condition. You cannot scrub the colour off your skin. Even the British have to be cured of this malady. Therefore Gandhi while enjoining caution begins by taking stock of the conditions prevailing in India, particularly regarding how she became enslaved both physically and mentally. For him we need to be clear about a few issues. "The English have not taken India; we have given it to them. They are not in India because of their strength, but because we keep them".[100] This is because our avariciousness attracted us to their ways and world views and we wanted to become rich as fast as possible. The princes and other elite fought among themselves, and while we did not trust each other, we did prefer to trust the Company Bahadur, an unscrupulous immoral corporation well 'versed alike in commerce and war'. The English came for the purposes of trade and making money. Only when this possibility is denied them is it possible to shake them off. Unlike the Englishmen, Indians lacked clarity of purpose. But while all this is apparent, Gandhi is cautious regarding sweeping generalizations. "It is my deliberate opinion that India is being ground down not under the English heel but under that of modern civilisation".[101] For him the only way to understand true civilization is by shunning materialism and acquiring a truly religious world view. This obviously means a creative harmony between the personal and the social, and a re-evaluation of the notion of civilization itself.

Gandhi however does not stop exploring for virtues. He clarifies "Civilization is that mode of conduct which points out to man the path of duty. Performance of duty means observance of morality. To observe morality is to attain mastery over our mind and our passions. So doing, we know ourselves".[102] While he agrees that short comings have persisted despite civilization, "we may utilize the new spirit that is born in us for purging ourselves of these evils".[103] The inspiration should be one of elevating the moral within us. However, such ethical concerns and hopes are not enough. Removal of the cause of the disease is the task for which one has to delve within oneself. "To believe that what has not occurred in history will not occur at all signifies inferiority".[104] The hatred of the English should actually shift to a rejection of their civilization. Thus a belief in oneself, a proper understanding of one's own civilization, shunning of crash materialism and acquiring a religious world view should in Gandhi's opinion help India become truly free. But this is not just a question of freeing oneself from the colonial yoke. Drawing parallels from Italy and Mazzini's efforts, Gandhi concludes that removal of troops will not necessarily improve the conditions of the people in terms of swaraj. The issue should be one of acquiring self-rule in the sense of welfare of all. Recourse to arms is involving in a war of attrition; such a war never really ends and always causes enormous damage to the co-laterals, people, and society.

While the *Hind Swaraj* does contain a lot of dos and don'ts, it also suggests alternatives. Gandhi suggests that instead of being preoccupied with differences, conflicts, violence, and antagonism, and so on, perhaps we should focus on the equally prevalent cooperation, love, compromise, and compassion. Our explanation and validation of history and events prefers to begin with an analysis of conflicts and confrontations. This is because of our pre-disposition to attribute causes of problems to 'others'. This fundamental is what Gandhi subjects to cross-examination. Resistance for him begins with systematically placing the self and the other as coparcener and partners in all social interventions. And the way forward is satyagraha-*atmabal*, or satyagraha as soul-force. It is not clear why Gandhi prefers to translate satyagraha as passive resistance in the English version although he had already changed to the more nuanced satyagraha by 1908 particularly when he is arguing in terms of what he defines as satyagraha. After all, *Hind Swaraj* is the call of the social as the inner voice!

Very broadly, the *Hind Swaraj* lays down the contours of a prospective equity-based social discourse by individuals within a social formation. The discourse aspires to ensure autonomy for the individual in the social edifice. As such, Gandhi explicitly articulates the composite role of an interlocutor. In a way this is a composite civilizational dialogue where civilization is a network of cogent distinct entities. While the content seeks to articulate the socio-political role of an interlocutor grounded on an elaboration of the local political economy, it is not a 'Memorandum of Understanding', just discernment. This distinction remains with Gandhi in terms of his relationship with all institutions such as the family, ashram, or the congress party. Lastly implicit in the *Hind Swaraj* is the question 'why should I help others'? As such it can become an initiation theme for a social worker, volunteer or a *satyagrahi*.

Social service

For Gandhi social service is serving our fellow beings, "in order that we may see a glimpse of God through them; because they have got the same spirit as we have, and unless we learn that, there is a barrier drawn between God and ourselves; if we want to demolish that barrier, the beginning is made by complete identification with our fellow beings". Social service is what helps us understand and recognize our level of incompetence and thereby helps push the bar. While separately the terms social and service stand for a configuration and an ethos, together they represent a structured process between provider and beneficiary. It is this structured process of involvement which aids in liberating us from the arduous constraints and contingencies of day to day personal survival.

But this two-way process between provider and beneficiary is not a deal exchange or reciprocation. For Gandhi, "Action is my domain, and what I understand, according to my lights, to be my duty, and what comes my way, I do. All my action is actuated by the spirit of service".[105] Providence, competence, a sense of commitment and an inner urge, all seem to be behind his desire to not just serve but also use the process to probe and find a meaning for his own 'being'. Gandhi however also argued that the renunciation involved in selfless serving is to give up the possessiveness of the individual so as to acquire *moksha*. For him spiritual freedom and longing for *moksha* was an all absorbing goal encompassing everything. This obviously requires self-control and renunciation; "service of humanity alone could generate the disinterested self-control essential for spiritual emancipation".[106] Freedom he felt lies in A*nasakti*, selfless service. But this is not easily obtained. Gandhi explains, "I am an humble aspirant for perfection. I know my way to it also. But knowing the way is not reaching its end".[107] The path is exacting, one of action and of service to humanity. The nub of Gandhi's world view, the social context of which revolves around swadeshi, sarvodaya, swaraj, and construction programme is his commitment to social service or *Anasakti*. While accepting the social processes of transition and transformation, he refuses to be hustled on to some highway of modernization and development. For him social transformation has to be through processes of conscious intervention and involvement. This brings up the characterization of Gandhi as being an intrepid itinerant social worker.

For Gandhi the urge for freedom and moksha is generic to human beings and is engrained in our selves. The import of this is that since the urge for freedom is contemporary and in conjunction with society, the ultimate of freedom which is *moksha*, too, has to be a contemporary discourse. Consequently the grammar of the discourse of *moksha* has to be service to others. "Through the selfless embodiment of ahimsa and satyagraha, Gandhi believed theophilanthropists (*friends of God and man*) could ameliorate human misery whilst freeing themselves from worldly hopes and fear. Freedom, he felt, lies in *anasakti*, selfless service".[108]

Social service for Gandhi is to come to terms with the distinct notions of 'love' and 'compassion'. You love to give and to take. Love is never one way. When it is one way it is infatuation. Compassion on the other hand is a one-way process of giving without expectations. As such when Gandhi uses the term love-force, he is suggesting that all such relationships are two-way.

In South Africa, Gandhi was able to illustrate and indicate the legitimacy of satyagraha as a potent tool of non-violent resistance and an enabling practice for the attainment of swaraj. He emphasised a couple of very insightful qualities. Firstly, satyagraha is not a question of transitory win or loss. It is an all-encompassing mission and always a march forward. As such it is an ongoing succession of awareness building events. However its essential import is in how it encourages local involvement and participation because it cannot be a transplant sustained by non-local initiatives. Further, to be genuinely awareness building, such participation has to ensure that they are associative-evolutionary in nature and not coercive or mediatory. Secondly it has to become free from dependency particularly from that of mediation by any individual or even group of leader/s. Andrews had pointed out this problematic to Gandhi when he was in South Africa.

Satyagraha to be sustainable and faithful to self-realization has to acquire a local narrative independent of the individual intervention or agency of individual *satyagrahis*. But contradictorily it has to be initiated and sustained by individuals. The *satyagrahi* has to march to a more outreaching inclusive call of which their involvement in satyagraha is the beginning. This is what can be characterized as the 'dichotomy of the threshold'; the inside has to be sustained while the outside has to be investigated. While the outside is not external and ignorable for the social in an individual, it is not the same for the personal in the same individual. Similarly while the local community has to be self-sustaining, creating and sustaining its own creativity and crafts-persons, it has to be able to relate, understand, adopt, and adjust with the outside world. In all of this, the threshold, however, should not become the site of contention and skirmish. This is a crucial aspect Gandhi was probing because satya and ahimsa, the core of satyagraha, have to be inclusive and transparently so. Gandhi's discontinuing of action and even withdrawing satyagraha is a pointer to the need to be clear about the nature of action in satyagraha. The purpose of his narrative is a mutuality of the insider and the outsider. In other words, he refuses to surrender to the dichotomy of the threshold along with the notion that 'contesting the other' is vital to action mediating social transformation. Gandhi recognized the debilitating influence of the brooding challenge of contesting the other and how it impacts the *satyagrahi* and the people. Perhaps Gandhi could afford to be large hearted and liberal. Can other *satyagrahis* and particularly *satyarthis* involved in satyagraha afford to be generous? People find it extremely difficult to comprehend the intrepid and itinerant nature expected of a *satyagrahi*. In particular for them the trouble is with the itinerant nature of the leadership and the fact that while fearlessness has to be acquired through constant honing, it is not in the giving of anybody. This becomes particularly tiring when satyagraha and its minimalism considers period of continuity of a satyagraha as being flexible. When action prolongs itinerant tends to get confused with 'enforced presence' and intrepid with 'stubbornness'.

Satyagraha has a threefold thrust: intentions, intervention, and involvement. Intentions are based on information and a philosophy or world view which acts as a guiding principle. For Gandhi, the world view articulates around satya, ahimsa swaraj, and satyagraha. While Raj Kumar Shukla gave the initial information about conditions prevailing in Champaran, Gandhi meticulously collected and documented relevant evidence and information.[109] He then used this information to arrive at relevant knowledge to be able to plan his actions. This two step strategy of first gathering information and then arriving at relevant knowledge became the basis of his specific plans and intentions of resisting the planters and the government. The significance of this strategy of creating knowledge after gathering information is to ensure that plans and intentions are transparent.

Intervention on the other hand is the actual conversion of intentions into action (plans). These need clarity about policy i.e. principle or course of action proposed to be adopted. These are programmes and strategies which depend upon knowledge of the local conditions. Here knowledge is the product of analyzing information gathered. Intervention by a *satyagrahi* is accommodative in that it reaches out to everyone; there is no 'other'. Intervention in many ways is akin to a policy decision. However, it is prone to be afflicted by procrastination due to its proclivity to involve everyone.

Involvement on the other hand is the individual's actual practice or application of ideas, beliefs, and methods based again on analysis and knowledge not mere information. For the *satyagrahi* this is essentially based on wisdom or distilled knowledge. This essentially refers to a proper understanding by an individual of how the implementation of action plans impact the attitude of those involved. Essentially involvement is inclusive and as a narrative of resistance, a response to the problematic of 'what we want' and 'what we don't want'. As a matter of fact the *satyagrahi* examines, 'do we really know what we want'? Further she is also conscious of this process of seeking clarity becoming rhetoric of vested interests? We cannot forget that even after 100 years, the issues of ownership of land, access to education, health, drinking water, sanitation, and communal harmony remain as they did when Gandhi went to Champaran to initiate satyagraha!

Involvement begins with acknowledging the mutuality and the support that one can provide another not in exchange for what the other can or has done but as a response to the over-all nurture one receives as a package of being. It presupposes a vision and mission for an individual and for society, and it also suggests alternatives in accordance with which one could transform society. In Gandhian Parlance, this vision as well as mission of involvement is sarvodaya. Therefore involvement cannot be a sporadic reaction to a situation. It needs preparation and has to be pragmatic and realistic. The preparation indicates choice while pragmatism indicates chance. Thus while on the one hand it is resistance to untruth, it nevertheless has to be a constructive effort which should be need-based and not interest- or wants-based. Thus, involvement as sarvodaya takes satyagraha, swaraj, and swadeshi as its practice. Involvement in many ways is a *Sadhana*, the means of accomplishing self-knowledge. And as one grows in self-knowledge, it becomes a spontaneous and natural expression of one's own self, i.e. of self-relization. Involvement therefore is an engagement with four cardinals: mediating the relationship between the personal, the family, and the social; the question of social transformation and the role of the state; the role of non-state forums in social transformation; the means and ends conundrum. A reading of swadeshi, swaraj, sarvodaya, ahimsa, and satyagraha in terms of their process orientation helps us come to grips with all these issues of involvement. To illustrate, why for instance is there an element of apprehension even coercion in the relationship between the individual, the family, and society? It is because the relationship is hardly transparent often burdened with hidden agendas. On the other hand, the role of the state is clear; it is coercive.

This in turn means moving from the moral to the more pragmatic issue of participation and conscious intervention which presupposes motives and intentions. Conscious intervention seeks social participation along certain lines. The problem is with selecting the best approach because some argument (and every argument will have some takers) can negate at least some aspects of any and every orientation and world view. The only thing that cannot be negated is one's own self. Not surprisingly since leadership is a crucial element in intervention, Gandhi focused on the individual and not on some vanguard, elite, or proletariat, not even on an exemplar. Participation therefore is action-based i.e. bound by the specifics of time, space, and expectations. Participation during the freedom movement had resistance at its core. Accordingly participation has to be inclusive and a process of construction and confrontation, methods amply demonstrated by Gandhi. For him participation and resistance is not a response to some 'we-they' syndrome.

Gandhian thought gives primacy to action. And action is to be chosen on the basis of its being desirable. The problem is in defining 'desirable'. One way is to describe it at three levels; the first is how inclusive is it in terms of involvement; the second refers to the comprehensiveness of the action in terms of taking into account all factors implicit and explicit that constitute the action; and the third refers to how it measures up to the issue of consequences and thereby truth. Above all, the worth of an action should be judged by the goodness of the consequent state of affair. Since all social actions are mediated events which end up as consequences and over a period give scope for further actions, a veritable action event consequence continuum unfolds. Desirable actions are those which establish goodness in the milieu which they influenced and are contingent upon. Social intervention can thus become satyagraha with goodness at the core. *Satyagrahis* don't solve problems they enable people to seize the occasion. Every action has to be a narrative by and of the people. While the *satyagrahis* as interlocutors do write the prologue, the epilogue remains dialogical and a narrative of and by the people. The involvement of the *satyagrahi* is necessary but never sufficient. They can only create the competence to seek adequate justice. But acquiring justice has to be an act of tyaag both by the *satyagrahi* and the people; this entails a conscious giving up of something to acquire something else which necessitates a paradigm shift for both. For the *satyagrahi* in terms of social intervention this corresponds to the issue of the professional and the volunteer. It also raises the vital question of the relationship between competence and expectation which generally is one of tense symbiosis; while they coexist, they don't depend on similarity of context for their origination and signification. The volunteer looks at these as contingent to aid intervention and participation while the professional looks at them as qualifications in a bargaining engagement. It is generally understood that credibility of a person depends upon a harmonious blend of the two.

Competence is common to both the professional as well as the volunteer. Purity of motive is never enough. The enigma is in the expectations. A volunteer involves in an activity because she wants to. The professional on the other hand has a wide spectrum of expectations and is more accommodative as far as project selection and involvement is concerned. A volunteer involves because of her commitment to the activity. This does not mean that she would like to pauperize herself in the process. Her commitment is towards a task that calls for creating a vibrant community. Self-satiations and self-realization emerges from the involvement leading to a consolidation of her social-centric commitment. On the other hand for a professional, involvement is a means to 'acquire access' which then delivers tangible self-satiation. The professional is fully involved takes pride in his job. But the job and self-actualization remains distinct leading to personal-centric commitment.

Thus the professional's skills and competences are available for hire by anybody while the volunteer's are not. The volunteer is always bothered about the consequence while the professional need not. While a professional is a mercenary, a volunteer will remain critical and selective. Further since the volunteer remains concerned about consequences, her capacity to use experience to judge outcomes keeps enhancing, changing, and sharpening. A synergy emerges between her work and the worksite, and she develops an organic link with the labouring community. This is crucial for a person aspiring to influence social transformation and interventional activities. By making herself personally a part of the process of change, her relationship goes beyond exchange to that of harmonious give and take. Consequently while expectations and returns go beyond the narrow domain of exchange value, resilience matures beyond the strictly personal to include the social as a necessity.

Thus the volunteer tries to remain committed to the holistic impact of actions. She tries to be inclusive in her approach, avoids expediency, and meticulously abstains from moral justifications for promoting her self-interest. Moreover when there is a conflict of interest in terms of the impact of a strategy on the community, the volunteer while enjoining caution, will take a personal stand regarding commitment. The professional on the other hand will prefer to remain neutral and preferably abstain from taking value-based social positions which might necessitate going beyond the requirements of the profession. For Gandhi the norm is clear, "unrestricted individualism is the law of the beast of the Jungle ... willing submission to the social restraint for the sake of the well – being of the whole society enriches both the individual and the society of which one is a member".[110]

Lastly the volunteer tries to cultivate detachment, i.e. she makes a sombre appreciation of the link between contribution and returns for the self as distinct from the impact of the intervention on the community. Some of the above might sound very demanding and idealistic, but for a social worker and particularly a Gandhian, the issue is to recognize these and internalize them with '*shradha*' and '*nistha*', that is, with respect and a sense of responsibility. The individual in the process of becoming a professional begins by acquiring a skill; mastering the skill gives the individual a profession. This profession soon becomes an adjunct of the individual. For the professional this adjunct then tends to become the medium and the inspiration which creates a world view for the individual via professionalism. Very soon this world view mediates the professional's search for meanings. The adjunct starts dominating and takes over the narrative of social involvement on behalf of the individual. The volunteer on the contrary tries to recognize these insidious characteristics of the adjunct. The volunteer tries to distinguish the essential from the incidental in terms of what Gandhi would recognize as truth from the contingent so that something that is added to another thing but not essentially a part of it doesn't end up becoming the driving force. For the volunteer the profession remains just a skill, albeit crucial. It is another matter that a volunteer by making social work a profession can create in social work an adjunct and end up like the professional, a slave to the adjunct; in the process, they can misuse the high status that society attributes to the social worker. Few are able to handle the strenuous obligations of being a *yogi, saint,* or *mahatma*! For Gandhi when consciousness is prefixed to work/service it becomes social work/social service. Such a social worker is no more an ordinary *pracharak*.

Travails of a world view

Prospecting a world view is a difficult discourse. As an interface between hope and conviction, doubt always plays a mischievous role. Doubt assumes a category of profoundness because only time can tell about its impact. But then to wait and do nothing is denied us. However we do want to decide about 'what we want as alternatives to live a better life'. We know that society is crawling with consequences of events which have tried to fuse hope and conviction. We also know that to understand this progeny of our creativity and action we need both hindsight and foresight. Further the pressure only increases when circumstances allow very little time for us to contemplate and respond. While history will follow, the problem is how to respond in the immediate present. Gandhi's swaraj, swadeshi, sarvodaya, and constructive programme via social work help us respond to the demand of the immediate present. He helps at two levels: firstly at the level of the individual's preoccupation with the personal and the social, and secondly at the level of the interface between the moment and history. Regarding this Gandhi begins with the known immediate given society. Since for him there is no 'Other' he focuses on the neighbour, neighbourhood, and neighbourliness. He encourages us to go beyond and preferably try and transcend the restrictions of the threshold which creates an 'other'. This call for sociability and socialness is a call to be creative critical and inclusive. In economic terms it means a sharp shift from exchange and surplus orientation to satisfaction of sustainable needs. In political terms it means transparency in intervention and involvement practices. And in cognitive terms it means imbibing and applying the dharma of self-service and self-realization foregrounded on ahimsa and satya. Above all, it excludes longing, particularly of specific mentifact such as beliefs, values, ideas, etc.

Future always seeks solace in memory. While the moment tries to choose from alternatives to articulate itself, memory encroaches with suggestions regarding the right choice. But the moment is distinct from memory. Memory actually is dead recall. Moment while articulating itself has no memory of itself because it is ceaselessly in the creation mode with no interlude for memory. Since the moment cannot afford to have a memory of its own, under the tutelage of the prevailing hegemony, it tends to adopt an annotation or justification of memory. Further through such elucidation the moment can either be creative, or mystify memory to suit its ambitions, thereby manoeuvring participants in an event. For instance a past can be dissected to separate content from context wherein a leader is debunked as a stooge. Again, when people fall in love the moment pervades; it is only when marriage is contemplated that we find memory coming in with religion, etc. Moment as bearer of memory in unfolding of events tends to encourage anthropomorphism. At times even Gandhi faltered. The curbing of a river which Gandhi uses as illustration in his articles on 'sarvodaya' is illustrative of this.[111] Gandhi argues, "But the flow of wealth, like the course of a river, can be regulated. Most of the rivers run out their courses unregulated, their marshy banks poisoning the wind. If dams are built across the rivers to direct the water flow as required, they will irrigate the soil and keep the atmosphere pure".[112] This regulating comes as a double-edged sword which can cleave both ways and on either side. Should it cleave on the side of surplus or scarcity, labour or leisure, wants or needs? Sarvodaya comes with its clutch of problems. This includes, for instance, the problem of hegemony of the local, consensus, conservation, reification, and of course that of development and concern about the future. The last is particularly pertinent because under the garb of concern for others, euphemistically termed as 'serving others', concern often allows service to transform into authority and then power. The preacher-server soon progresses into a leader and then into 'the leader'. Soon his discourse becomes one of heads I win tails you lose, wherein the social as defined by the leader becomes the over-riding paradigm as also the measure of all intervention and involvement in processes of social transformation. Soon all relationship between nature, labour, and product; those between the personal and the social; and those between scarcity and abundance, labour and leisure, self-help, and sharing are all evaluated against ambiguous performance criteria whose definition remains the exclusive preserve of the leader. Perhaps this is why Gandhi chooses to remain an intrepid itinerant social worker, always incisively interrogating claims, be they economic, political, or socio-cultural. He remained constantly vigilant and cautious about the delusion of freedom and choice, particularly when made under ambiguous definitions of development, faith, involvement, and leisure. For him freedom and choice had to correspond effortlessly with the often conflicting notions of wants and needs, ends and means, rights and duties, and give and take. While analyzing necessity and compulsion, Gandhi would urge caution because compulsions emerge as crisis and remain susceptible to manipulation. Perhaps this is why for him sarvodaya is not *antodaya*. A*ntodaya* as service has this inclination of becoming leader sensitive. Gandhi sought to separate the action from the potential selfishness inherent in the endeavour.

Accordingly swadeshi for Gandhi was not just a question of consuming or not consuming Indian products. It was more an idea of recovering the idea of India as local, sans the parochialism of region, religion, or nation. The 20th-century Indian milieu for all practical purpose was a moth-eaten frayed brittle social formation albeit with a resilient core. Split at many levels it was certainly seeking cohesiveness and a vigorous identity. Taking his que from earlier thinkers, Gandhi sought to find such an idea through a bold combination of ambition or motivation and empathy or responsiveness. Swadeshi was one such strategy. By inserting the qualities of conscious thinking, being, and purpose, Gandhi converted swadeshi into a conviction regarding the local which while eschewing antagonism towards any country avoided chauvinism. Swadeshi by denouncing the prevailing order and renouncing any association with that, which is unacceptable to the local, is an announcement of praxis of rural-mindedness and sociability of the neighbourhood. This in many ways was also a strategy to help the local re-appropriate its body, soul, and uniqueness. Similarly, *Hind Swaraj* was not to appropriate a house that the British built.

For Gandhi, swadeshi was not a question of the efficacy of the quality of proximity within a social milieu, nor was it an issue of egoism or altruism. It was a question of a sustainable cohesiveness which did not depend on external forces for its actuality. Given the trauma of colonial rule the moot question was one of necessity, choice, and acts of determinism which influence the local milieu. Thus, "when you demand swaraj, you do not want swaraj for yourself alone but for your neighbour too"[113] is how Gandhi understood. Swadeshi by questioning the hegemony of the overarching market system designed by the imperial power, sought to address not just some of the splits in the polity but also inculcate an element of patriotism to reclaim a sense of identity for the people. While encouraging certain restrictions it did not deny any necessity. Its stress was on discretion while choosing. Encouraging entitlement and endowment, swadeshi "was not the universality of the use of an article which goes under the name of swadeshi but the universality of participation in the production or manufacturing of such articles".[114] Swadeshi thus embodies service as self-help and self-realization.

Notes

1 *An Autobiography* (2004, 275).
2 *MPWMG*, Vol. I (104).
3 *An Autobiography* (2004, 127).
4 Tridip (2012, 11).
5 Parel (2007, 118).
6 *MPWMG*, Vol. I (109).
7 Ibid. (110).
8 Ibid. (116).
9 Ibid. (117).
10 *CWMG*, Vol. 50 (215).
11 Ibid., Vol. 37 (265); Vol. 13 (94); Vol. 48 (415) quoted in Dasgupta (1996, 36).

12 Dasgupta (1996, 39).
13 *CWMG*, Vol. 8 (316–460).
14 Diwan and Lutz (1985, 11–12).
15 Parel (2007, 74).
16 Ibid. (72–76).
17 *CWMG*, Vol. 8 (316).
18 Ibid. (317).
19 Ibid.
20 Ibid. (318).
21 Ibid.
22 Ibid.
23 Ibid.
24 Ibid. (319).
25 Ibid. (336).
26 Ibid.
27 Ibid. (348).
28 Ibid. (360).
29 Ibid.
30 Ibid. (361).
31 Ibid.
32 Ibid. (368). Italics added.
33 Ibid.
34 Ibid. (369).
35 Ibid. (384).
36 Ibid. (419).
37 Ibid.
38 Ibid. (420).
39 Ibid. (456).
40 Ibid. (457).
41 Ibid. (421).
42 Ibid. (457).
43 Nandy (1992, 135).
44 Sarukkai (2016, 1731–32).
45 Parekh (1991, 56).
46 Ibid. (57); *Young India* (Apr. 30, 1931).
47 *MGTEW* (2008, 258).
48 Parekh (1991, 59).
49 *Harijan* (Aug. 22, 1936).
50 *Young India* (Jun. 14, 1928); *MGTEW* (2008, 116).
51 *Young India* (Mar. 12, 1925).
52 Parel (2009, 116).
53 Suhrud (2012, 22–23); Parel (2009, Introduction).
54 Suhrud (2012, 23).
55 *MGTEW* (2008, 264).
56 *MPWMG*, Vol. III (1987, 327).
57 *MGTEW* (2008, 258).
58 *MPWMG*, Vol. III (1987, 326–27).
59 Ibid. (331).
60 Gandhi (1957, 66).
61 Mukherjee (1993, 76).
62 Sharma and Suhrud (2010, 9).
63 Ibid.
64 Ibid. (10).
65 Ibid. (98).

66 Ibid. (7).
67 Ibid. (10).
68 Ibid. (29); Suhrud (2012, 25).
69 Sharma and Suhrud (2010, 6).
70 Ibid. (9).
71 Ibid. (92).
72 Ibid. (6).
73 Ibid.
74 Ibid. (17).
75 Ibid. (9).
76 Ibid. (10). Italics added.
77 Ibid. (11–12).
78 Ibid. (13).
79 Ibid. (15).
80 Ibid.
81 Ibid. (66).
82 Ibid. (82).
83 Ibid.
84 Ibid. (84).
85 Ibid. (87).
86 Ibid. (89).
87 Ibid. (18).
88 Ibid. (19).
89 Ibid. (40).
90 Ibid. (41).
91 Ibid. (42).
92 Ibid. (44).
93 Ibid.
94 Ibid. (50).
95 Ibid. (52).
96 Ibid. (21).
97 Ibid. (29).
98 Ibid. (*fn.* 25, 29).
99 Ibid. (30).
100 Ibid. (34).
101 Ibid. (37).
102 Ibid. (56).
103 Ibid. (58).
104 Ibid. (60).
105 *MPWMG*, Vol. I (1986, 4).
106 *Harijan* (Mar. 3, 1946).
107 *MPWMG*, Vol. I (1986, 4).
108 Ibid. (17).
109 *Harijan* (Mar. 2, 1946); also see Pouchepadass, J. (1999).
110 *CWMG*, Vol. 69 (258).
111 Ibid., Vol. 8 (419).
112 Ibid.
113 *Harijan* (Mar. 1, 1935); *CWMG*, Vol. 60 (254).
114 *Young India* (Jun. 17, 1926).

8

GANDHI IS GONE, BUT GANDHIAN THOUGHT REMAINS

Hadh chale so maanwa, behadh chale so saadh;
hadh behadh dou taje, ta kar mati agadh

– *Kabir*

[Within limits walks the ordinary man, the spiritual man walks in
areas beyond limits;
But he who discards (restrictions of) limits and
no-limits, unfathomable is his intellect.]

Itinerant, intrepid social worker

In relation to social transformation and transition, while Gandhi was deeply conscious of the significance of vision, his mission was left to the demands of his quest for truth and the temporal transactional promptings of satyagraha. He had no enemies to decimate but lots of ideas to disseminate. For him the old folksy seeing, seer, seen sequence meant that while God sees everything, including us mortals, mortals too see everything, including God so as to be able to revere him; only in the case of us mortals it remains deemed, i.e. considered or imagined seen. Seeing thus takes centre stage with the deemed referring to the fact that all of us see differently because all are not equally blessed. Gandhi reduces this rather esoteric sequence to a more manageable doer, doing, and done continuum. The doing in this being transactional comes with mundane accountabilities which the transcendental seeing could avoid. Since doing is action, for Gandhi the sequence of doer, doing, and done is the structuring of satya. Further, with doing being human, onus is not difficult to attribute. Gandhi then adds another qualification. While religion is the spiritual articulation of a free society, swaraj is its secular credential. While swaraj is not to be misunderstood as swarajya, religion and swaraj between them makes the heuristic universal. The issue then becomes one of a relation between amity and the ideal. For Gandhi love and discipline are not incongruous. As such, the constraints of amity provide the basis for ahimsa without which no genuine love is possible; the problematic lies in the emotional content of related issues such as detachment, routine, and service. While detachment means harbouring no pre or post involvement expectations, routine refers to involving as per one's competence, and service indicates abjuring the notion of other. In the process of living very often these three tend to become tactical issues with different emphasis thereby creating tensions between them. These tensions manage to put love and discipline in oppositional roles. At the root of course is the problematic of expectations.

Recognizing that one can never transform absolutely from a *satyarthi* to a *satyagrahi*, throughout his life Gandhi strove to comprehend, examine, elaborate, and disseminate the rejuvenating significance of satyagraha. At a personal level, it meant coming to terms with the individual and the social within, and at the social level it meant recognition of the edifying binary of give and take.

Gandhi evolved from a *satyarthi* to a *satyagrahi* and then continued to mature while refining the concept of satyagraha. He continued to grapple with personal inconsistencies; but unlike others he remained transparent about them. Gandhi was a thinker-activist. This meant he did not have projects to implement; rather he had ideas to acquire and share. Both as an activist and a thinker he chose to live a certain lifestyle constantly searching for universally applicable principles so as to live unswervingly. Living for him was neither a chore nor an end in itself. Gandhi's method is *agraha*: obsessive holding firm to and insisting on means so that the ends lead to satya and ahimsa. For him it was not just a question of the goodness of his actions in terms of consequences, but also that his actions affirmed that goodness should be intrinsic to actions. Actions "arose out of his unwavering conviction that constructive thought and timely action are inseparable. If skill in action can clarify and correct thought, soul-searching deliberations can purify action".[1] For him the path is one of systemic intervention, resolving contradictions and questioning the socially engineered creation of desires. While Gandhi recognized the pivotal role of the individual, he would not allow this to degenerate into individualism. Perhaps for him individualism seeks to convert the individual into an acquisition, an investment? When he insists that poverty is the only wealth of society, perhaps by simultaneously accepting that there is no 'other', he is cautioning that the individual after all is a lonely creature and that society is fated to systematically do away with all such lonely creatures! *Artha* and *kama* can never take away loneliness. That is the task of *dharma* which exposes the immorality of the implicit notion of material satiation. Moreover dharma is practice of satya. For Gandhi this practice is social work or the shedding of loneliness by systematically eradicating the idea of the 'Other'. This overcoming of loneliness through social work is what Gandhi considers to be the sum and substance of dharma and the path to *moksha*.

Social work however has to contend with a very intricate and intimate problematic. Gandhi had to deal with this all his life. In the transition from a *satyarthi* to a *satyagrahi*, while he gained a lot of insight such as ahimsa, satya, satyagraha, the significance of the dichotomies between ends and means, rights and duties, and so on, he also had to deal with a couple of issues which remained liminal. The first is the distinctness of the personal and the social within an individual and what this engenders for the individual as a person and as a social being. Secondly accepting that for an individual the nature and quality of living is determined by the congenial mutuality of the personal and the social within, how should the individual respond to the dichotomous demands of the two? Apparently s/he does this through what we have described as give and take. This give and take occurs within the individual and with society separately and is particularly visible when the individual makes choices from amongst alternatives.

For Gandhi this give and take was never easy because while for the *satyarthi* the driving force was the personal, for the *satyagrahi* it was the social. Moreover the agency to mediate this is the family which itself is the bearer of inner tensions. Society tends to encourage the social within the individual family members through conspicuous involvement in social activities, while values such as consumerism professionalism and so on encourage personal autonomy. Moreover the family is composed of individuals of distinct generations with distinct desires. Consequently very often the individuals in the family get confused about the harmony between give and take particularly because the social remains biased towards the present, while the personal opts for the whole and the resilient. Moreover, while facing a problem the social opts for cure, while the personal opts for care. Perhaps this is because the person looks at her life as a whole while the social segregates it into past, present, and future. At the root is the fact that while the social can ignore possessiveness, the personal cannot; urge for security remains primeval.

Gandhi found himself squeezed between the personal and the social. He had to choose between the dilemma of what Kabir said: "Aap he maali, aap he bagicha, aap he kaliyan todta"; and at another level is the paradox of "aap he dandi, aap he taraaju, aap he baithe tolta". Gandhi had to negotiate the razor's edge between predicament and incongruity. The savant of Varanasi was indicating both a dilemma and a paradox: one perhaps solvable and the other while perhaps solvable at the individual level, remaining impossible to solve at the social level. Every gardener knows that if buds are trimmed and only a few retained, each flower becomes conspicuously large. And if all the buds are left to flower the relative size of the flowers is smaller. The personal would prefer to trim the buds while the social would like all of them to flower. Of course if you have a particular ideology you can select the flowers you want to trim!

To resolve this Gandhi opted to shift agency from family to ashram. The tight-knit homogenous family 'we' with its elemental linkages became a premeditated heterogeneous open 'we' of social workers. Gandhi felt that if everybody recognized the benevolence, modesty, and compassion of service it would knit the grouping into a cohesive unit without having to pander to the individualism of the family. This problematically ended up with social work becoming the agency and the social worker as an individual retaining all the pulls and pressures of the personal and the social within. While Gandhi remained convinced about the logic of his idea he nevertheless moved out of the Sabarmati Ashram. It seems social service by itself does not solve the tension between the personal and the social within an individual. Being an activity whose terrain is society, and which is biased towards a cure to solve issues, it is soon hijacked by institutions maned by professionals/cadre/*karyakarta*. The social worker soon forgets that s/he can never be the judge, jury and prosecutor at the same time. Unfortunately very often the social worker is unable to choose between the individual-centric family and the social-work-centric ashram/party/institution. The institution permits her to dodge the personal. But this also means it keeps the person-oriented *satyarthis* whom s/he should help become *satyagrahis* at a distance. Unlike the flower obsessed bee, she cannot ignore the buds or the garden. In other words a social worker cannot sidestep the fundamental import of the family 'we' if she has to be receptive to the society 'we/us'.

An Assassination and a martyr

On 30 January 1948, an assassin's act became an event, a moment which created a martyr and an assassin. Creatures of convictions and circumstances, both martyrs and assasins are products of ideologies and mentors. However, when they make contact, i.e. when the actual act of assassination occurs, the ideology and the mentor of the protagonist might or might not be conspicuous at all. The protagonists of the act of assassination might have left their erstwhile mentors to hone their convictions perhaps by other means and wait for an opportune time to strike. Assassination is an act of personal choice and humility, beyond fasts, renunciation, and prayers. While its origination and objectives are social and ideological, its accomplishment and execution is utterly personal. Paradoxically while this split is absolute, it sustains an inclusivity wherein the mentor and the ideology continue to draw insights from the progeny, the martyr and the assassin. As to the act, it seeks to erase itself only to emerge first as memory and then as history. No one claims the act because it is prodigal. However the martyr claims followers while the assassin will encourage enthusiasts. The real benefactors will be the mentors and ideologies which nurture the proclivity which leads to such acts when apparently right is wrong and the wrong is right. On the face of it, assassination might seem to be an aberration from which one may not generalize. But its repeated occurrence in history denies us the luxury of avoiding this naked exposition of contorted lust for power. The two-fold problematic between the assassin and the mentors and ideologies is in understanding a peculiar invisible aspect of assassination: its perception of social impediments and the latent coveted privileges which encourage the assassin and amity and ideal demand re-assessment which the act is incapable of.

Gandhi himself had witnessed such a moment when he went to England in 1909 when Madan lal Dhingra sought martyrdom. *Hind Swaraj* was his reflection of that perhaps nihilistic moment. And history tells us that while Dhingra sought martyrdom, Gandhi himself became a martyr. Some might consider this seeking and being made an academic privilege. But for the practitioners of power politics and aspiring ideologies it provides space for manoeuvring and positioning, a situation which can be used as and when necessary. Even today in both the above mentioned cases it is not easy to identify the source of the inspiration behind the act. While riots are an old phenomenon of deliberate social blood-letting, mob-lynching generally wished away as acts by fringe elements is somewhere in between assassination and riots. This so called mob event occurs when apparently a spontaneous mob takes law into its own hand and as per its understanding delivers immediate justice which normally is death. Actually there is no mob. This alleged mob is never a fringe; it is composed of an assorted group of persons with shared ideology and mentors. Such amorphous groups always have elements primed to act. While this eclectic group is part of an on-going social narrative, the particular lynching might not be a pre-planned act. But even here while the event might seem to be unprompted and impulsive the assassin/s (individual or group) and the martyr/s (individual or group) have an ideology and mentors. By calling this event an act of a mob is to deny the existing, albeit for the time being, indiscernible inspirations and aspirations of the perpetrators and their mentors. Mob-lynching is an act by the increasingly utterly lonely social within us. The Indian social formation has still to come to terms with this phenomenon.

A discussion and a seminar

1947, the country had just passed through a traumatic partition with all the savagery communal passions can unleash. But society cannot wait. It has to go on; social transition and transformation cannot be blocked. Further, for this transition and transformation to be meaningful, society has to encourage criticism, dissent, and creative experimentation for which it has to be sensitive, unrestricted, and democratic. While the past cannot be ignored, effort has to focus on the present and the future. In effect the transition has to put the individual and institutions on the same page, sharing similar if not the same 'spirit' of aspiration. The congress party took over the state from the departing British. This meant it acquired authority over parliament and bureaucracy and by itself constituted a cabinet to mentor, monitor, and mobilize the necessary processes of change and continuity, not to mention that it had considerable influence over the constituent assembly which was mandated to scribe the Indian Constitution. In effect the congress party could build a swaraj. This meant it now had to be clear about what it wanted, not just what it did not want. To the solemnity was added Gandhi's fond hopes. "My ideal village still exists only in my imagination. After all, every human being lives in the world of his own imagination. In this village of my dreams the villager will not be dull – he will be all awareness. He will not live like an animal in filth and darkness. Men and women will live in freedom, prepared to face the whole world. . . . Nobody will be allowed to be idle or to wallow in luxury. Everybody will have to do body labour".[2] Behind this seemingly essentialist and simplistic representation lay a world view and a critique of unbridled competition, industrialization, consumerism, leisure, and of course the potential tension between the emergent hegemonic Indian state and local communities. "I will not want my house to be walled in all sides and windows to be stuffed"[3] is how he expressed his expectations. But, while the task was certainly difficult, as was his wont he remained pragmatic. "Civilization in which possession of a car will be considered no merit"; but at the same time "being a highly practical man I do not avoid railway travelling or motoring for the mere sake of looking foolishly consistent".[4] For Gandhi the ultimate in evil is 'consistent consumerism'.

In effect Gandhi was suggesting that swaraj is not a given. As a matrix of change it remains two dimensional unless it accepts the local people as the third; juncture, concept, and people makes an operational social ensemble. Infirmities start to emerge when we begin to consider the local as contrapuntal to the general and the abstract, and its moral authority as tentative. Gandhi wanted Indian swaraj to reflect an Indian understanding of what is and what ought to be. While he was certainly against some western style modernisation, he remained down to earth and pragmatic.

A few months into independence on 11/12 December 1947, a meeting of various Gandhian organizations was convened to go into the emergent independent government's attitude towards constructive programme and to decide as to whether the constructive workers should or should not form a separate body to participate in governance for the furtherance of their objectives.[5] Gandhi was firmly against constructive workers taking part in party politics and becoming part of the government. He was also not inclined to subsume everything under the state apparatus. Aware that most of the Sanghs were creation of the congress and while not being part of the government had the potential of coming together as a bloc, Gandhi advised caution. He was not for forming a rival platform to the congress. The problem is that he was also deeply suspicious of the intellectuals who had overtaken the congress. He would have preferred to disband the congress. But then he was a practical man. Recognizing that for the intellectuals who dominated the freedom struggle, constructive programme was just a strategy, he wanted the constructive workers to take a critical but creative look at the role of the congress, congressmen, and constructive work; "constructive work is not a strategy or a technique of fighting. Constructive work connotes a way of life'.[6] This meant that people involved in such programmes should be convinced and competent about their roles. Gaining such competence was to have been a major component of his perception of Nai Talim. Sadly this critical and creative line of thinking stopped with Gandhi. Some have argued that effecting such a termination was an intention behind his assassination.

"The objective of the constructive works organization is to generate political power";[7] exercising power will have to remain with the people. For him, "we must recognize the fact that the social order of our dreams cannot come through the congress of today".[8] "Today politics has become corrupt. Anybody who goes into politics gets contaminated. Let us keep out of it altogether. Our influence will grow thereby".[9] The problem as he saw it is the lure of office and ministership. The way forward was to "Think of the root and take care of it as much as you can, and make self-purification the sole criterion. Even a handful imbued with this spirit will be able to transform the atmosphere. The people will soon perceive the change and they will not be slow to respond to it".[10] Therefore the focus needs to be on the interlocutor, more so because the various Sanghs as institutions had not been able to coordinate and work together. So the first necessary step was to cooperate before merging into a body; 'let the props and pillars unite' was his advice. This he warned was not going to be easy. "The various Sanghs had worked separately and independently of one another till now. We tried to set up a co-ordinating committee for the purpose of *samagra gram seva*, but it did not work".[11] Setting forth the agenda for the constructive workers, particularly in terms of the perils and necessity of politics, he clarified, "you must not expect to get the Constitution you desire through the congress. . . . It should be enough if the Constitution you get does not actually stand in the way of constructive effort".[12] For him the efforts of the constructive workers and works should be that of researchers and as 'instrument for the building of democracy'. With the demise of colonial rule the task for Gandhi was to build a swaraj; this necessitated being wary of state power and of choosing whom to associate and work for.

This is what a group of Gandhi's colleagues and followers had to respond to when they decided to continue with the seminar which they had organized and where Gandhi was to preside. This was to be as a follow up to the above described discussions regarding constructive works with Gandhi. Unfortunately instead of continuing with the narrative of the ongoing text, each started writing a new chapter. And they ended up creating more 'props and pillars'! Interestingly the initiative for such individual enterprise came from a free flowing seminar which was organized after the assassination of Gandhi.

Challenges of swaraj

With independence the nature of the Indian milieu changed radically. The details and the nature of the emerging discourse between the oppressor, the oppressed, and the interlocutor changed. Gandhi was assassinated and it was for the Gandhian interlocutors to continue with the aspirations of satya, swaraj, sarvodaya, satyagraha, and ahimsa. The interlocutors in a changed milieu had to define their role and aspirations. As Acharya Ramamurti was to explain much later, "it was a question of power: capturing power, generating power and exercising power"; the interlocutor's role was to generate power.[13]

Six weeks after Gandhi's assassination some of his leading followers gathered at Sevagram to comprehend a couple of crucial issues: with Bapu gone whom would they go with the questions an independent India was asking, and what were they to do? The discussions were intense and illuminating.[14] The seminar recognized that while the various constructive workers sanghs were not able to attract the youth, the youth apparently were being attracted to competing ideologies such as Marxism. Moreover in a democracy people not only wanted to have a say in the processes of social transformation, they also wanted to become clear about possible alternatives and the choice abetting practices. The Indian state, Indian in every sense of the term, was the major challenging emerging concern, particularly because it provided conspicuous access to power without ensuring commensurate commitment to responsibilities. Rights, wants, take, and ends were becoming the guiding ethos. The seminar recognized that the young 'democracy' albeit an old civilization was in a hurry and looking for easy alternatives was not averse to borrowing from the all too forthcoming west. The debate regarding tension between the call of an old civilization and the urges of fecund modernization remained inconclusive.

The seminar while being careful about its association with the state recognized that with the British gone and the state acquired, maintaining society was not a choice. The question is who would monitor and perhaps mentor this. While participatory decision making processes can be very messy, the endemic problem of poverty, exploitation, and the complex problematic of region, tribe, caste, and community remained. This can easily be further complicated by the benign claims of development and underdevelopment, minority and majority, and so on. However a simple question emerged: will democracy be the handmaiden of constructive work/workers, or will politics, regulations, and decree define constructive work? The corollary as to how should the Gandhians relate to the sate remained unclarified and open-ended. In the debate synthesis regarding mentor and participant remained inconclusive.

Subsequently other than those who wanted to associate with the state, many Gandhians went to various places all over the country and established organizations, institutions, and even initiate movements such as Sarva Seva Sangh, Gandhigram, khadigram, Bhoodan, Chipko respectively. Essentially Gandhian, each of these nevertheless had a distinct learning curve. And each of them has left or is carrying a distinct narrative. But then they were not the only interlocutors mediating the Indian transition with an exclusive dream. There were many others of different persuasion, ideology, and commitment. While the Gandhians interacted with them and tried to understand different world views, the non Gandhian organizations in turn were also influenced by Gandhian thought. Some openly sympathised while others preferred not to.

Does this mean that the Gandhians and the non-Gandhians while sharing similar objectives were not able to gainfully debate with each other? In a way, in a democracy, which is a highly cultivated option, the answer would be both yes and no. Take the case of Anna Hazare moving from Ralegan Siddhi to Delhi, the emergence of AAP and it's taking the political path, and you recognize both the import and the constraints of Gandhian praxis. This is also in the context of the fact that while not many Gandhian organizations (there are some) seemed to be actively involved with the problems of the people, Gandhian perceptions are being adopted, albeit in a more contemporary sense. It is ironical that while Gandhi was very much of a political being, post-independence Gandhians on the contrary preferred to remain apolitical. Today's followers of Gandhi however are not averse to politics while abjuring party politics. As a matter of fact, if we try to carefully go into what Gandhi wrote and practiced, we can discern what we call modern (contemporary), secular (inclusive), and democratic (autonomous). But we might not get to know much about the state. Gandhi remained sceptical about the nature, role, and impact of the state as an institution of power. Perhaps this refers to the social within us and its awkwardness with give and take? Moreover the hierarchy favouring propensity of the state constantly puts the personal and the social within an individual at cross-purposes because the state prefers the social.

Tracing some Gandhian alternatives

Gandhi's method has four distinct albeit related aspects: uniqueness, the notion of the local, self-reliance, and ahimsa.[15] While all these pertain to the ethical, their significance lies in the fact that together they indicate a distinct world view, a world view which not only gives its adherents a frame of reference for organizing their lives, but also coaxes them into becoming constantly conscious of how their exertions affect the way they live and perceive both their existence and that of those around them. Together they form the foreground of a meaningful vernacular narrative.

The first aspect is that of uniqueness. Every community is a unique expression and a binding together of the wide spectrum of factors ranging from the environmental, the ethnographic to the anthropomorphic. History leaves its solitary mark; this solitary mark, a product of environment, economics, politics, culture, and religion, retains a significant role in every community's longings. Uniqueness is a quality every community needs, aspires, and builds upon, thereby gaining an orientation and identity.

The second aspect is the perception of 'local' which can be described "as a graspable historio-geographic entity". While contours of social formation i.e. country, kingdom, nation, changed, mode of existence also evolved from tribal, mobile pastoral systems to settled village feudal systems to migrant colonial mercantile systems, and then to present rootless motile urban systems. At the human psychological level the hub kept shifting from the clan, to the family to the individual. Thrust of any intervention has to recognize this evolution because for an individual the relationship between private life and the social formation is crucial. For instance in industrial-capitalist-market-systems the hegemonic forces would prefer a rootless individual and his urban habitat, permitting easy exploitation of an alienated individual by the system. Gandhi recognized this dilemma. He was clear that industrialization as practiced by the West would create a rootless human alienated both from community and human relationships, graduating into a split personality with the personal and the social of the individual at loggerheads. Since most of India still lived in villages and the family remained crucial, Gandhi focused on the village and family as the basic elemental site to help everyone articulate an easily recognizable identity. Every social project and practice whether economic, political, cognitive, or environmental, could easily emanate from this site. Not that this site was pristine pure; it was far from it. But it allowed one to secure ones identity and thereby consciously and in a discerning fashion relate to the rest of society.

The third is self-reliance. While in uniqueness and local identity the focus remains on the social, in self-reliance Gandhi sought to bring the self on par with the social. While he has no illusions about the nature of social structures and forces, he nevertheless tries to encourage every human being to become capable of reducing dependency. This he thinks is possible if people recognize the pivotal and innovative relationship between wants and needs, rights and duties, ends and means, and give and take.

The fourth is ahimsa or *krodha-tyaag*. This is where Gandhi makes the human being paramount, where he encourages people to go beyond futile polemics, such as simultaneously trying to prioritize and reconcile the conflicting claims of social integration and self-assertion. When he spoke of trusteeship, or of not hating anybody he was trying to arouse a subconscious quality among people; this quality is the normally dormant quality of 'ahimsa', a secular manifest of the more emotional "love".

Thus while trying to eliminate caste class and sectarianism Gandhi would begin by identifying the role of the human being in the structuring of such practices. He would then prefer to change and win over the human being while eliminating the practice and the structures which upheld it. As far as the human being was concerned Gandhi preferred to give in and felt that this should be the essential sensitivity when social intervention is designed. For him the issue was to recognize one's own identity, understand the local milieu with which this identity is able to organically link, sustain it preferably through self-help, and imbue this with ahimsa as a non-negotiable ethos culminating in self-recognition. For him an individual is progressiveness incarnate.

Back to the present

Intervention and involvement we have seen entails clarity regarding purpose of agency and action. In this Gandhi stands out because whenever he initiated an intervention he placed himself squarely within it, sometimes too conspicuously. He also allowed himself the liberty of the dialectics of process, of happening and happenstance, of going forth and holding back. But above all he was clear that intervention serves interests; it is for the interlocutor to be clear about these. The urge for clarity can avoid unnecessary rhetoric, particularly about intentions. This becomes crucial when we also realize that within our unstable, volatile, and immensely discriminatory milieu, we still have to resolve fundamental issues such as who for instance is an Indian. Given that the Indian narrative of hegemony is still evolving, our institutions such as the parliament, judiciary, and so on remain cluttered. While the Indian soul seems to be soft the self is haughty, we are still struggling to distinguish the grammar, meaning, and rhetoric of tradition, history, and aspiration. Or perhaps this is a new game of an old civilization! India is certainly an old civilization; but to judiciously assimilate and use this moral and visionary heritage we need to dispassionately align with the present, a period of intensely debilitating self-doubt and enormous sycophancy. We have to be clear about what is it that we want; expediency will not help.[16]

But this will be a demanding task. At every stage of transition and transformation we will have to be able to respond to complex sets of issues. To illustrate, we have to respond firstly to the prevailing poverty of means, ideas, and resources restricting our meaningful aspirations. Secondly we have to overcome our continuing to remain wrapped in a confusing and shifting sense of morality wherein we tend to indiscriminately use power and authority thereby perverting the social milieu. We have to overcome our tendency to allow love, relationships and history to become a brooding menace by confusing form, substance and symbols. And above all we have to get over our tendency of cultivating a myopic attitude towards others particularly the West wherein our understanding and responses keep fluctuating erratically between fears of being smothered which spawns insular and parochial notions of nationalism and abject capitulation ending up with us accepting modernization as the ultimate panacea. Nation building has to be an exercise in systemic involvement in the discourse of making social choice. And perhaps, if we go by what Gandhi thought, this has to be more than the first past the post, ballot exercise.[17]

Social transformation is a process of continuity, change, and choice. To make this sustainable at the economic front it requires selecting strategies of resource mobilization, consumption, and production processes; at the political level, it means initiating participatory processes to mediate society's authority to make choices; at the cultural front, it means being sensitive to the vernacular while ensuring its universal validity. This will necessitate bringing together the compatible and the complimentary, generating a "we" feeling by stressing the participatory and the collective; helping people assert, liberate, and energize themselves; trying to convert the spontaneous and the innovative into systematic involvement; and articulating the significance of empowerment, that is, effective but non-exploitative access to structures and processes which are necessary for meaningful aspirations to be attained.

Intervention and involvement can then become meaningful as awareness events of enlightenment and emancipation. But to consolidate, exponents and supporters of such events must cognize their own transition from *satyarthi* to *satyagrahi*. Involvement and intervention must try to anticipate and mediate 'awareness events'. Giving scope to expectations, opportunities and potentials, they have to consciously articulate a world view by bringing together elements, forces, individuals, and institutions. In the Gandhian schema this is a three-fold approach. The first is creativity, integrity, and accountability, hall mark of craftsmanship. The second is to recognize the interdependence of seeming binaries such as means and ends, rights and duties, want and needs, give and take, man and machine, and so on. At the core of this understanding is the need to come to terms with binary of 'I' and 'Me'. The third is the abiding role of satya and ahimsa. In practice this means preparation, analysis and a bias towards process orientation that is learn, create, and learn to create once again.

However for this approach to consolidate it has to negotiate with the state, the so called free markets and the call of modernization presented through the plans of developmental experts. Gandhi worked simultaneously on two parallel fronts of involvement – the constructive and the confrontationist. In his scheme of things these remain distinct even in the distant future. Thus he would not speak of development or empowerment. For him the domain of the private and the universal remain distinct albeit coaxial. For Gandhi, intervention, as also social planning is a process of continuous monitoring. However, while it is a process of deliberation it is not one of conspiracy. This means being aware of a lot of things but responding selectively albeit transparently. Further monitoring our social existence means judging – judging others, judging ourselves, and judging oneself. This not only means forsaking dependency, it necessitates accountability, fearlessness, and self-reliance – a vibrant coalescence of I, me, we, us and they.

In terms of practice for Gandhi this meant concurrent involvement at two level – that of appreciation and of application. Appreciation refers to perspective and awareness building i.e. articulation of a perspective and inculcation of systemic and holistic thinking – ahimsa, satyagraha, sarvodaya, etc. Application on the other hand stresses the twin themes of co-operative endeavour and general management of social discourse – khadi, swadeshi, trusteeship, etc. In many ways these are distinct modules although there is many a grey zone. While appreciation refers to the constructive and application to the confrontationist, their message is in that they permit every individual space and choice at all levels, personal and social.

In all this the typical in Gandhi's position is that while at the personal level the constructive/ appreciation can merge with the confronting/application modules, at the social and universal levels they remain distinct. This is because mediating the harmony between the personal and the social is a constantly surfacing "expectation and consumption profile", which tends to remain distinct for the individual, the family, and society. The stress here is on the term evolving, because, the problem with evolving "expectation and consumption profile" is that it is not just a matter of individual or societal will. It is an "emergent profile" depending as much on individual will as on social initiatives and contradictions i.e. the systemic.

A contemplative dialogue

The inevitable necessity of existence sounds tautological, but it is always the point from where we start. Circumstances force our hand and we respond. The point is do we do this consciously or is it as a matter of course. Most often at this threshold of chance, choice, and response, we find ourselves pre-occupied, prone to procrastination and pre-occupied with the varied demands of the immediate. This is where Gandhi with his understanding of morality and conscience differs. He responded to chance, but chose to consciously evolve from the humdrum of the necessities of existence; from a *satyarthi* he knowingly evolved into a *satyagrahi*. We have referred to him as an intrepid itinerant mystic social worker. Sounds quaint, but then, this is what the progression of Mohan to Mahatma was. It was a long haul. Gandhi stayed in South Africa for twenty years, and it is this stay which made the essential Gandhi. Of course after his return he kept evolving, honing his ideas through contemplation and action.

What stands out is the alacrity with which Gandhi was able to seize the element of chance. But equally important is his sagacity of choice that is selecting his responses. While potential opportunities emerge, it is always the individual who chooses to respond in specific ways. The nature of the choice is what informs as to how intrepid we are, and the specificities describe the itinerant, that is our capacity to avoid fixity. And both if we notice demand consistency, commitment, and competence, qualities which have to be scrupulously acquired. Further it is during this painstaking process of acquiring consistency, commitment, and competence that we come to recognize the complex relationship between the personal and the social within us, particularly as to what comes first in this symbiotic interdependence. This can either lead to unnecessary tension between the personal and the social, or we can accept that communities don't act, people do. But we must also realize that while personal interests fade away with time and or death, social interests remain. However, it is the markers or memories which both interests leave behind which act as milestones in the transition of human 'living'. It is this living which craves the mystical, the ineffable as meaning; a meaning which for the individual is always in the present and for society always either in the past or the future.

It was this quest for memories markers and meaning which necessitated an invocation, an act of contemplation. And this is when Gandhi suggests the very mundane binary of give and take, but of course in his quaint manner with the mystical '*vaisnava jana to tene kahiye je pida parayi jane re, para dukhe upkara kare to ye mana abhimana na ane re*' [call those people godlike who feel the pain of others; help those who are in misery, but never let self-conceit enter their minds]. The mystic of Gandhi the social worker refers to the travails of the common people and their daily existential bargaining with the godlike social of their beings. Gandhi had a distinct approach to the problematic of poverty and abundances as also of labour and leisure. It was a constant dialogic of informing and being informed, of give and take. For human beings, given their capacity to think, poverty and abundance are not given, they are crafted, that is, deliberately designed and made. It is during this crafting that the personal and the social within us become engaged in a tense discourse of alienation, consumerism, service, individualism, etc. Exploring the Gita, Gandhi was able to rediscover the significance of enstasy or "experience of nothing except an unchanging, purely static oneness".[18] We wonder as to why Gandhi took the religious spiritual path? Perhaps for him it was not religion but the path of dharma which while recognizing the essentialism and consequentialism of *artha* and *kama*, encouraged the capable within us to prospect that 'next step'. But while he seems to have done it with élan, it was never an easy process. And while he did not always succeed, his resilience and wit kept him going; luckily for the *jignasu* in him, success was not a *Sarai*. He constantly searched for the qualities of internal sustainability which maintained social processes. In this he drew strength from his abiding faith in the efficacy of satya and ahimsa. However God for him is not a theory, it is an engagement. Reckoning with reason, seeking to have the last word, Gandhi put it thus, "for men like me, you have to measure them not by the moments of greatness in their lives, but by the amount of dust they have collected on their feet in the course of life's journey".

I began my quest with the problematic of our not being able to find or perhaps evading our social memories. Invoking Gandhi brought out the intrepid itinerant mystic evolving from being a *satyarthi* to becoming a *satyagrahi*. Besides, now that I can reflect, it appears the sentinel-apostle of truth has, what is more, left behind a resonance which continues to reverberate with a cadence from somewhere deep within which seems to tell that vigilance about the immediate however trivial, and hope however lonely, necessitates being alert to thought, action, and predicament. Therein perhaps reposes the memory of the Phoenix from Sabarmati.

Notes

1 Iyer (1989, 123).
2 *CWMG*, Vol. 81 (319).
3 *Young India* (Jun. 1921).
4 *Harijan* (Oct. 14, 1939).
5 *CWMG*, Vol. 98 (34–43).
6 Ibid. (35).
7 Ibid. (36).
8 Ibid. (37).
9 Ibid. (36)
10 Ibid. (38).
11 Ibid.
12 Ibid. (39).
13 Banerjee (1999).
14 Gandhi and Snell (2007).
15 Banerjee and Ghotge (2001, 17–18).
16 Ibid. (102–19).
17 Ibid. (102-19).
18 Zaehner (1968, 143).

GLOSSARY

abala weak
abadhya unrestrained
adharma amoral, unrighteous
advaita non-duality, monism
agraha insistence, obstinacy
ahimsa non-violence
anasakti selflessness, selfless action
antiyaja untouchable
aparigraha non-possession
ashram a spiritual community
asteya non-stealing
atman the universal self
avatar incarnation of divinity
bapu father
bhajan devotional hymn
bhakti devotion, faith
bhangi member of a caste associated with scavenging
brahmachari a follower of brahmacharya
brahmacharya fidelity, the first of the four stages of life
brahmin caste name
buddhi discrimination
charkha spinning wheel
chitta pure perception
dalit oppressed caste
dasanudasa slave of a slave
deva a celestial being
dharma duty, righteousness, religion as ethics

duragraha   obstinacy
grihastha   householder
gunas   attributes
harijan   literally 'child of god', the name Gandhi gave to the untouchables
hartal   boycott, cessation of work
jiva   the individual soul
jnana   wisdom
kama   pleasure
karma   moral law
karyakarta   activist
lakh   a hundred thousand
lokasamgraha   the welfare of the world
mahatma   great soul
mama   mine
mantra   a sacred incantation
maya   cosmic illusion
moksha   liberation, enlightenment, salvation
mumukshu   seeker after moksha
nirvana   emancipation from conditioned existence
patha   trail/track
praja   nation according to Hind Swaraj
prakriti   nature
prarthana   prayer
prithvi   earth
purushartha   human effort; a goal or aim of life
ramarajya   the rule of Rama
sadhana   spiritual discipline
sadhu   ascetic
samaj   an association; society
samatwa   *equality*
sanatana – dharma   eternal religion(Hindu religion)
sangha   a voluntary association
sanyasa   renunciation
sarvodaya   welfare of all
sarai   Inn
sat   ultimate reality
satya   truth
satyagraha   non-violent resistance
satyagrahi   on who offers satyagraha
satyarthi   a truthful person
shastra   Hindu scriptures
shruti   revelation (vedic texts)
shmriti   that which is remembered
shuddhi   ritual purity

shudra   menial caste
swadeshi   self-sufficiency and self-reliance
swaraj   self-rule
swarajya   one's own country
takli   spinning wheel
tapas   penance
yagna   sacrifice
yama-niyama   abstentions-observances
yoga   spiritual discipline

BIBLIOGRAPHY

Primary sources

The Collected Works of Mahatma Gandhi, (*CWMG*), 90 vols. New Delhi: Publications Division of the Government of India, Navajivan, 1958–84.
The Essential Writings of Mahatma Gandhi, (*TEWMG*). Edited by Raghavan, N. Iyer. New Delhi: Oxford University Press, 2009 (1991).
The Gospel of Selfless Action or The Gita According to Gandhi. Translated by Mahadev Desai. Ahmedabad: Navajivan, 1970.
Harijan. Ahmedabad, India, 1933–48.
M. K. Gandhi: An Autobiography or The Story of My Experiments with Truth. Translated by Mahadev Desai. Ahmedabad: Navajivan Publishing House, 2004 (1927).
Mahatma Gandhi: The Essential Writings, (*MGTEW*). Edited by Judith M. Brown. Oxford: Oxford University Press, 2008.
The Moral and Political Writings of Mahatma Gandhi, (*MPWMG*). Edited by Raghavan, N. Iyer; Vol. I. *Civilization, Politics, and Religion*. Oxford: Clarendon Press, 1986; Vol. II. *Truth and Non-Violence*. Oxford: Clarendon Press, 1986; Vol. III. *Non-violent Resistance and Social Transformation*. Oxford: Clarendon Press, 1987.
satyagraha in South Africa. Translated by V. G. Desai. Ahmedabad: Navajivan, 1928.
Young India. Ahmedabad, India, 1919–32.

Secondary sources

Ambedkar, B. R. *Annihilation of Caste*. Bombay: Kokil, 1937.
Ambedkar, B. R. *Ranade, Gandhi and Jinnah*. Jullundur: Bheem Patrika Publication, 1943.
Ananthamurthy, U. R. *Hindutva or Hind Swaraj*. India: Harper Perennial, HarperCollins publishers, 2016.
Armstrong, Karen. *A History of God*. New York: Ballantine Books, 1993.
Arnold, David. *Gandhi: Profiles in Power*. Harlow: Longman, 2001.
Aron, Raymond. *Power, Modernity and Sociology: Selected Sociological Writings*. Edited by Dominique Schnapper and new essays translated by Dr. Peter Morris. Hants, England: Edward Elgar Publishing House, 1988.

Bakshi, Rajani. *Bapu Kuti: Journeys in Rediscovery of India*. New Delhi: Penguin Books, 1998.
Bandyopadhyay, Sibaji. *Three Essays on the Mahabharata: Exercise in Literary Hermeneutics*. New Delhi: Orient BlackSwan, 2016.
Banerjee, Samir. *Bas Eak Kadam Aur*. Shimla: Indian Institute of Advanced Study, 1999.
Banerjee, Samir. *Notes from Gandhigram: Challenges to Gandhian Praxis*. New Delhi: Orient BlackSwan, 2009.
Banerjee, Samir and Sanjeev Ghotge, ed. *Contributions Towards an Agenda for India*. Shimla: Indian Institute of Advanced Study, 2001.
Banerjee, Samir and Aman Namra, ed. *Sangathan, Shaktivardan Aur Gandhi Vichar*. Shimla: Indian Institute of Advanced Study, 2001.
Baxi, Upendra and Bhikhu Parekh. *Crisis and Change in Contemporary India*. New Delhi: Sage Publications, 1995.
Beckert, Sven. *Empire of Cotton: A History of Global Capitalism*. London: Penguin Random House, 2014.
Benoit, Madhu. 'The Mahatma and the Poet'. *Gandhi Marg* 19 (1999).
Bhattacharya, Sabyasachi. *The Mahatma and the Poet*. New Delhi: National Book Trust, India, 2008 (1997).
Bhattacharya, Sabyasachi. *Talking Back: The Idea of Civilization in the Indian Nationalist Discourse*. New Delhi: Oxford University Press, 2011.
Bilgrami, Akeel. *Secularism, Identity and Enchantment*. Ranikhet: Permanent Black, 2014.
Biswas, S. C., ed. *Gandhi: Theory and Practice, Social Impact and Contemporary Relevance*. Shimla: Indian Institute of Advanced Study, 1990.
Bondurant, Joan V. *Conquest of Violence: The Gandhian Philosophy of Conflict*. Berkley and Los Angeles: University of California Press, 1969.
Bose, Nirmal Kumar. *Studies in Gandhism*. Ahmedabad: Navajivan, 1972.
Brown, Judith M. *Gandhi: Prisoner of Hope*. Delhi: Oxford University Press, 1989.
Brown, Judith M. and Anthony Parel, ed. *The Cambridge Companion of Gandhi*. New Delhi: Cambridge University Press, 2011.
Chakravarti, Arindam. 'The Deadly "Mama", The Perils of Possession'. *Studies in Humanity and Social Sciences* XX, no. 1 (2013): 55–77.
Chakravarty, Bidyut. *Non-Violence: Challenges and Prospects*. New Delhi: Oxford University Press, 2014.
Chandra, Bipan. 'Gandhiji, Secularism and Communalism'. *Social Scientist* 32, no. 1/2 (Jan.–Feb. 2004): 3–29.
Chatterjee, Margaret. *Gandhi's Religious Thought*. New Delhi: Macmillan, 1983.
Clymes, Augustine and A. K. Sharma 'Gandhi and the Contemporary Challenges: The Emergence of New Social Movements'. *Gandhi Marg* (Jan.–Mar. 1995).
Dada Dharmadhikari. *Philosophy of sarvodaya*. Mumbai: Popular Prakashan, 2000.
Dalton, Dennis. 'Gandhi: Ideology and Authority'. *Modern Asian Studies* III, no. 4 (1969): 377–93.
Dalton, Dennis. *Gandhi's Power: Non-violence in Action*. New Delhi: Oxford University Press, 1993.
Dasgupta, Ajit K. *Gandhi's Economic Thought*. London: Routledge Research, 1996.
Dev, Dutt. 'Sarvodaya, Our Times and Gandhi' in S. C. Biswas ed. *Gandhi: Theory and Practice, Social Impact and Contemporary Relevance*. Shimla: Indian Institute of Advanced Studies, 1990.
Diwan, R. and M. Lutz, ed. *Essays on Gandhian Economics*. New Delhi: Gandhi Peace Foundation, 1985, 11–12.
Doornbos, Martin and S. Kaviraj, ed. *Dynamics of State Formation*. New Delhi: Sage Publications, 1997.

Fagg, Henry. *Back to the Sources: A Study of Gandhi's Basic Education*. New Delhi: National Book Trust, 2002.
Framarin, G. Christopher. 'Good and Bad Desires: Implications of the Dialogue between Kṛṣṇa and Arjuna'. *International Journal of Hindu Studies* 11, no. 2 (Aug. 2007): 147–70.
Gandhi, G. and Rupert Snell, ed. *Gandhi Is Gone. Who Will Guide Us Now?* New Delhi: Permanent Black, 2007.
Gandhi, M. K. *Satyagraha in South Africa*. Translated by Valji Govindji Desai. Madras: Triplicane, 1928.
Gandhi, M. K. *Self-Restraint and Self-Indulgence*. Ahmedabad: Navajivan, 1947 (1928).
Gandhi, M. K. *Hindu Dharma*. Ahmedabad: Navajivan, 1950.
Gandhi, M. K. *Basic Education*. Ahmedabad: Navajivan, 1951.
Gandhi, M. K. *From Yerwada Mandir. Ashram Observances*. Translated by V. K. Desai. Ahmedabad: Navajivan, 1957 (1932).
Gandhi, M. K. *Voice of Truth*. Edited by S. Narayan. Ahmedabad: Navajivan, 1969.
Gandhi, M. K. *sarvodaya*. Edited by B. Kumarappa. Ahmedabad: Navajivan, 1984.
Gandhi, M. K. *Gandhi on Women: Collection of Mahatma Gandhi's Writings and Speeches on Women*. Ahmedabad: Navajivan, 1988.
Gandhi, Rajmohan. *The Good Boatman: A Portrait of Gandhi*. New Delhi: Penguin Books, 1995.
Gandhi, Rajmohan. *Mohandas: A True Story of a Man, His People and an Empire*. New Delhi: Penguin, 2006.
Gandhi, Rajmohan. *Why Gandhi Still Matters*. New Delhi: Aleph Book Company, 2017.
Ghosh, B. N. *Beyond Gandhian Economics: Towards a Creative Deconstruction*. New Delhi: Sage Publications, 2012.
Gier, F. Nicholas. 'Gandhi: Pre-Modern, Modern or Post-Modern?' *Gandhi Marg* (Oct.–Nov. 1969): 261–81.
Gier, F. Nicholas. 'Ahimsa, the Self and Post-modernism'. *International Philosophical Quarterly* 35, no. 1 (Mar. 1995): 71–86.
Gopal, Sarvepalli. *Radhakrishnan: A Biography*. New Delhi: Oxford University Press, 1992.
Govindu, Venu Madhav and Deepak Malghan. *The Web of Freedom: J. C. Kumarappa and Gandhi's Struggle for Economic Justice*. New Delhi: Oxford University Press, 2016.
Green, Martin. *Gandhi: Voice of a New Age Revolution*. New York: Continuum, 1993.
Green, Martin. *The Origins of Non-violence: Tolstoy and Gandhi in their Historical Setting*. New Delhi: Harper Collins, 1998.
Guha, Ramachandra. *Gandhi Before India*. New Delhi: Penguin Book, 2013.
Guha, Ramachandra. *Gandhi: The Years That Changed the World 1914–1948*. Gurgaon, Haryana, India: Penguin Random, 2018.
Gupta, Dipankar. 'Gandhi Before Habermas: The Democratic Consequences of Ahimsa'. *Economic and Political Weekly* XLIV, no. 10 (Mar. 2009): 27–33.
Gupta, Som Raj. *The Word Speaks to the Faustian Man*, Vol. I. New Delhi: Motilal Banarsidas Publishers, 1991.
Guru, Gopal. 'Ethics in Ambedkar's Critique of Gandhi'. *Economic and Political Weekly* LII, no. 15 (Apr. 2017): 95–100.
Guru, Gopal and Sundar Sarukkai. *The Cracked Mirror. An Indian Debate in Experience and Theory*. New Delhi: Oxford University Press, 2012.
Hardiman, David. *Gandhi in His Time and Ours*. New Delhi: Permanent Black, 2003.
Hardiman, David. 'Towards a History of Non-violent Resistance'. *Economic and Political Weekly* XLVIII, no. 23 (Jun. 2013): 41–48.
Hay, Stephen, 'Gandhi: Guide to a Better Human Future'. In *Gandhi, Freedom and Self-Rule*, edited by Anthony J. Parel, 139–52. New Delhi: Vistaar Publications, 2000.

Hick, John and Lamont C. Hempel. *Gandhi's Significance for Today*. London: Palgrave Macmillan, 1989.
Hiltebeitel, Alf, *Non-violence in the Mahabharata*. London and New York: Routledge, 2016.
Hingorani, Anand T. *The Role of Women*. Bombay: Bhartiya Vidya Bhavan, 1964.
Hunt, J. D. *An American Looks at Gandhi: Essays in Satyagraha, Civil Rights, and Peace*. New Delhi: Promilla & Co. Publishers, 2005.
Hyslop, Jonathan. 'Gandhi 1869–1915: The Transnational Emergence of a Public Figure'. In *The Cambridge Companion to Gandhi*, edited by Judith M. Brown and Anthony J. Parel. New Delhi: Cambridge University Press, 2011.
Ignatius, Jesudasan. *Gandhian Theology of Liberation*. Anand: Gujarat Sahitya Prakashan, 1987.
Iyer, Raghavan N. *The Moral and Political Thought of Mahatma Gandhi*. New York: Oxford University Press, 1973.
Iyer, Raghavan N. 'Gandhi on Civilization and Religion'. In *Gandhi's Significance for Today*, edited by John Hick and Lamont C. Hempel. London: Palgrave Macmillan, 1989.
Jordens, J. T. F. *Gandhi's Religion: A Homespun Shawl*. London: Palgrave Macmillan, 1998.
Kapila, Shruti and Faisal Devji, ed. *Political Thought in Action: The Bhagavad Gita and Modern India*. New Delhi: Cambridge University Press, 2013.
Katha Upanishad. Shankaracharya. Calcutta: Vedanta Press, 1987.
Kaviraj, Sudipta. 'On State, Society and Discourse in India'. In *Rethinking Third World Politics*, edited by James Manor. London: Longman, 1991.
Kishor, Giriraj. *Pahela Girmitiya*. New Delhi: Bhartiya Gyanpeeth, 1999.
Kishor, Giriraj. *The Girmitiya Saga*. Translated by Prajapati Sah. New Delhi: Niyogi Books, 2010.
Kishwar, Madhu. 'Gandhi on Women'. In *Debating Gandhi*, edited by A. Raghuramaraju. New Delhi: Oxford University Press, 2006.
Kolge, Nishikant. *Gandhi Against Caste*. New Delhi: Oxford University Press, 2017.
Kumar, Krishna. *Political Agenda of Education: A Study of Colonialist and Nationalist Ideas*. New Delhi: Sage Publications, 1991.
Kumar, Krishna. 'Mohandas Karamchand Gandhi (1869–1948)'. *Prospects* 23, no. 3/4 (1999): 507–17.
Kumarappa, Bharatan, ed. *Basic Education*. Ahmedabad, Inida: Navajivan, 1951.
Kumarappa, Bharatan. *Towards New Education*. Ahmedabad: Navajivan, 1953.
Kumarappa, J. C. 'Handicrafts and Cottage Industries'. *Annals of the American Academy of Political and Social Science* 233 (May 1944): 106–12.
Lath, Mukund. 'The Concept of Anrsamsya in the Mahabharata'. In *The Mahabharata Revisited*, edited by R. N. Dandekar. New Delhi: Sahitya Academy, 1990.
Lipner, Julius. *Brahmabandhab Upadhyay: The Life and Thought of a Revolutionary*. New Delhi: Oxford University Press, 1999.
Mahadevan, T. K. 'An Approach to the Study of Gandhi'. In *Gandhi: Theory and Practice*, edited by S. C. Biswas, 45–61. Shimla: Indian Institute of Advanced Study, 1990.
Malhotra, S. L. *Lawyer to Mahatma: Life, Work and Transformation of M. K. Gandhi*. New Delhi: Deep & Deep, 2001.
Mukherjee, Partha. 'Sarvodaya After Gandhi: Contradictions and Change'. In *Contemporary Crisis and Gandhi*, edited by Ramashray Roy. New Delhi: Discovery Publishing House, 1986.
Mukherjee, R., ed. *The Penguin Gandhi Reader*. New Delhi: Penguin Books, 1993.
Mukherjee, Subrata and Sushila Ramaswamy. *Facets of Mahatma Gandhi Vols. I to IV*. New Delhi: Deep & Deep Publishers, 1994.
Nandy, Ashis. 'The Culture of Indian Politics: A Stock Taking'. *The Journal of Asian Studies* 30, no. 1 (Nov. 1970): 57–79.

Nandy, Ashis. 'Cultural Frames for Social Transformation: A Credo'. *Alternatives* XII, no. 1 (Jan. 1987): 113–23.
Nandy, Ashis. *From Outside the Imperium*. New Delhi: Oxford University Press, 1992.
Nandy, Ashis. *Bonfire of Creeds: The Essential Ashis Nandy*. New Delhi: Oxford University Press, 2004.
Nandy, Ashis. 'Towards a Third World Utopia'. In *Traditions, Tyranny and Utopia: Essays in the Politics of Awareness*. New Delhi: Oxford University Press, 1992.
Narayan, Shriman. *The Selected Works of Mahatma Gandhi Vols. 1–6*. Ahmedabad: Navajivan, 1968.
Nauriya, Anil. *The African Element in Gandhi*. New Delhi: National Gandhi Museum, 2006.
Nayar, Sushila. *Kasturba, Wife of Gandhi*. Wallingford, PA: Pendle Hill, 1948.
Panthem, Thomas and Kenneth L. Deutsch, eds. *Political Thought in Modern India*. New Delhi: Sage Publications, 1986.
Parekh, B. *Colonialism, Tradition and Reform*. New Delhi: Sage Publication, 1989.
Parekh, B. *Gandhi's Political Philosophy: A Critical Examination*. London: Palgrave Macmillan, 1991.
Parekh, B. *Gandhi: A Very Short Introduction*. Oxford: Oxford University Press, 2007.
Parel, Anthony J., ed. *'Hind Swaraj' and Other Writings*, Cambridge: Cambridge University Press, 2009 (1997).
Parel, Anthony J., ed. *Gandhi, Freedom and Self-Rule*. New Delhi: Vistaar Publications, 2000.
Parel, Anthony J. *Gandhi's Philosophy and the Quest for Harmony*. New Delhi: Cambridge University Press, 2007.
Parikh, Nilam. *Gandhiji's Lost Jewel: Harilal Gandhi*. New Delhi: National Gandhi Museum, 2001.
Patel, Sujata. 'Construction and Reconstrucion of Woman in Gandhi'. In *Debating Gandhi*, edited by A. Raghuramaraju. New Delhi: Oxford University Press, 2006.
Pouchepadass, Jacques. *Champaran and Gandhi: Planters, Peasants and Gandhian Politics*. New Delhi: Oxford University Press, 1999.
Prabhu, R. K. and V. R. Rao. *The Mind of Mahatma Gandhi*. Bombay: Oxford University Press, 1945.
Pradhan, R. C. 'Making Sense of Gandhi's Idea of Truth'. *Social Scientist* 34, no. 5/6 (May–Jun. 2006): 36–49.
Puri, Bindu. *The Tagore-Gandhi Debate on Matters of Truth and Untruth*. New Delhi: Springer, 2015.
Pyarelal. *Mahatma Gandhi: The Early Phase*. Ahmedabad: Navajivan, 1965.
Radhakrishnan, ed. *Mahatma Gandhi: Essays and Reflections of His Life and Work*. Mumbai: Jaico Publishing House, 1998.
Raghuramaraju, A. *Debates in Indian Philosophy: Classical, Colonial and Contemporary*. New Delhi: Oxford University Press, 2006.
Raghuramaraju, A., ed. *Debating Gandhi*. New Delhi: Oxford University Press, 2006.
Ramachandran, G. *Whither Constructive Work?* Wardha, MP: All-India Village Industries Association, 1951.
Rao, K. Raghavendra. 'Globalising Gandhi Against Global Crisis: Perils and Problems'. In *Gandhi and the Present Global Crisis*, edited by Ramashray Roy. Shimla: Indian Institute of Advanced Study, 1996.
Ramamurthi, Acharya. *Marx and Gandhi*. Ahmedabad: Vimal Prakash Trust, 1992.
Rawls, John. *A Theory of Justice*. Cambridge, MA: Harvard University Press, 1971.
Rothermund, Dietmar. *Mahatna Gandhi: An Essay in Political Biography*. New Delhi: Manohar Publishers and Distributors, 1992.
Rothermund, Indira. 'The Individual and Society in Gandhi's Political Thought'. *The Journal of Asian Studies* 28, no. 2 (Feb. 1969): 313–20.

Routlegge, Paul. *Terrains of Resistance: Non-violent Social Movements and the Contestation of Space in India*. Westport: Prager, 1993.

Roy, Ramashray and Ravi Ranjan. *Essays on Modernism, Democracy and Well-Being: A Gandhian Perspective*. New Delhi: Sage Publications, 2016.

Sachs, Wolfgang, ed. *The Development Dictionary: A Guide to Knowledge as Power*. New Delhi: Orient Longman, 1997.

Sarukkai, Sundar. 'The "Other" in Anthropology and Philosophy'. *Economic and Political Weekly* 32, no. 24 (Jun. 1997): 1406–1409.

Sarukkai, Sundar. 'Inside/Outside: Merleau-Ponty/Yoga'. *Philosophy East and West* 52, no. 4 (Oct. 2002): 459–78.

Sarukkai, Sundar, 'The Sociality of Science'. *Current Science* 111, no.11 (Dec. 2016): 1731–32.

Shah, Ghanshyam, ed. *Re-reading Hind Swaraj: Modernity and Subalterns*. New Delhi: Routledge, 2013.

Sharma, J. and A. Raghuramaraju, ed. *Grounding Morality: Freedom, Knowledge and the Plurality of Cultures*. New Delhi: Routledge, 2010.

Sharma, Suresh and Tridip Suhrud, trans. and ed. *M K Gandhi's Hind Swaraj: A Critical Edition*. Hyderabad: Orient Blackswan, 2010.

Sorabji, Richard. *Gandhi and the Stoics*. Oxford: Oxford University Press, 2012.

Suhrud, T. 'Gandhi's Key Writings: In Search of Unity'. In *The Cambridge Companion to Gandhi*, edited by Judith M. Brown and Anthony Parel, 71–92. New Delhi: Cambridge University Press, 2011.

Suhrud, Tridip. *Reading Gandhi in Two Tongues*. Shimla: Indian Institute of Advanced Study, 2012.

Surendra, L., Klaus Schindler and P. Ramaswamy, ed. *The Stories They Tell*. Madras: Earthworm Books, 1996.

Sykes, M. *The Story of Nai Talim: Fifty Years of Education at Sevagram 1937–1987*. Wardha, MP: Nai Talim Samiti, 1988.

Tendulkar, D. G. *Mahatma Vols. 1–8*. New Delhi: Publication Division of the Government of India, 1951–4.

Terchek, Ronald J. *Gandhi: Struggling for Autonomy*. New Delhi: Vistaar Publications, 2000.

Thapar, Romila. *Ancient Indian Social History: Some Interpretations*. Hyderabad: Orient Longman, 1984.

Thomson, Mark. *Gandhi and his Ashrams*. Bombay: Popular Prakashan, 1993.

Tidrick, Kathryn. *Gandhi: A Political and Spiritual Life*. London: I. B. Tauris, 2008.

Veeravalli, Anuradha. *Gandhi in Political Theory: Truth, Law and Experiment*. London: Routledge, 2014.

Vivekananda, S. 'Work and Its Secret'. In *The Complete Works of Swami Vivekananda*, Vol. II. Calcutta: Advaita Ashram Publication Department, 1963.

Weber, Thomas. *Gandhi as Disciple and Mentor*. New Delhi: Cambridge University Press, 2007.

Zaehner, R. C. *The Bhagavad Gita*. Oxford: Clarendon Press, 1968.

INDEX

abadhya 36
adhikaritva 124
affection 148–52
ahankara ego 58
ahimsa 2, 14, 86–92, 188
Ambedkar, Dr B. R. 141
Ampthill, Lord 40
Anasaktiyoga or The Gospel of Selfless Action (Gandhi) 123
Andrews, C. F. 17, 46
anti-Gandhian 2
aparigraha (non -possession) 32, 130–1
Arnold, Sir Edwin 116
artha 49
arthi 19
ashram 61–64; Phoenix Ashram 16, 31, 32, 39, 43, 46, 47, 62, 63, 73, 146, 193; Sabarmati Ashram 62, 63, 182, 193; Tolstoy Farm 39–48, 62, 63, 73, 90, 111, 123, 147, 148, 158
Asian community 30
Asiatic Act 34, 38, 95
assassination, 8, 39, 40, 47, 72, 158, 183–6
atma, atman 112, 129, 131
Autobiography, An (Gandhi) 112

Baker, A. W. 22
Bakshi, Rajni 3
Bhagavad Gita 35, 53, 110, 120, 125–30
Bhoodan 9
Bible 110, 118
Blavatsky, H. P. 114
Boer War 26, 31, 56–7, 71, 121
brahmacharya 14, 15, 33, 72–9
Brahmin 114, 116, 134, 135, 142

bread-labour 103, 148, 152
BrihadAranyaka Upanishad 111
British Constitution 23
British government 8
Buddha 115–17
budhau 5

caste system 134–7; *see also varna-ashrama vyavastha*
Catholics 110
Champaran 33, 94, 172
Chipko 9
Christian 22, 23, 25
Christianity 110, 115, 118–20
Christian Missionaries 120
civil disobedience 34
civilization 61, 68, 71, 73, 131, 141, 142, 157, 159, 160, 161, 162, 164, 165, 167, 168, 169, 184, 187, 189
civil society 7, 8, 95, 143
communal politics 38
Congress, Indian National 165
Congress, Natal Indian 27, 44
Constructive Programme 94, 146, 175, 185
contraception 81
craftsperson 148–52
culture 67, 94, 141, 151, 188

Dada Abdulla case 15, 22, 70
darshana 7
Das, Tarak Nath 40
democracy 8, 12, 187; hegemonic authority and 12; radical notion of 9
dharma 7
Dhingra, Madanlal 39

Index

Doke, Joseph (Reverend) 40
Draft Ordinance 33

education 11, 25, 80, 146, 164, 167, 172
England 21–26; Indians living in 39; liberal intellectual milieu of 120; liberalism 108; parliamentary system of 167; Royal Assent from 33
enstasy 128, 192
evolutionary revolution 11

fast 7, 43, 46, 76, 100, 101, 103, 152, 164, 168, 183
food 46, 60, 76, 78, 88, 103, 118, 119, 131, 141, 148

Gandhi, Harilal 25, 38, 42, 55, 86
Gandhi, Kasturba 20, 25, 33, 38, 39, 42, 44, 46, 47, 54, 55, 73, 76, 82
Gandhi, Manu 144
Gandhi, Rajmohan 3
Gandhian interlocutor 9
Gandhian orientation 10
Gandhian praxis 9
Gandhigram 9
Gandhi's assassination 8
Gandhi's journey 2
Gandhism 3, 7
gender 79–82
Gita *see* Bhagavad Gita
give and take 40, 41, 56, 58, 59, 60, 71, 86, 90, 99, 125, 127, 141, 152, 174, 176, 181, 182, 188, 189, 190, 192
Gokhale 17, 66

Habib, Haji 39
himsa 57
Hind Swaraj 4, 12, 16, 39–48, 147, 157–69
Hindu: ashram system 75; scriptures 32; society 136; *vrata* 101; *yama niyama* 101
Hinduism 32, 62, 110, 114, 115, 116, 117, 120, 125, 138, 140–2, 155
Hindu-Muslim unity and differences 36
humanity 53
humility 2, 3
humility and humbleness 20

imperialism 29
indentured labourers 23, 25, 32, 34, 44, 47, 51, 52
India: ancient civilization of 162; Church in 118; civilization 141; civil society in 7; Gandhi to return 41; multi-religious country 116; post-independence democratic 9; *satyagrahi* in 12; socio-economic milieu 134
Indian community 29, 37
Indian Opinion 16, 30–2, 35, 40, 146
interlocutor 54–6
intrepid social worker 180–3
Isa vasyam 7, 134–9

Kabir 2, 11, 111, 115, 116, 182
Kallenbach, Hermann 41, 42, 45, 47
kama 49
karmabhoomi 15, 52
khadi 117, 155, 191
khadigram 9
Koran 110
kshatriya 134–6
Kumarappa, J.C. 8

labour 148–52
Laxman-rekha 7
The light of Asia (Arnold) 116
Lutherans 110

machinery 151, 152, 161, 164
mamakara possessiveness 58
martyr 183–4
Marxist comrades 2
Mashruwala, Kishorelal 8
meditation 131–3
Mehta, Jeki 47
Mehta, Pranjivan 40, 43
Mia, Essop 35, 37
moksha 48, 62, 82, 85, 92, 108, 112, 121, 170, 181
monetary-finance system 52
money-grubbing 25
Muslim 22, 36, 38, 42

Naidoo, Thambi 35
Narayan, Jayprakash 9
Natal Indian Congress 27, 44
Natal legislature 37
Nehru 8, 9
Nirvana 117
niti 7
non-violence *see* ahimsa
non-violent revolution 11
nursing 32, 65, 70

passive resistance 16
Pearson, W.W. 46
phalatyaag 59
Pietermaritzburg 16, 22, 56, 64, 70
Polak, Henry 30
political movements 40
political spectrum 7

Index **205**

possessions 57–8
post-independence democratic India 9
post-*satyarthi* Gandhi 67
poverty 21, 39, 57, 85, 101, 112, 131, 147, 150, 181, 187, 190, 192
Prasna Upanishad 5
prayer 131–3
Protestants 110

racism 22, 29
Radhakrishnan, Sarvapalli 67
Ramamurti, Acharya 8
Ramanama 114
Ram Sundar Pandit's case 34, 35
Raychandbhai 23, 73
religion 23, 35, 36, 42, 58, 62, 82, 83, 88, 89, 95, 108–13
Ruskin, John 31
Rustomjee, Parsee 26, 31

sadhana 15, 120
samabhava (equability) 32
samata 7
samatvam 7
sanyasi 48, 49, 62, 73, 103
sarvodaya 11, 12, 35, 41, 53, 94, 103, 112, 120, 146–8, 152, 170, 172, 173, 175, 176, 186, 191
Sarva Dharma Samanatwa 133–4
Sarva Seva Sangh 9
satya 14, 82–6
satyagraha 14, 15, 92–100
satyagrahi 48–49, 100–4; contingent nature of 17; Gandhi conceptualizes the role of 100; Gandhi returns to India 51–3; *Hind Swaraj* 162–9; impacts 171; in India 12; involvement of 173; morality and wisdom 100–4; phase from 1904–1914 12; renunciate 63; in South Africa 12; virtuous and practicing virtue 56
satyagrahi phase 15, 29–34
satyarthi: England 21–26; Indian community 23; of individual preparation 17; orientation training of 17; phase from 1893 to about 1903 15; to *satyagrahi* transformation 11–12, 48, 53; significance of 18, 19; South Africa 21–6, 114
satyarthi phase 15, 16, 18–21, 121
scrutiny 44
sectarianism 11, 189
self-defeating 3
self-goals 2
self-in-society 48
self-liberation 19
self-realization 19, 31
self-reliance 188

self-respect 31
self-sufficiency 32, 120
serve society 56
Shaivism 110
Shastras 120, 141
social activism 30
social clarity 5
social formation 188
social service 30, 57–8, 170–5
social transformation and transition 11
South Africa: British Indians in 87, 160; Gandhi as *satyarthi* 21–6; Gandhi left 17; Gandhi's involvement in 65; Indian community in 42, 96; Indian independence movement 53; Indians in 16, 30; Indian struggle in 101; *satyagrahi* phases 12, 53; social transformation involvements in 122; society 23; socio-economy 52; struggles in 10; Trappists in 118
SS *Kildonan Castle* 40
sudra 91, 134–6, 141
swadeshi 2, 7, 12, 58, 103, 120, 146, 152–8
swaraj 14, 157–62; challenges of 186–8

Tagore, Rabindranath 3, 6
TARA (Transvaal Asiatic Registration Act or the Black Act) 33
Thoreau, Henry David 34
Tolstoy, Leo 40, 73, 111, 123, 147, 148, 158
Trappist monastery 23
travails 175–8
trusteeship 11, 48, 139, 189, 191
Truth 36, 37, 56, 69, 71, 82–5, 87, 89, 95, 101, 108–13, 115, 118, 119, 132, 133, 140, 159
tryst with faith 114
tyaag 15, 59–61
tapascharya 85, 158

uniqueness 188
Unto This Last (Ruskin) 31, 56

Vaishnavism 110
vaishya 134–6
varna-ashrama vyavastha 134–7
varnadharma 140
Vidushak 5
Vivekananda, Swami 68

women 44, 79–82
worship 131–3
Wyllie, Sir Curzon 39

yajna 58, 59, 79, 157

Zulu rebellion 16

For Product Safety Concerns and Information please contact our EU representative GPSR@taylorandfrancis.com
Taylor & Francis Verlag GmbH, Kaufingerstraße 24, 80331 München, Germany

www.ingramcontent.com/pod-product-compliance
Lightning Source LLC
Chambersburg PA
CBHW070830300426
44111CB00014B/2509